THIN LIZZY
SOLDIERS OF FORTUNE

ALAN BYRNE

THIN LIZZY
SOLDIERS OF FORTUNE

ALAN BYRNE

PUBLISHING

fIRE
fLY

PUBLISHING

First published in 2004
by Firefly Publishing

Firefly Publishing is an imprint of SAF Publishing Ltd
and Helter Skelter Publishing Ltd

SAF Publishing Ltd.
149 Wakeman Road,
London.
NW10 5BH
ENGLAND

email: info@safpublishing.com

www.safpublishing.com

ISBN 0 946719 57 8

Printed in England by the Cromwell Press, Trowbridge, Wiltshire.

ACKNOWLEDGEMENTS

Thin Lizzy – Soldiers Of Fortune was a five-year labour of love. At times I had good reason to believe that I may never hold the final book, at given points it seemed unbeatable, and other times I felt unbeatable.

As with all adventures such as this, something new is found, something old re-told and sold in a fresh wrapper – capturing Philip Lynott's essence was one hell of a cauldron. So many interviewees speak with such deep affection for the man, that it seems impossible to escape the aura that remains so long after his death. He is sorely missed in human terms.

The following are the people who made available their time and effort for this project, for your indulgence I thank you. Their input, no matter the size, was and will continue to be greatly appreciated.

The Cast…

Brendan Shortall, Brush Shiels, Deirdre Costello, John D'Ardis, Darren Wharton, David Mallet, Roddy Cleere, Ted Carroll, Adam Winstanley, Soren Lindberg, Paul Mauger, Robbie Dennis, Anne Minion, Brian Robertson, John Alcock, Scott Gorham, Snowy White, Brian Downey, Jerome Rimson, Gus Isadore, Tony Visconti, Robin George, Steve Johnson, Paul Hardcastle, Peter Hince, Brian May, Mark Stanway, Robbie Brennan, Laurence Archer, Denis O Regan, Kit Woolven, Mark Nauseef, Chris Tsangarides, Jon Stone, Graham Cohen, Liz Devlin, Patrick Murphy, John Slater, Eric Bell, Smiley Bolger, Philip Chevron, Jim Fitzpatrick, Jackie Hayden, Frank Rogers, Joe Staunton, Gay Woods, Marco Mendoza, Dave Flett, Junior Giscombe, Andy Gee, Fish, Johannes @ Record Heaven, Tony Johns, John Earle, Marian Parry, Betty Wray, Shay Healy, David Heffernan,

THIN LIZZY

P.J. Heraty, Philip Tapsfield, Graham Parker, Jacky Smith (Queen fan club), Chris Mansbridge, Randy Bachman, Tracey Ganapathy, Marcus Connaughton, Paul Brady, Terry O Neill, Patrick Byrne, Midge Ure, Magnus Rouden, Paul Jenkins.

'Extra Special' thanks go to Philomena Lynott for immeasurable help, direction and patience during the course of this project.

To those who made available their private archives of both audio/visual material and newspaper clippings etc, my thanks for your efforts, patience and time. Special mention goes to Phil Osborne (the ole Scot), Nick Sharp and Graham Hart, Tony and Philip Went, Par Olsson, Phil Birch, James ' The Real Canadian' Taylor, Adam Winstanley and Black Rose. Roddy & Margaret Cleere for patience and generosity of spirit, also, to Mrs Deirdre Murphy (translations). Many thanks also to those who have helped promote this project via the Internet, supporter websites etc.

Mum, Dad (all Ireland Champion, no less) and Sarah B….unflagging support, antagonism, experience, ass kicking and for always trying to push me in the best direction.
Niamh 'El Dalo' Daly for the supreme effort with the *Soldiers Of Fortune* CD-ROM'.

The following can be held responsible for support/tantrums/ pandemonium/proof-reads/shoulders and ears… These are the people who never let me overheat, those who were here and there through the soft, semi-erect and hard times I salute you…
David 'Oberon' O Brien, Shane 'Percy' Murphy, Brian 'Internet' Donovan, Brian 'Baz Ads' Barrett, Lorraine 'No Name' Kelly, Michael 'Keats' Keating, Harpo, Owen 'Fuji' O Connor, Mark 'Plane Proposal' Murphy, Phil 'O' Osborne, Sandie Gibson, David 'Harry' Manning, Zeppo, Mark Hayes, Stephen Dempsey, Andrea, Colin Meade (Bed and Board) and all at the Meade compound (Mary's Vineyard), Pat and Delores Kelly (No more late calls), Jason 'Toaster' Byrne, Groucho, Richard 'Probin'' Hoban, Chico, Johnny Fox, Willy Owens, Ginger Tompkins, Flash, William 'The Great Converter' Arnold, Niamh 'El Dalioso' Daly, Fiona Nagle, Lisa 'Captain' Farrell, Andrew 'Photos' Oliver, Lisa 'el punko' Murphy, Bernie 'Blunt' Sharp, Sinead 'Obi Wan' Tobin, Peter McDwyer, All at Quest International Carrigaline, Co. Cork, Eire and Don Hegarty at Glaxo Smithkline, Ringskiddy, Co Cork, Eire.

A million thanks must go to my publisher, Firefly and Dave Hallbery, everyone at SAF and Helter Skelter, for faith in the project and ultimately giving it a home.

If I have let anyone out it is without intention, everyone's help was greatly appreciated.

Dedications tend to be difficult in certain situations but the following people are most deserving of the mantle. Though no longer here to see this project, come to fruition, you are always in my thoughts and the most important part of my memory bank.

This book is sincerely dedicated to the memory of Jack, May, Bridget and Tommy…See ya later!

Good luck,
Alan Byrne, 2004

INTRODUCTION

The sight of Philip Lynott sauntering through the streets of his native Dublin is an image fondly recalled by the city's populace. In life and in song, Phil often praised Dublin and its characters. That city, and Ireland in a wider sense, was the source of much of Philip Lynott's inspiration.

Glen Corr, the house in which Lynott used to live, is just a short walk from St. Fintan's cemetery, the place where his body is now buried and where fans from around the world come to pay their respects. Phil's grave, originally marked with the cross of the cowboy until the cemetery authorities insisted on something less ostentatious, now has a flat gravestone designed by Jim Fitzpatrick, a long-standing friend and neighbour of Philip's, as well as the designer of some of Thin Lizzy's best known album covers. The stone's inscription translates from Gaelic to read: 'Sleep In Peace, Our Black Rose'. Strewn beside the grave, are numerous valedictions, mementos and dedications.

A short walk from St Fintan's will take you to White Horses, the house that Phil gave his mother Philomena on her fiftieth birthday and where she still lives. A warm welcome awaits anyone asking after Phil and a room is preserved in his memory. Platinum, gold and silver discs adorn the walls along with a life-size cut out of Phil in his *Solo in Soho* pose, as well as many other portraits of the singer, some specially commissioned and some sent by fans from around the world. Phil's extensive vinyl collection takes up much of the space, while personal photograph albums document his life away from the spotlight.

Beyond the family shrine, Philip Lynott's memory is still present in many of his old haunts. Numerous watering holes still display a commemoration of one or more of his visits.

In recent years the emergence of the *Hot Press* Hall Of Fame has opened another avenue for fans to investigate the history of Thin Lizzy, as well as hosting memorial gigs by tribute acts. There was an extensive turnout for the unveiling of the Philip Lynott wax model at the Dublin Wax Museum, including former Thin Lizzy drummer Brian Downey who dropped in to say a few words and pose for photographs along with a number of Phil's old friends and colleagues.

The oft-mooted plan to erect a statue of Phil in Dublin seems to be finally nearing fruition after many years of hard work. Meanwhile, a regular flurry of Lizzy-related releases help keep Phil's flame burning across the globe, including a well-received live album, tribute discs, spoken word recordings and a variety of other packages.

As with many other rock acts, the internet has facilitated a flowering of organised fan activity and Roddy Cleere's *Roisin Dubh* [or "Black Rose"] Trust Website is particularly notable in keeping Phil's memory alive.

There is even a new incarnation of Thin Lizzy on the road featuring Scott Gorham and John Sykes. Though this line-up has taken some flak for going out under the Lizzy name – and clearly Sykes' vocals are not a patch on Lynott's – the shows have often been warmly received.

Talk of a Lynott biopic based around Philomena Lynott's memoir *My Boy* have been circulating for years, and Ferndale Films have recently taken up the option. They are currently in pre-production with Noel Pearson at the helm, a director renowned in Irish film circles whose previous credits include *In The Name Of The Father* and *My Left Foot*. Many actors have been rumoured to be taking part including Holly Hunter, Elaine Cassidy, with American actor Gary Dourdan rumoured to have been cast as Lynott.

A film would further add to the myth of Philip Lynott – for some a hero on a par with the great figures of Irish history he wrote and sang about. Man or myth, I wanted to celebrate one of the most original musicians to ever take to the stage, as well as the band he played with.

Def Leppard, Bon Jovi, Metallica, and more recently the band who have brought rock and roll back to the mainstream, the Darkness, all harnessed the raw energy that made Thin Lizzy so accessible. It is indeed a tribute to the Thin Lizzy legacy and that of their frontman Philip Lynott. And so what follows here are the adventures of his band, Thin Lizzy...

1

BIRTH OF A COWBOY

Philomena Lynott was born by gaslight in Dublin on October 30, 1930. She was raised as one of nine children in a Catholic family in the Dublin suburb of Crumlin.

"We were poor yet we were a very happy family," Philomena recalls. "Everybody went to church on Sunday and everybody had their bath on Saturday night with our Sunday clothes all laid out for us. Everything had to be ready for school and it was a time for great obedience for your elders. You never gave a smart answer back to your mother or father.

"I remember my mother getting our first radio called a Telefunken. At night-time back then without radio we just read books, did our homework or went to our dances."

Throughout the build up to the second World War, emotions had been running high across the neutral Eire. Philomena recalls the rude awakening.

"Sometime during 1939, which also happened to be the year my school opened in Crumlin, I can remember walking up the road one day with a jug of milk. There weren't any bottles in those days and a woman hit me over the head with a newspaper and exclaimed, 'go home and tell your mother the War has broken out'.

"If your family was really poor, in those days you left school at thirteen. There was never any talk about going to college... I left school at thirteen and went to work in a home for elderly people, shuttling to and from work on my bike."[1]

After the war, many Irish youths were tempted by the enticement of advertisements to seek work on the British mainland and beyond and in 1947, Philomena joined this exodus and moved across the water.

"England was being rebuilt after the war," Philomena remembers. "There was plenty of work in England and even the bus conductors were women. At this time people were just starting to come alive again."[2]

Philomena started work as a trainee nurse, settling with ease into her new surroundings and quickly making friends. The dancehalls beckoned again and it was at just such an event that Philomena made the acquaintance of a tall dark-skinned man named Cecil Parris. Philomena gladly accepted his offer to dance with her and they continued to meet during the course of the following months. The reaction from some of Philomena's friends towards her new romance was far from positive – the first of her many encounters with racial prejudice.

Before long, Cecil's job with the services necessitated his return to London. It was around this time that Philomena discovered she was pregnant.

Her son, Philip Parris Lynott was born on 20 August, 1949 at the Halham Hospital in the West Bromwich part of Birmingham. Cecil had proposed marriage but Philomena declined his offer. "He was a fine man who never denied being Philip's father," she says, "But life just didn't happen that way."

In terms of the morals of the time, the situation was traumatic – to be an unmarried mother was bad enough for the Catholic community, but to have a half-caste child in 1940s Britain was enough to invite scorn.

"When you had a baby back then out of wedlock you were a very sinful person, a person of no morals," Philomena explains. "I can't blame the man... As the old saying goes it takes two to tango. As sad as it was, I remember dreading having this baby and I didn't know what was to become of me, whether I'd live or die. When I had Philip, in those days he was termed illegitimate, a bastard, and you were shunned by society and men wouldn't go near you.... To be shunned kills the spirit, and for years I walked around with my shoulders creased. They call it walking around with a hump in your back. And then one day I just shed the hump and I walked tall and held my head high. Now I don't give two damns about anybody, for nobody is better than me and nobody is beneath me. And if I don't owe you money, well then that's about it really, isn't it?"[3]

Despite employment, including a spell at a centre for unmarried mothers where Philomena once again became the victim of racial intolerance, she found she was increasingly unable to manage the bills and baby-sitting costs. Initially Philomena's parents back home in Dublin were wholly unaware of her circumstances in Britain, but eventually she informed them of her situation and did as much as she could to try and heal any possible rift. She decided to return to Dublin to ask her mother if she would raise Philip, while she resumed her job in England, regularly sending over money to keep the child. Much to Philomena's relief her mother agreed.

Philip was nearly three years old before he met his grandparents. Many of his early childhood experiences following his move to Ireland provided the backdrop for some of his songs, and the real lack of an authority figure meant he could get away with more than most of the kids of his age. This situation was made worse when the only male authority figure, Philip's grandfather Frank, died in 1964. The resulting liberal upbringing possibly provided the opportunity for the young Lynott to develop his craft, but it may also have contributed to his undoing.

For the moment however, Philip was in a household full of love and he was as happy as any other child growing up in Dublin in the fifties and sixties.

"He was an amazing character," Philomena recalls, "because by the time he was old enough to realise, nobody was going to sit him down and say, 'You have no daddy'. He grew up being aware that there was only a mammy coming home to visit him in Ireland. He never really asked me until he was about fifteen and I said, 'He was a fine man your father', and I outlined our circumstances. It didn't bother him because he had become his own character. He had become a bit of a celebrity in Dublin by just being black. Philip was different, full of himself, kids always wanted to come around and play with him and that made him feel special. His character overcame any stuff like being illegitimate."[4]

When the time came for Philip to go to school, it was his Uncle Peter who kept an eye on him, claiming that, "For a short period of time he was subjected to a torrent of abuse, but it settled down and Philip came to be accepted by the other kids there." But it was through another Uncle of his, Tim, that Philip developed a keen interest in music and started writing his own songs. A lot of these pieces never went beyond the bedroom, but they provided a creative outlet for the young Lynott.

As with any other Irish youngster of the time, the youthful Lynott was pre-occupied with cross-channel soccer, which led to endless games of street football on Leiglin Road in Crumlin. On one such occasion Patrick Byrne can recall the time when one rather acerbic neighbour decided to curtail the youngsters playing ball.

"I can't recall his name but I can certainly recall his actions. We grew up around the same area and anyone who was interested in kicking a ball joined in. Now there's always one neighbour who wants to be a killjoy, and the ball constantly made its way into his front garden, purely by accident of course! Eventually he threw the ball back over the trees punctured. So, needless to say his front garden became an absolute wreck with sods all over the place by the next morning. Phil Lynott played his part, indeed he got as stuck into it as we all did."

In his mid-teenage years Philip finally emerged as lead vocalist in a band. While his uncle Peter had begun playing guitar and singing with a local Dublin band The Sundowners, Philip got roped into playing for the Black Eagles. They were managed by an old neighbour by the name of Joe Smith whose sons Danny and Frankie also played in the band. Joe had the notion of also getting Peter to play with the Black Eagles, but after failing to enticee Peter from his Sundowners' position he opted for the younger Lynott.

Philip's aunt, Mrs. Betty Wray, vividly remembers an early band performance in a hall at Mount Argus.

"Phil had asked if we would like to go and see him perform. As we got closer to the hall, we could hear music playing, then a male voice started singing. I remember thinking the singing was so good that it must have been a professional singer hired for the night. On entering the hall you can imagine my amazement to see little Philip up there. He was still only a teenager at the time but we felt he had found his vocation."[5]

The Black Eagles provided Philip with excellent experience in front of an audience. Their most popular gigs were held at St. Anthony's Hall as well as St. John of Gods where Philip occasionally played an acoustic set along with future Thin Lizzy drummer Brian Downey.

Downey recalled the time that they got to know each other.

"Yeah... it was in school maybe around 1965 that Phil and I hooked up. You could always make him out down on the schoolyard cause he'd be surrounded by a gang of guys. At this time I wasn't actually part of that gang but it wouldn't be long before the initiation began. Eventually we started going to the same clubs and concerts together. To be honest he was one of the most interesting characters around Dublin. He'd hang around the record shops looking for obscure songs to do. I mean, even in the schoolyard he used to sing things that nobody else used to sing and he always sounded great. He used do Ray Charles's 'Crying Time', I remember him being really into that. His record collections always seemed to be full of records that you wouldn't get on this side of the world. To my knowledge he sent away to America to get some of the stuff, but it was quite obscure."[6]

One event organiser, Paddy Murphy, also recalls the era:

"I remember Phil Lynott fairly well. We used to make up an old rickety stage for his band and they'd play sometimes for nothing. The odd time they'd make a couple of quid but never much more than that. They seemed like a really nice bunch of kids and they were always willing to please, I can only guess that our appreciation went some way as their reward."[7]

By the mid-sixties, Philomena had started a new relationship with a man named Dennis Keeley. The two of them took over the running of a hotel in Manchester called the Clifton Grange. With no experience, the two agreed to try to turn its fortunes around by attracting a certain type of clientele. It would become home to both the famous and not so famous, the important and the self-important. It was a mix that led to it becoming known as "The Showbiz". Philomena recalls…

"Philip came over two or three times a year and I went home two or three times a year. It was a great excuse to see each other. He'd arrive over and ask straight away, 'Who famous have you got here?' and I'd have all different bands, footballers, snooker players. I think that made him feel special because when he met up with other musicians in London they'd say to him that they had stayed in his Ma's place in Manchester and it was great fun. I remember too when I would get a call from a band that Philip had been talking to and they hadn't been making an awful a lot of money from their gigs. Philip would call me to ask if I could do a special for them and more often than not I would accommodate them. I look back on my time in the Clifton Grange as a lot of fun really, it was a mad house. Everyday there was something different and funny happening, I mean even to use the term "hotel" is quite ridiculous because a hotel is run to order. Our clientele would generally keep late hours, going on from doing their own gigs to catching another gig by friends, maybe then moving on to a club and then to a curry house and then back to the hotel bar which would be open all night. And so therefore breakfast was more or less served at midday or one in the afternoon. But if one lazy little rascal didn't arrive down until 2 pm wanting his breakfast he just helped himself, it was like being in your own Ma's kitchen when you think about it, they were fabulous times."[8]

Philip made friends for life at the hotel including a Canadian named Percy Gibbons who took Philip under his wing and told him how his band The Others Brothers had made their way on the music scene. Gibbons recalls…

"Philip would love to get words to rhyme and a lot of the ideas that came from the Clifton Grange days ended up on Lizzy albums, especially the first two, *Thin Lizzy* and *Shades Of A Blue Orphanage*. I felt privileged to know I could trace those songs back to their roots."[9]

Graham Cohen, one of many regulars at the hotel, became a close family friend and confidant of the ShowBiz scene.

"I went in there one night after finishing work in another club. I was about eighteen or nineteen when I started there. The way the hotel ran was with a hotel license which permitted residents to drink all through the night and day if they so pleased. In Manchester the clubs were run differently, all had full liquor licenses that closed up at 2 am. Consequently we opened the Clifton Grange bar at two in the morning so we weren't competing with the clubs. We captured everyone after they'd been thrown out of everywhere else. It wasn't open to the general public as such. Purely residents, though they were allowed to bring in a guest if they wished which was often the case and we ran right through the night. Back in those days the cabaret scene was huge. Bursting with a big circuit of people who were nearly always our clientele. Some of the guests went on to be huge names and others just fizzled out."[10]

On one of her many trips home to Dublin, Philomena made a surprise trip to see Philip in action with the Black Eagles.

"Philip was playing down at Mount Argus," she recalls, "and I sneaked on down there and I hid behind a priest. Philip was never shy, anybody who gets up onstage and gives a performance in front of a crowd of people has 'it', if you know what I mean. He was still only about fifteen or sixteen and he was doing it. Philip had been in bands since he was about eleven. The manager of the Eagles (Mr. Smith) picked Philip because he looked good and that gave Philip a lot of experience on the stage. I remember he gave them all black polo necks and they looked great. When I look at the photos today they all look fabulous. Philip loved it with the Black Eagles, they got to travel around Ireland and he was having a ball."[11]

As time passed, the Black Eagles eventually split into different factions. Both Joe Smith's sons departed for other careers and even Joe lost interest. It was at this point Brian Downey replaced Nick Higgins as drummer of the Black Eagles.

Of the many groups and showbands that graced and oft disgraced the music scene in Dublin, one man in particular shone through as the next great Irish hope. His name was Brush Shiels. Garrulous by nature, with a professional aloofness, Brush recalls the days of playing the scene in Dublin during the late sixties…

"There were loads of clubs to play in back in those days, The '72, The Go-Go, The Apartment, The Scene and of course the Five Club. The Five Club was organised more or less by Terry O Neill and ourselves, whilst the

72 Club was run by a guy known as Uncle Bill. It was all about playing seven nights a week. Even in the showband scene everything was wide open. I don't think it's ever been as good since [1968-71]. It was geared towards trying new things, which you can't do now."[12]

Towards the end of the touring life of the Black Eagles, bookings had started to come in for gigs the length and breadth of the country, but with so many line-up changes they struggled and eventually disbanded. Not, however, before they had befriended Ted Carroll who managed a variety of bands around at that time.

"On the night I first met Phil Lynott," Ted recalls, "the Black Eagles turned up, the gear was set up by a couple of guys and then just as they were due on stage at eight o'clock, the band came trotting in from their van with their instruments. They were dressed in their stage gear and jingled their way to the stage because they were all wearing bell-bottom jeans complete with little jingle bells sewn onto them. We were intrigued to see that their lead singer was a tall skinny black kid who a year or so later I was to learn was named Philip Lynott. Phil and the boys gave a confident performance that night, running through Small Faces' and Yardbirds' covers and we would certainly have re-booked them, but we lost the use of the hall and decided to call it a day. It would be two years before I had contact with Phil again and this was when he accepted an invitation to join a new group, Skid Row, which I was setting up with Brush Shiels."[13]

In order to please the family, Philip enrolled at the Clogher Road Technical College, where he was to learn a trade. Brian Downey also enrolled as a student and the two renewed their friendship.

On leaving the Technical College at eighteen years old Lynott still had music in his heart and a venomous will to succeed in the music business. Even so, when a generous neighbour offered him a job as a fitter and turner at Tongue & Taggarts iron foundry in Crumlin he accepted.

Lynott hated the job, which paid him two pounds and five shillings per week. It was in stark comparison to the gigs he had been doing with the Black Eagles where he cleared ten quid at a minimum. This disparity led to Philip's early retirement from his apprenticeship and paved the way for his future.

Quitting the foundry caused problems at home in Leiglin Road. Philip's Granny was particularly disgusted about his views toward regular employment. There was also the issue of his friends, who she viewed as "undesirables". It was considered best for all concerned if Philip found more suitable accommodation. The continuous ignoring of his uncle's curfew at least provided him with a comical couplet in "Dancing In The Moonlight":

"It's three o'clock in the morning and I'm on the streets again,

I disobeyed another warning I should've been in by ten."

Philip moved into a rented flat in Clontarf, overlooking the Northern corner of Dublin Bay frequented by other folks in the music scene. Here, following the demise of the Black Eagles, Philip wiled away his time with a variety of throwaway groups including Kama Sutra, gigging at the usual places and keeping a watchful eye on the other hopefuls.

Ted Carroll remembers how Lynott was in the frame when Skid Row was being formed.

"In the interim, I had been managing a group called Rockhouse, featuring Paul Brady on lead vocals and Vox continental organ. Brush [Shiels] at that time was playing with a Country and Western group called Rose Tynan and The Rangers. Brush used to come to see Rockhouse and would bemoan having to play boring C&W, saying he would love to be in a band like Rockhouse, who were, it has to be admitted, shit hot. Paul Brady, who was also at UCD at the time, failed his first year exams and was dragged home by his parents to concentrate on his studies. Rockhouse folded, and their lead guitarist Brenny Bonass and me decided to have a go with another group, the Uptown Band and we recruited Brush Shiels to play bass. He suggested that we get Phil Lynott in as lead vocalist. I drove up to Crumlin to Phil's Grandmother's house where he lived (they didn't have a phone, in fact not many people did in those days) but there wasn't anybody home. I left a message for Phil to get in touch, but nothing happened, so, we brought in someone else as lead vocalist, a guy called Dick O Leary."[14]

Phil had left home by then, so the message never reached him, but it wasn't long before Lynott crossed the path of Carroll and Shiels once more...

"The flower power revolution was upon us and the Uptown Band soon became one of the hottest bands around the Dublin clubs, thanks to hundreds of Gladioli – they were ritually tossed to the punters at every gig. Our light show was the best (the only one) in Dublin at the time," Carroll explains.

But a band coup soon saw Carroll replaced by Larry Mooney who promised to get the band more money and better gigs. However, Brush disapproved of Larry Mooney and decided that he wanted to leave and form a new band with Carroll as manager.

"This time there were no mistakes!" Carroll continues. "We kept after Phil, until I got him to agree to come down to a rehearsal. Phil arrived and started rehearsing with the rest of the band, Brush on bass, Bernie Cheevers on lead guitar and Noel Bridgeman on drums. Brush said, 'Phil is our man, he looks good and will click with the chicks, me and Bernie and Noel can take care of the guys and the musos.'

"The band rehearsed in the basement of a condemned house in Phibsborough. We managed to get an electrician friend down to hot-wire the place so it was quite cosy, with light, heating and power. Noel was a friend of Brush and this was his first band. We had been toying with the idea of bringing in Brian Downey, but he had joined another band, however Noel worked out well and he was in."[15]

Very quickly they gelled and various friends who dropped by rehearsals spread the word around the clubs that the band was going to be great. But they still needed a name and after votes were cast Skid Row was chosen.

Initially, Skid Row managed to construct a set riddled with covers from the repertoire of the Yardbirds, Hendrix, the Doors and most prominently the Beatles. The tunes ranged from "Hey Jude" and "Strawberry Fields Forever" to "Eight Miles High" and even Clapton's "Sky Pilot". Lynott had yet to take up the bass guitar and with him fronting the band Ted Carroll had plenty of reason to believe the right ingredients were all in place. Brush continues the story…

"He was a bit inhibited at the beginning as a front man. I remember he was going out with some girl at the time called Carol. I told him she was having the wrong effect on him musically and that it would be best that she stay away from the gigs. I reckoned that he should be concentrating more on the girls in the audience. He did turn into a great showman though and he had good presence, we were all working hard with Skid Row and were putting on some great shows." [16]

Whilst the band continued rehearsing, Ted Carroll quickly got them a string of gigs around town. With Brush and Philip's contacts, the band was guaranteed maximum exposure. "By February 1968 they were one of the top groups in Ireland," Ted re-affirms.

Around this time Philip began seriously considering the possibility of including some original material in Skid Row's set, a move which would separate the band from an ever growing list of Irish musicians.

"I remember talking to Brush and suggesting that we should get into writing our own material," Lynott later confessed in *Hot Press*. "Once it had been suggested to Brush, he just had to do it. It was a challenge to him, which is something he can't resist. That was how we began writing our own stuff."[18]

After arranging a show in Dublin at UCD it was decided to put some thought into how to get the audience to react more to the band. Brush recalls…

"One time we saw this movie together starring Sidney Poitier and Tony Curtis called *The Defiant Ones* where two jailbirds, one white man and one black man, are handcuffed to each other after escaping from prison.

Of course the Tony Curtis character turns out to be a racist and the two of them end up hating each other. Philo and myself had the idea that we would pretend to have a row onstage, literally make a scene. The first time we tried it was at UCD and it was a big success. We tore his shirt just a fraction before the show, so that when I grabbed it would easily come off him. Granny's Intentions were top of the bill but they had no chance after that. As all this was going on Bernard Cheevers was playing guitar with his teeth. Ted used to have this backing tape with the sound of cars flying down a road and ending with a big crash and this was used as our grand entrance to the stage. Call it what you want, it worked for us."

At the peak of the band's fame they were offered the opportunity to record a single at Eamonn Andrews' studio. The result of that session was the first true Skid Row composition.

"We only wrote about four or five songs together," Brush reveals. "He was full of ideas. The first thing we wrote and recorded was a song called 'Photograph Man'. You could see that he could write. He got better as time went on and he figured out a way of exploiting it with Lizzy."[19]

There was little positive feedback to "Photograph Man". Ted Carroll had plagued London record companies with the song, but couldn't convince anybody to take a chance. After about six months in charge Ted quit to concentrate on his other career as a booking agent. By the spring of 1968 the band were in disarray and Noel Bridgeman decided to move to Germany. Being without management Bernie Cheevers too opted for a career change. He decided to take up an apprenticeship with Guinness, thus rendering the band little more than a shell.

The first replacement was of 19 year old drummer Robbie Brennan, an engineering student and former member of Paul Brady's Roots Group.

"I was in a band that was being managed by Ollie Byrne who knew Brush and he asked me if I'd like to join Skid Row," Robbie Brenann recalls. "I wasn't there long though before they felt that they were having trouble with Phil's singing."[20]

In the latter stages of 1969 Phil had to finally agree he was singing so far off key that something drastic needed to be done. Whilst he prepared for a trip to Manchester to get his tonsils removed, the band continued to soldier on without him. By the time Phil returned, his card was marked.

"We hung around a lot in those days whether we were playing or not," says Brush, "and I didn't like letting him go. It worked both ways – to get to the next point he had to go it alone, and Skid had to step ahead without him. I thought we sounded better without him and the decision was as straightforward as that. After he was thrown out I still saw him four or five days a week for about six months as I was teaching him bass. Sometimes he used to play Canned Heat's 'On The Road Again' while I was on harmonica. All I gave him was the basics of handling bass, which enabled him to put his own stamp on how he wanted to play it. I was just trying to make sure he got a gig somewhere around town when he was kicked out. A chip on the shoulder is great motivation and it meant he had to work a lot harder than he would have done before. He ended up practising bass day and night."[21]

"When Phil told me he'd been kicked out of Skid Row I was delighted. I was out of a job at the time, so I thought it was a perfect time for us to start thinking about putting a band together again," recalls Brian Downey.[22]

So after being ejected from Skid Row, Phil continued writing. Meanwhile Downey was having similar experiences with his blues band Sugar Shack.

"We had a hit on the Irish charts with a song called 'Morning Dew', it got to number16. We mainly played the club circuit in Dublin. We had a great manager in that he was well aware of the commercial aspects of the market. Because we wanted to stick to the blues it became difficult to play the type of music we wanted to play when we were on the road. This in turn led to arguments which we couldn't sustain, hence the demise of the band so soon after our chart success brought me back into the fold with Phil."[23]

In late 1969 Phil and Brian formed a band called Orphanage with Joe Staunton, a left-handed lead guitar player and Pat Quigley, another bass player. Phil played rhythm guitar using a Fender Mustang he had borrowed. One of the other people to pass through the band was Terry Woods, who would remain a close friend of Philip's to the end of his life.

"We always had guest musicians joining us on stage such as Terry Woods from The Pogues and that was great," says Joe Staunton. "Gary Moore had recently arrived down from Belfast to join Skid Row and although he never played with us, the two of us got an apartment down in Fairview that we shared for over a year. He was still only seventeen and he was a phenomenal guitarist even then. The idea of floating members came from a novel idea that Phil had. He had such a wide variety of influences and he mixed around with a lot of people. Elvis and Hendrix are documented as his main influences but his scope was such that he wanted to incorporate everything into the band in order to garner further appeal."[24]

Orphanage played their first gig at the Five Club in Hartford Street. For all the wrong reasons Joe recalls vividly his introduction to the world of gigging...

"I was so wound up, because it was my first real band and these guys were the seasoned players. It was a very shortlived band but we had the best of times. I can always remember playing at the Franciscan Hall in Limerick because Phil had done this interview and he had finally got my name right for the media. It usually turned up in the reviews as 'Stuntan' or something like that. So after the gig and the interview we all legged it for the stairs to go down and meet the chicks but of course I fell from the top to the bottom with such excitement and into the arms of a Franciscan brother."[25]

The name of the band was drawn straight from Lynott's roots.

"I thought of the name Orphanage partly because I could have ended up in an orphanage," Lynott told *Hot Press*. "For a woman in Ireland in the fifties, having a kid out of wedlock, and a black kid in particular, keeping it was hard. There were other reasons, the pad where I first met Tim Booth, Orphan Annie, Tim Goulding, Ivan Pawle and that lot – that was called the Orphanage. Also it seemed like a good moody name."[26]

Orphanage recordings are almost non-existant, though many of the songs would resurface later in Lynott's career.

"There was an a capella group called The Press Gang and the first recordings we did as the Orphanage was done with those guys in a basic four track studio that used to be on Dominic Street," confirms Staunton. "We did a blues number called 'You Fool, You Fool' and I wish I had a copy of those recordings but they vanished quite a while back. One must also remember that there was great competition for gigs back in the Orphanage days. Dr. Strangely Strange were great buddies of Phil's. Phil played a song with the Orphanage called 'Donnybrook Fair' that he co-wrote with those guys though I don't think it was ever put down on tape. Because Orphanage didn't last that long we never got that much material down on tape. We were only together for about six months or so and we were hardly what you could call a fully fledged professional group."[27]

While Orphanage were kicking their heels in the republic, a Belfast boy was the trying to find his way out of the show band circuit. His name was Eric Bell.

Born on 3 September 1947, Bell was in the Irish showband The Dreams at the same time that the Orphanage was treading the boards around Dublin. After a brief flirtation with Van Morrison's Them in the early sixties he headed off to play in a variety of bands that included Shades Of Blue and The Blue Beats. After short spells in a succession of other groups, Eric found himself back in the stressful world of the showband. He takes up the story:

"Everybody knew that the showband scene was where the money was made, and so off I went touring up and down the country with the Dreams. The money was good but there wasn't really any satisfaction with playing this type of music, for me anyway. With the sixties coming to a close I felt that the same should happen with my time as part of The Dreams. I had money saved but I didn't own an amp. So here I am trying to get out of the showband scene without the proper equipment to start up a new group."

It was clear that Bell had decided to move on.

"At the last gig I was presented with the amp to mark the beginning of my transition from showband freak to a real musician. I thought it was a nice touch and it wasn't really something that had to be done. So my departure was on nothing but good grounds."

Throughout the fall and winter of 1969, Eric began traipsing around the group circuit in Dublin. After various attempts to get in with the "in crowd" he ended up in the Bailey pub off Grafton Street one night in December.

"I was relieved to find another Belfast man in there by the name of Eric Wrixon. I hadn't planned on meeting him in there but he too had been part of the showband scene for so long. At this stage I was quite low on funds and managed to buy a half-pint of Guinness. So after exchanging pleasantries we decided that we were both on the same wavelength and a real group without artistic boundaries was what we both really wanted."[28]

Wrixon's pedigree was as long and colourful as Bell's – they had both played with Van Morrison's Them. For Bell, the same night was also his introduction to acid.

"The two of us swallowed half a tab each," remembers Bell. "For whatever reason we decided to keep the night going and chose the Countdown Club for our next stop. We knew a guy at the door and so we could get in for free, and I hadn't got a clue what band was meant to be playing that night. It turned out to be Phil and Brian with Orphanage. There are little things like that thrown throughout Lizzy's career which to me mean that this band in whatever format were going to make an impression on the music world. By the time we got in, Orphanage was already into their set whilst we were sipping cheap sherry in paper cups that were on sale at the venue. This was the night I met Phil Lynott and this was the night after a drug-fuelled introduction that we, together with Brian, decided to form a band that were to become known as Thin Lizzy. Philip still wasn't playing bass, but I was totally mesmerised by Brian's drumming and said to myself, 'I've got to get that guy for the band I'm going to form.' After talking for about ten minutes or so, while they took a break in the dressing room, I decided to stop beating around the bush and asked if they knew any bass players and drummers that may be interested in starting up a group. They were a bit vague and as I probably got the vibe they weren't interested themselves, I made my way to the exit but not before we exchanged phone numbers. As I was about to leave Phil shouted out, 'Look Eric, Brian and me will start a band with you under two conditions.' Number one was that we did some of his songs and, number two was that Phil played the bass. From there on in we were a band."[29]

Although a kick in the teeth for the other members of Orphanage, there was no ill feeling toward Phil or Brian for leaving. Joe Staunton recalls...

"When the group disbanded we were all very close and I kind of took it personally because I thought that they felt I wasn't up to their standards. At the same time after that we all kept in touch and Phil always inspired me so much to continue playing that I'm still doing it today. Even when Lizzy were riding high in the charts and when he'd come home he'd always look me up and we'd meet for a few drinks and it'd be great. He knew he had something that I hadn't but his encouragement is something that I'll never forget."[30]

2

EARLY DAYS

Christmas came and went and the band toasted the new year, not with gigs, but with rehearsals while the local press awaited the launch of the new "Bell/Lynott supergroup" as it was referred to in Pat Egan's beat column in the *New Spotlight* weekly music magazine. The envisaged three-piece now looked as if it might be a four-piece with Eric Wrixon coming in on keyboards. The band started rehearsals in the most miserable of circumstances. Eric Bell confirms:

"Our first rehearsal wasn't the most encouraging as we battled to scale the fence to get into a disused hall to practice. Worse again on a typical Dublin winter night which was so cold I can recall my eyes were the only visible part of my body."[1]

"The first session really was desperate but the germ was there. We used some of Skid Row's gear and it was very funny because Philip had decided to bring along his bass guitar. So we started a blues number… I was playing in C, Philip was in A, and the keyboard player, Eric Wrixon, didn't know whether he was playing a piano or a harp. Brian was the only one who seemed to know what he was doing. But there was something more – a good energy, nice dynamics, and we had nothing else going on at the time so we stuck it out."[2]

In January 1970 Terry O' Neill became manager of Thin Lizzy. O'Neill, hailing from Phibsboro in Dublin had actually been a drummer since about the age of twelve in a band called The Visitors:

"I first met Philip and Brian at St. Peter's Hall in Phibsboro when he was with the Black Eagles. From what I can recall, they played there regularly on Saturday nights while The Visitors, who eventually became The H Group, played there every Sunday night at a teenage hop."

O'Neill had originally been a roadie for the initial incarnation of Skid Row before Lynott convinced him to work for Lizzy when they formed. In October of 1970 O'Neill left, selling his interest in Lizzy to Brian Tuite and Peter Bardon.

However, the band had yet to decide upon a name. It was after rehearsals at the Countdown Club when the gear was being packed up, that they started throwing around a plethora of possible ideas. Book and film titles were considered. Eric Bell describes how Tin Lizzie became Thin Lizzy:

"I basically just said, 'What about Tin Lizzie?' [The name of a character in *The Dandy*] But the reaction was dreadful. All I could hear was someone saying, 'No, no'. At that point the only name we could come up with was Gulliver's Travels. So a little while later we went back down through all the names we had come up with and were worth repeating and Tin Lizzie was one of them. I had this idea that I'm from Belfast and down in Dublin they say t'in instead of thin and t'ick instead of thick. So I said if we call the band Thin Lizzy people will come out to see us in Dublin and say, 'Oh we're going to see Tin Lizzy tonight' and we'd say no its not Tin Lizzy it's Thin Lizzy, so we'd get some controversy going with the name. Everyone thought it was a great idea and the name stuck."[3]

Jim Fitzpatrick maintains that Lizzie also refers to a blonde girl called Liz Igoe who was one of the most stunning looking girls in Dublin at the time. He thinks that Lynott added the Tin because it scanned better. Fitzpatrick also remembers talking to Lynott about the old famous automobile, a Tin Lizzy. "He was really chuffed when I told him their slogan, 'Any colour you like as long as it's black.' Somewhere along the line it mutated into Thin Lizzy which was appropriate anyway."[4]

Whatever or wherever the source, the name stuck and a press release on 18 February, 1970 finally announced Thin Lizzy to the public. The band took some time out to play some relatively low-key gigs before their official debut at none other than the Countdown Club on 5th March. Because these gigs were interspersed with Eric and Phil touring the folk circuit to make a little extra money, it is difficult to ascertain which dates took place and which didn't.

After their inaugural gig at The Countdown, Eric Bell still has vivid memories of being with Phil in Dublin whilst the band continued to prepare for their big break:

"I remember waiting for Phil by Abbey Mooneys, it was so cold – I mean it wasn't natural. I'll always recall Phil lugging around his guitar case, which resembled a coffin, it was so big. There wasn't any handle on it so he had to use his two hands to lug this thing to wherever we would be rehearsing. Looking back on it now seems so ridiculous but that's what we had to do."[5]

It wasn't only falling into place musically, Ted Carroll had also returned to the fold after a stint in England trying to build up his record business.

With Lizzy becoming hot news in the press, interest soon filtered through to EMI Ireland. As a result they played an industry showcase gig at St. Aidan's Hall on July 4. Though well down the bill behind Granny's Intentions and the Urge, Lizzy never doubted their ability as musicians nor their faith in the material Phil was writing.

Rumours abounded that Pink Floyd producer Norman Smith was flying in especially to catch the new band's performance. Lizzy won out on the night and earned themselves a chance to record a one-off single for EMI. The resulting session was recorded at Trend Studio under the watchful eye of studio owner John D'ardis. Back in the early seventies Trend Studios was off Baggot St, near St. Stephen's Green. Originally D'ardis worked at the Eamonn Andrews Studios as a lowly paid junior engineer until starting Trend Studios, which is now situated on Princes St in Dublin. D'ardis recalls his first introduction to Lynott:

"Lynott showed up with two great guitar players, Eric Bell and Gary Moore to try and cut some demos. Unlike showband material, his was all original and completely different. I liked his voice and his style, and as I was writing songs at the time, I eventually asked him to demo one of mine. The first single, 'The Farmer' was actually recorded here at Trend Studios. He had a problem with the b-side in that none of the other songs were beyond their rough demo form and the single was due to be issued. So he asked me if he could use the song he had demo'd for me called, 'I Need You'. From what I can recall there was only a pressing of about 500 copies and because of later success, the item has become a much sought after collectors item."[6]

Before the eventual release of "The Farmer", the band concluded that a keyboard player didn't quite fit in with their plans and, as finances were tight, Wrixon was eased out of the band.

'The Farmer' came out on 31 July and managed to sell 283 copies, whilst the remainder were most probably melted down and recycled. Now it has been known to fetch prices in the region of £800 by Lizzy enthusiasts. The failure of the single left a lot of disappointment within the Lizzy camp.

However, the management, now consisting of Ted Carroll, Brian Tuite and Peter Bardon, maintained their faith in the material young Lynott was coming up with.

By September 1970 Lizzy was attracting interest from abroad. Frank Rogers, brother of singer Clodagh and A&R man at Decca had originally arrived in Dublin to check out Ditch Cassidy and his band. The gig at the Zhivago Club didn't quite go to plan as Ditch had an enormous fight with his band members, and they in turn refused to back him at the audition. Lizzy found themselves as a hastily arranged substitute for Ditch's backing band, playing for about half an hour or so. Rogers recalls the event with relish:

"While I was at Decca working as a label manager I got a call from Brian Tuite about a guy called Ditch Cassidy, who was Ireland's answer to Joe Cocker. So he got Cassidy and Lizzy together for a showcase gig, which of course never includes a big audience. It was a free flight and accommodation situation, so of course I went over to Ireland with Neil Slater, another producer, to check Ditch out. Lizzy was backing Ditch and after Ditch had finished I asked Lizzy to play something. They played a few originals and I think they threw in a Hendrix number. But I thought they were great, they projected well and to be honest I was fascinated by Phil, with the huge afro and his pencil-thin frame. Immediately I wanted to sign them and I did. Basically I rang Decca and said I thought I had found something, which they took my word on and the deal was wrapped up pretty quickly. Back in those days there was a little more leeway for a guy like me to make those kinds of decisions. A&R men back then could make a judgement and have it seen through by the record label they were working with."

In turn Rogers decided to shelve plans to sign Ditch and instead focused his attention on Thin Lizzy. He convinced the producer Scott English to go over to Ireland to check the band out for himself. In a few short weeks a second audition was set up at the Peacock Theatre on Abbey Street where an electrifying performance from Lizzy signalled a change in their fortunes. Rogers duly signed the band to Decca and had Scott English handle the production.

On the 2 January, 1971 Thin Lizzy travelled to London to record some material for their new label. On the ferry they had an extraordinary stroke of luck, as the increasingly influential DJ, John Peel, happened to be returning from a short break in Ireland:

"Well that was a strange thing indeed because I was coming back from one of my regrettably few trips to Ireland. I'd only been there for a week, driving around looking at things – and on the ferry on the way back this bloke came up to me and said, 'Hello you're John Peel, aren't you?' And I admitted this was true and he said, 'We're in a band and we're going to be playing in Britain and it's the first time we've been over here' and so on. Then he said, 'Keep an eye out for us' and of course that bloke was Phil Lynott from Thin Lizzy."[7]

The band didn't waste a second of their time in London and were in the Decca studios in West Hampstead with producer Scott English by the 4th January. English was no stranger to fame having written the Jeff Beck single "Hi-Ho Silver Lining" amongst other notable hits. The band's first album was recorded in a mere five days and finished by 9th January, The session was engineered by Peter Rynston. Scott English then mixed the album over a period of two days.

Just after Christmas 1970, Ted Carroll took on the full-time role of Lizzy manager along with Brian Tuite and Peter Bardon. Though he had been monitoring the bands' progress over the last six months he now felt the time was right to renew his acquaintance with Lynott. Carroll recalls Brian Tuite and his constant worrying:

"Not many people know this, but at one point we were working so hard, and Brian was driving through Dublin one day and started feeling quite ill. He promptly drove to a local hospital. He then quite calmly explained to the staff that he was suffering from a heart attack. And would you believe it, he was having a mild heart attack! It could only happen to Brian."

With an album under their belts, Lizzy returned for a few Irish dates, but they were still at a loss for a title for their first recording. As deadlines drew near the only suggestion thus far was "The Friendly Ranger" but this was dropped in favour of an eponymous title. The release of the album was set for the 30 April.

John Slater, who worked at Decca as a record sleeve co-ordinator between 1964 and 1978, recalls a youthful Phil Lynott coming in to his office to discuss the cover artwork.

"I certainly remember the more amusing parts of the meeting, that's for sure. I was taken aback when we met because there standing in front of me was a tall Irish black man, it didn't seem to fit. The lingo he was coming up with was very hippie in style, 'man this' and 'man that'… but he was full of ideas. His first notion was for a burning hand coming out of a freshly dug grave! He wasn't interested in doing it with a cartoon twist, it had to be real life. First of all I'm thinking how am I going to talk him out of this? In the end we managed it, though it was looking dodgy for a time. Because of their name, Thin Lizzy, we thought it might be best to play on the whole American automobile angle. In the end that's what we did settle on, though we couldn't find the right car so I think we ended up using a Vauxhall Victor or something like that."[8]

Somehow lack of communication between record company and the band meant the initial album cover artwork arrived back with the wrong title, as Philip Tapsfield of the Decca Art Dept. recalls:

"One of our in-house artists, David Ansty, designed their sleeve. He actually did the sleeve with the name 'Tin Lizzy' instead of "Thin Lizzy". When they came in Scott English was with them, a big guy with a beard, he had the tapes wrapped in silver foil, which we of course we thought was something entirely different, but he assured us it was to protect the tapes from rogue magnetic fields."

Apparently rather than trying to correct the error, Decca executives initially tried to persuade the group to change their name. After refusing, the release of the album was delayed by a week while the artwork was corrected.

With all the hassle of getting the album cover right, Ted Carroll in particular winces at the memory:

"I can't say I was a fan of the first Thin Lizzy album cover. Walt McGuire, the Decca American counterpart commissioned different artwork for the first album and got it. It now seems to be a collector's item."[9]

Indeed, the US version, which wasn't released until the latter part of 1971, has a miniature cartoon Model T Ford (a Tin Lizzy) driving over a naked female hip. The US back cover features a fish-eye view of the band taken in Dublin the previous autumn by Roy Esmonde.

The majority of the album was credited to Lynott and was almost a personal ode to both his upbringing and his professional situation. The album standout without a doubt is "Look What The Wind Just Blew In". As Shay Healy, producer of the RTE Documentary, *The Rocker* later commented:

"One thing that always struck me about Philip was his use of clichés, he took songs such as "Look What The Wind Blew In" and turned it into a tale of teenage conceit and bluff all at the same time. The image of the young man in his prime, being outwardly casual with a girl as well as maintaining a dismissive streak. He never hid the fact that his romantic outlook was at the forefront of many of his songs and this transcended to the people and they more or less ate it up because it was so easy to identify with."[10]

Lyrically, Lynott was still somewhat naïve. Tracks such as "Remembering" and "The Friendly Ranger At Clontarf Castle" sound fragmented. Also, long self-indulgent instrumental breaks attempt to add muscle but in fact hold back the immediate impact of some tracks. A more simplistic approach would have worked better. Perhaps a lack of studio direction didn't help. "Eire" was, of course, a salute to the homeland and recognition of its inspiration to them as musicians and to Philip as chief songwriter.

"Diddy Levine" highlights Philip's reluctance to let go of the circumstances of his upbringing. Sooner or later, everybody who had some impact on Lynott would be carefully woven into his poems and songs. For instance "Saga Of The Ageing Orphan" is almost a namecheck riddle. It was a pattern that would be religiously followed throughout his career, especially in his latter years. "Clifton Grange Hotel" is an obvious tribute to his mother's hotel. After spending a great deal of his summer holidays there during both his formative and latter teenage years, Philip had met an alarming array of different characters and these inspired an apt lyric.

In later years, some of Lynott's songs seemed too contrived to ring true, but these early recordings are both innocent and honest. "Ray Gun" is Lizzy's voyage into what became Rory Gallagher territory, not strictly blues but made seemingly all the more simple by Eric Bell's playing.

The initial UK pressing was 2000 copies. As a debut, the album was strong, but with its Celtic overtones the likelihood of gaining decent exposure in England was always going to be slim. Their following, though steady, had not yet gained sufficient momentum to push the album anywhere near the charts, though it did get significant airplay on Kid Jensen's Radio Luxembourg show. Jensen would prove to be an extremely useful ally in the early days as Ted Carroll recalls:

"The major bonus for this record was the fact that Kid Jenson worked so hard to promote it, making it his number one album on the Radio Luxemburg charts, that was a great break for us. Also John Peel was instrumental in hoisting it upon the unsuspecting listener. Those guys gave Lizzy the kind of break you needed back in those days."[11]

The reviews of the album were mixed, though this didn't deter a band already hungry for success. An English tour was booked to promote their first record, and Ted Carroll remembers that there were a few problems:

"Our first gig in England as Thin Lizzy was upstairs at Ronnie Scott's," Ted Carroll recalls, "for which we got paid five quid. On the other hand our second gig was supporting Status Quo at the Marquee. This was the gig we remembered for all the wrong reasons. It was Easter week and Phil had a fender bass with a huge hole through the body of it and he broke a string. All the shops were closed – so he ended up borrowing one from Quo. Similarly, it was suggested to Brian Downey that he could use their drum kit as well, except for the snare, which was his own. This would help speed up the changeover. So all the rest of the gear went into the back of the van and minor worries dismissed. We finished the gig and by the time we got to the van we discovered that all our gear was stolen, including Phil's bass, which was being bought on a hire purchase basis. He was like a dog over that."[12]

Lizzy were already demonstrating the sort of determination to prove that nothing was going to step in their way. Clearly Lynott had an ego to match his height, but his nature rarely reached the point of sheer arrogance.

According to Frank Rogers, the band knew that they needed adequate representation if they were going to progress further:

"A guy called Peter Walsh ran an agency at the time and Lizzy were sorely lacking in this department. We were really desperate to get an agent, so I took a test pressing of the album to a guy who used to work there called John Salter, but he wasn't too sure about it. There was also a junior representative there called Chris Morrison and he just went mad for it. Soon after that he came on board and started getting bookings for the band."

Another adopted Dubliner Smiley Bolger, roadied for the band for a while. Bolger recalls the circumstances of the band's first UK tour:

"I was reporting for *Spotlight* magazine at the time and I was travelling around with them doing gigs, London to Manchester for £50. That's the way it went at the time. Everyone back then was given a couple of quid a day to live on. I was helping out here and there with the lights while Peter Eustace was taking care of sound and with all this going on then I had to review the gig later – nothing biased going on there at all, I may add."[13]

Peter Eustace, the main Lizzy roadie from the beginning of their career right through to the bitter end, had also started to work for them around the same time:

"I actually started working for the band doing the lights and moving equipment around before I settled into the position of sound man. Basically they couldn't get anyone else to do the job. Because they didn't really have enough money for lights Phil wanted to keep me on sound. Even at that point Phil used to take a great interest in the sound and what was going on. He was a perfectionist, a hard working perfectionist."[14]

By the time negotiations started for their second Lizzy record in the summer of 1971, their main Irish competition Skid Row had just released their second album for CBS entitled *34 Hours*. It was the follow-up to their self-titled debut release in the early months of 1970. Though both albums were received rather modestly, they do serve as primary examples of Irish rock 'n' roll. At this time Lizzy were perceived as more as a folk-rock outfit. Compared to sheer raw energy of Skid Row there was too little rock and roll and too much pining for the homeland in their songs.

"Early Lizzy when I saw them were alright," remembers Skid Row mainman Shiels. "I thought 'Whiskey In The Jar' was a terrible load of cobblers. We didn't see that as playing, being musicians that is. We never saw Lizzy as posing any threat to the progress of Skid Row. We were both three-pieces and that's where the resemblance ended. A couple of tracks off the first album were good but that's about all. I suppose I was impressed but there was nothing really there that overwhelmed me."[15]

Within the Skid Row camp all was not well. Their young, gifted guitarist, Gary Moore was becoming extremely disgruntled with the band's emphasis on showmanship.

"I left after the second album," Moore recalls, "because I felt that they were starting to concentrate more on going down well with the crowds as opposed to playing well. At that stage of the proceedings Brush would be prepared to go out and do anything just to get a response from the audience. He was more interested in playing 'Johnny B. Goode' at ninety miles an hour, taking his shirt off and bouncing his bass off the floor and his chest, which is all well and good, but at the time I was very much into wanting to play."[16]

Another potential big break was almost lost when Ted Carroll arranged for Radio Luxembourg DJ, Kid Jensen, to see Lizzy live:

"Kid Jensen drove up from London with me to see the band live for the very first time. We stopped for a meal on the way and arrived at The Country Club at about 8.15 p.m. just in time to hear the final strains of Lizzy's last number. They had originally been due to go onstage at 8.30, but had to go on early because Albert Lee's band, Head, Hands and Feet, who were 'getting it together in the country' at a nearby cottage, had been booked at the last minute. They had become regulars at the bar downstairs and had promised to play a gig for free and this was the last chance to do so, as they were returning to London the following week. Afterwards Kid Jensen and his girlfriend drove back to Manchester and partied with Thin Lizzy until the early hours in the bar at the Clifton Grange Hotel. However Kid had to return to London the following morning, as he had to be back in Luxembourg in time for his Sunday night show and so could not stay to see Lizzy play the Manchester Apollo."

Meanwhile Lizzy were becoming frustrated about the progress of their second album. Decca wasn't ready to release a new album and a compromise was reached whereby the band recorded four new tracks for a proposed EP. The EP was recorded rather briskly at Decca's West Hampstead studios over the 14th to 16th of June. Entitled 'New Day' it was released on August 20th and it neither impressed the record company or the public. Ted Carroll remembers the confusion surrounding the "New Day" cover:

"We asked Decca to release it in a picture sleeve, but they refused because of the cost. So the band decided to do their own sleeve. Some guy called Rodney, who was recommended to us by a friend who worked for a booking agency in Bristol, was enlisted to furnish the artwork. We decided to go the whole hog and make the cover a gatefold (possibly the first 7" ever released in the UK). A friend called Tony Bradfield, who we knew from around the club scene, printed the sleeve in Dublin. We printed 2000 covers and shipped most of them to the Decca pressing plant in New Malden. However they arrived late and the first 500 copies went out without the picture sleeves."[17]

The "New Day" EP consisted of "Dublin", "Things Ain't Working Out Down At The Farm," "Remembering Part 2" and "Old Moon Madness". Although it did not make the charts, the EP would leave its mark on those who consider it a defining moment of Lizzy's Decca years. Frank Rogers:

"The 'New Day' EP came about as a result of the promotions department. They felt that if they didn't have product to work on for the band, they couldn't increase their profile. With only one album out every year, the hype will only last so long, and with Lizzy on the road, it was hard to keep their name on the lips of the public. It now changes hands for about 100 quid a pop."

Shortly after the EP was completed, Lizzy returned to Ireland for well-received shows at the National Stadium and at a free concert in Blackrock. The band was supported by Elmer Fudd and Mellow Candle amongst others, and Pat Egan confirmed that the Stadium gig was "the best money's worth at a Dublin concert for years." Brendan Shorthall, a Dubliner who worked in the media back in those days recalls the day Lizzy came home:

"There was a big buzz around and I remember people saying that Phil and the boys were after making it to the big time. They had recorded an album but it was in Ireland that their biggest fanbase lay. I heard all sorts of stories that the band only flew in after some serious conversations with record company people and the rumour was that it was just bullshit. The amount of hype surrounding them was extremely significant but when confirmation hit the streets that they really were going to play, the fans were delighted. I remember it clearly to this day and will never forget the almost surreal atmosphere of the whole event."[18]

Convinced that they had the right producer in Nick Tauber, Decca tried coercing the band into recording at De Lane Lea studios in Wembley, where Queen were working up material for their debut release. Brian Downey is one who felt that the band should have returned to the Decca studios at West Hampstead:

"The drum sound at De Lane Lea was terrible, and in fact the whole album still sounds flat to me."[19] Downey's argument is backed up by listening to the self-titled debut album from Queen.

After the relative commercial failure of the Lizzy debut, the pressure to produce a successful second album was mounting. After failing to secure the production services of Martin Birch, who had worked with Fleetwood Mac and Deep Purple, the band settled for Decca's choice of Nick Tauber.

The band had little time to write material due to their winter touring schedules, but pressure from the record company dictated an album was to be out before spring 1972. Having chosen the strongest tracks for their debut, as well as putting songs towards the EP, it left Lizzy with little new material as sessions began in late 1971.

Time and money were short, and unreliable transport wasted any opportunities to sit down and write whilst touring the UK. Ted Carroll recalls one such incedent on the M1 after a gig in Chester during September:

"The engine in the transit van, which had been bought off Grannies Intentions for 100 quid, started knocking on the way home after the gig and we had to keep stopping to let it cool down. It finally gave up the ghost on the M1, somewhere in Northamptonshire. We called the AA who towed us to a deserted garage, and we then had to wait for about an hour for a taxi, which took us home to London. The cost was 25 quid and after we got paid 20 quid for the gig that left us with a net loss of a fiver, not including petrol, oil and repairs to the van."

The new material sounded far too dilute when it hit the shelves early in 1972. The band chose to title the album after their two previous bands, hence *Shades Of A Blue Orphanage*. Of the nine songs, all but one is credited to Lynott. The opening track "The Rise and Dear Demise of the Funky Nomadic Tribes" was indicative of the fashion for tracks with extremely long titles. Downey opens with a catchy beat, but as the only group composition it lacks focus and is a consortium of half-baked ideas and is an extremely indulgent album opener. However the album's saviour comes in the shape of one of Lynott's best early compositions, "Buffalo Gal". Lynott's vocal is stretched – at given points sounds like he might explode – but he maintains the understated nature of the song and portrays an extremely picturesque yet elegiac version of his wild west. Lynott also can't help but make reference to personal aspects in his life when he sings, "Dry your eyes and I'll apologise for all the lies."

The album unfortunately takes the first of a few fatal downward spirals in the well-intentioned but unsuccessful Elvis tribute "I Don't Want To Forget How to Jive". It is a loose affair with Lynott trying his best early Elvis lingo. Lines like "I don't want to forget how to jive, I just want to be alive…" sound severely ad-libbed. It would be several years before Lynott would eventually succeed in producing a better tribute.

"Sarah (Version 1)" is a heart-felt and melancholic ode of admiration to Lynott's grandmother as well as a reflection of his childhood circumstances. The album continues with "Brought Down" where the game of love is once enjoyed, then cursed by the tribulation of a pain too much to overcome. "Brought down and I don't think I can get up again," sings Lynott. Riddled with namechecks – Dr. Strangely Strange, one of Ireland's leading bands at the time come in for a mention – Lynott sounds desperate as the song starts to fade. His moorings lost, he is struggling to get back on his own two feet – a theme that would be re-visited in the years to come, though under entirely different circumstances.

"Baby Face" on the other hand is a basic straightforward rocker in the Ritchie Blackmore vein. If anything it's an amusing tale about a 'chick' of the day. Ironically, it was around this time Ritchie Blackmore of Deep Purple fame tried to woo Lynott into a super-group he intended to call Baby Face. Apparently the recording of *Shades* had nearly ground to a halt because of this intervention. Lynott eventually decided to ride his luck with Lizzy, as opposed to jumping on Blackmore's bandwagon. Lynott's decision to concentrate on his own material was a wise one, as Blackmore's proposed supergroup did little more than jam around in the De Lane Lea studios.

"Chatting Today" was a left-over track from the first album.

"Phil had told me about the songs he had written," Eric Bell remembers, "and we suggested that he come over to my flat to listen to them. One of the very first songs he played me was 'Chatting Today'. I could hear how I could complement his songs with my style of guitar playing and it was great, the chord changes, everything seemed to fit."[20]

"Call the Police", another standout from the album, is a slinky number relying heavily on Bell's excellent riffing and Lynott scatting around the lyrics. Johnny – a familiar name in Lynott compositions of later years – makes his debut. Johnny would later become Lynott's alter ego – an escape route when questioned about the autobiographical lyrical content of his songs. Writing in the third person the lyrics ooze classic Lynott chaos.

The album closes with the rather revealing lyric of "Shades Of A Blue Orphanage" describing Phil's childhood or, more pertinently, how he now perceived it as a young adult. The under-age drinking, lurking around on corners, looking for trouble in the back streets, gazing at heroes up on the silver cinema screen. Larger than life figures held a close association for the young Lynott and it would be one of the most intensely autobiographical songs to ever appear on a Lizzy album as Lynott gazes back across the land-scape of his youth.

In a short interview with Robert Brinton of *Disc* magazine, Lynott con-fided his thoughts on writing the album.

"I am into developing the melodic side, it's important but that's not to say I'm or the band are going to do it at the cost of the feeling we try to put into our music. *Shades* was really an experiment with a number of sad and blue songs, relating to a certain time in our past. The climate has changed towards the singles market. There's a new market now unaffected by the old image stigma. The young people are into sounds. Most places we play we get a really good response. When you're on the road it gives you a chance to pick up on it..."[21]

Nevertheless, the general consensus among band members was one of mild disappointment with the album. The title was one that unhinged old roots, so for the cover the band considered something from the local library archives that might compliment the album's content. The band agreed on the orphanage theme and the art department at Decca decided to follow the idea through. John Slater confirms:

"I went through a list of material, which I deemed to be suitable, and made the proposal to them. I found this photograph of a few children posing in rags and they went with it, but the guy who was in charge of European marketing objected to it. He felt that the cover resembled people, or in this case children, from a concentration camp. Of course this subject hit a little too close to home for the man was Jewish and that idea was rather quickly deleted. However it did remain for the British prints and the band felt happy enough to go with it."[22]

By the time winter gave way to spring the band were in extensive rehearsals for a tour to support their new album. They were getting paid so little for English gigs, that short Irish tours were always scheduled to supplement their income. Indeed this was a ploy that Lizzy and Lynott used wisely for their duration as a band. There was no single issued to promote the album, so for the moment Lizzy's live shows were the only way to raise their profile. The more often they played live, the more exposure, hence the likelihood of increased record sales – it was a subject that was becoming a topic of discussion within the Decca boardroom.

Lizzy's tour to support the album release ran throught Feb/Mar '72, with Arrival, Worth and Barabas. Worth did part of the tour and Barbaras filled the remainder of the gigs. All the bands travelled on a large single decker coach and used the same PA, as Ted Carroll recalls:

"During the course of the tour, romance blossomed between Diane Birch, one of the singers with Arrival, and Eric Bell. They ended up together for quite some time after the tour had finished."

Released on the 10 March, Lizzy's second LP, like its predecessor, failed to make an impression on the British charts. But the reviews in general were upbeat and the college circuit beckoned once again. On 16 March they set out on a two-month trek across Britain that would take them well into the summer.

The band returned to Ireland in mid-July to gear up for a ten-day tour.

Further bookings ran into October, though not without the occasional venture into the studio to work on material for their next album. During their busy touring schedule the band would relax by toying around with the old traditional Irish standard "Whiskey In The Jar". By the end of August they were in Europe for a series of dates in Germany, Belgium, Holland and Switzerland before returning to the studio to master the tracks for their forthcoming album in early October.

Towards the end of July '72 Brian Tuite and Carroll had decided to try and find someone in the UK to take over from Brian as co-manager. Tuite wanted to concentrate on his business interests and although Lizzy were still popular at home and starting to build up a following in the UK, progress was slow, and Tuite was tired of having to continually lend money to the band.

Carroll approached Status Quo's manager Colin Johnson about a deal. He had been working out of Billy Gaffe's office (Rod Stewart's manager) above the Marquee club on Wardour Street. Johnson was initially interested, but wanted to see the band live again. Carroll then asked Lizzy's agent Chris Morrison to arrange a gig as soon as possible at the Marquee so that he could be sure that Johnson would make a decision as quickly as possible. Carroll remembers:

"After I explained why I wanted the gig, Chris responded, 'What's wrong with me? I've worked my ass off getting the band gigs and you want to take them to Colin Johnson.' Chris was managing a band called Danta, an afro rock band who had a single on CBS that hadn't sold, but because of the band's fire-eating conga drummer, they had plenty of gigs. I had thought of Colin Johnson as a potential manager because he already managed a successful band and because I believed that he would be able to shoulder the financial burden, until Lizzy was able to become financially secure."

Carroll quickly agreed with Morrison as he had seen how hard he had worked with filling Danta's gig dates, and aside of that, as Carroll remembers, "Chris used to telephone CBS every day when Danta had their single out to check up on sales figures." Carroll reasoned that even though Morrison had no money, he would ensure that the band had enough dates to make ends meet.

After the lack of success of the second album, Carroll and Morrison decided that they would try to negotiate a release from the deal with Decca Records, so that they could secure a new deal and raise money to help finance the band. So after a discussion with Frank Rogers at Decca, it was decided that Lizzy would record just one more single and if that wasn't a success, they would be let go.

By now Decca were pressuring for a single release. The management convinced the group to record their rocked up version of "Whiskey In the Jar", despite Lynott's reluctance. He had his mind set on one of his own compositions "Black Boys On The Corner" with "Whiskey…" making up the B-side.

"Originally we were going to bring this old Irish ballad out as the A-side in Ireland and flip it as the B-side in England," Ted Carroll explains. "But we were so happy with the arrangement that it was the A-side in England as well."[23]

"Whiskey In The Jar" and "Black Boys On The Corner" were recorded in studio 4 at Tollington Park in just one day in October with the arrangement of "Whiskey" being jointly accredited to all three members.

Around this time a German guy waltzed into the band offices in London with an unusual proposal.

"When we moved to London it was very rough, we were virtually starving," explains Eric Bell. "To keep the band on the road we needed so much money each week for roadies and for the office. Basically this guy spoke with our manager and he said he wanted us to record an album of Deep Purple's greatest hits. He wanted us to call the band Funky Junction. So, we were booked into a London studio but Phil said he couldn't sing like Ian Gillan. We knew someone from Dublin who played with the band Elmer Fudd, called Benny White and they played a lot of Deep Purple covers. I think he brought over the keyboard player from that band as well. So we ended up paying them something like 60 quid each plus expenses to come over and record the album. We actually ended up writing some stuff as fillers for the album ourselves. I even did my interpretation of a Hendrixesque "Danny Boy". When the album emerged it was called *Funky Junction Pay Tribute to Deep Purple*. Either way we got paid and the money earned from that venture went straight back into the office to keep us going for another while."[24]

The album itself has now become a collector's item and is hard to track down. Exorbitant amounts of money have been known to change hands for it these days.

Up to now Ted Carroll and Brian Tuite had been managing the band on a shoestring budget, and though they had released two albums, Thin Lizzy's profile was no bigger. It would be difficult for them to last playing in this division and Carroll wisely saw the need for progress in order to salvage their career. He offered to buy Brian Tuite out in order to search for another partner to lift Lizzy up another division. Tuite accepted the offer and a chance conversation with Chris Morrison, the band's booking agent, brought about a new co-manager for the band. Morrison promptly got the band a prestigious slot supporting one of the hottest glam rock outfits of the day – Slade. With the tour set to begin in early November the new management went full steam ahead into national promotion. The tour featured a three-band bill in the guise of Lizzy as openers, Suzi Quatro next and Slade headlining. Lizzy were only given a short but sweet 45-minute slot, but the tour would prove a turning point for both the band and their management.

With a string of hit singles and albums Slade had already achieved the adulation that Lizzy craved. Lynott always thought he was destined for super stardom and he was eager to get there as soon as possible. Patience was the buzzword amongst management. If they could turn Slade fans' attention to Lizzy they could well be onto a winner. Downey claims Lizzy were 'incidental' on the bill, and the first night at Newcastle did little to disprove his theory.

"Slade were the real bees knees at the time of that tour," according to soundman Peter Eustace. "We were just stunned by this band that would go out there and get everyone going. In Newcastle, Lizzy went on, came off and I believe it was Chas Chandler [Slade's geordie manager] who went into the dressing room and just went crazy at the band. He said, 'You know, if that's the kind of show that this band puts on you can just forget it, you're just off the tour.' Even in the early days Philip didn't do a lot of moving. He'd say nothing between songs, basically he was very shy. That is the guy that I remember on stage, shy but very charismatic. He actually broke down in tears at this criticism that night, but from then on he knew he had to get his act together. From that point on he started to chat with the audience and to do that he had to trust the audience. He had to give them what was inside him and I don't think he had ever really done that with anyone before in his life. The audience took to this, this sincerity and this sort of humility and that was quite unusual…"[25]

On 14 November the band returned to the BBC studios for a couple of sessions. Primarily used for promoting their latest single the band recorded dazzling versions of "Whiskey In The Jar" and "Gonna Creep Up On You" before making their way to Manchester for a gig at the Free Trade Hall. Manchester was still Lynott's second home, as Philomena continued to run her successful hotel enterprise. Naturally this became their digs anytime the Lizzies found Manchester on their gig list.

"There would be big parties thrown after the gig back at the hotel, when they were playing in Manchester," Graham Cohen recalls. "You'd have your usual guys around, Downey would be in one corner and then Philip would be in another and the girls would be screaming all over the place – within reason of course. Those times though were always electric when Lizzy hit town, something extraordinary in fact."[26]

Just after playing the Top Rank venue in Doncaster on November 22nd with Slade and Suzi Quatro, everyone decided to drive to Glasgow immediately after the gig so as to get some sleep before the next show at Green's Playhouse. Lizzy raced off in the long wheelbase 35cwt Ford transit which they shared with their equipment, PA and road crew of Pete Eustace and 'Black' Charlie. Once more, as Ted Carroll recalls, it was never quite plain sailing:

"The van broke down between Carlisle and Glasgow at about two in the morning leaving the band stranded in the middle of nowhere. Just as we were about to give up hope of making it to the gig the next day, help arrived in the form of Slade's road crew in their seven tonne truck. They stopped, hooked a rope to the Lizzy-mobile and towed the band into Glasgow. We finally arrived at the bed and breakfast stopover at about half seven in the morning, just in time for breakfast. The next day we arranged for the band to rent a truck from Avis and they all squeezed into the cab for the next two dates on the tour, Edinburgh and Southampton. After Southampton there was a break for a few days, so I drove the truck back up to Glasgow and collected the repaired Lizzy-mobile. Then I returned it to the band in London, in time for them to finish off the last two dates of the tour in Cardiff and Bristol."

"About three weeks before the tour was due to start, we heard that Suzi Quatro had been added to the tour and RAK records wanted her to use our PA. We agreed, and charged RAK 300 quid a week. Up until recently Lizzy were still using a 400watt system with 4x100 watt columns. We heard about a new top class 1200watt system, that had only been used once for a UK tour by the Everly Brothers. We managed to buy it for 1400 quid although that didn't include the mixing desk, so we bought a 6 channel mixing unit to link up with the one we already had, and some multi-channel cable and hooked the whole lot up and prayed that it would work. So with Suzi using our PA it was paid for in one fell swoop.

When we first discussed purchasing this larger PA, once crucial element in the whole deal was physical size. We got exact dimensions from the company that was supplying the rig and I very carefully calculated that we would be able to get the new PA, band's gear and the band and two roadies into the Thin Lizzy 35cwt transit van. This was essential, as we couldn't afford to hire a larger truck. I calculated that if we got rid of the second row of seats in the van, we would have room. We had a double seat from an old tram that had come out of Grannies Intentions' old van and had been lying around my flat. This would only take up half as much space as the row of seats we had removed."[27]

All involved with the Lizzy organisation testify to the importance of the

Slade tour. To capitalise on the exposure, Decca whisked the band into the studios to produce a follow-up to *Shades*. In the meantime, they released "Whiskey In The Jar", much to the disgust of the band, who thought it was sending out the wrong signals. It had taken so long for Thin Lizzy to build an identity with their audience and now this was in danger of being destroyed by a rocked up version of an old traditional Irish ballad about trigger-happy highwaymen.

"Whiskey" was too long to be considered for radio airplay. The edited version, however, lost some of the daring mystique of the song and actually cut out the lyrical and adventurous climax of the tale. The recording also features Lynott with a very husky tone, reminiscent of Rod Stewart.

The single was issued about a week or so into the tour and began its slow climb up the charts, so slow in fact that it wasn't until the following year that it would breach the top forty in Britain. It would be Lizzy's first chart entry and again their cause was championed by Radio Luxembourg DJ, Kid Jensen.

Lynott's mixed feelings at the success of the single was probably borne out of ego. Even though he had composed some rather touching and idly pleasant songs, commercially accessible material was conspicuous by its absence. The record company considered they needed a hit, and if that happened by exploiting the band's Irishness and playing on the "paddy" angle, then so be it. After all, it was about time that they started to re-coup on their serious financial outlay.

By Christmas "Whiskey in the Jar" hit the No 1 spot in Ireland and stayed on the chart for over four months. Meanwhile in England it would take just a couple of more weeks to end their chart drought and stabilise the band's stature in the industry. Eric Bell remembers how they nearly keeled over upon hearing the news via telegram that the song sat at No 23 in the UK charts. Within a short time it climbed to No 6 on the English charts, helped a little by their management's ingenious notion of sending miniature bottles of whiskey to influential DJ's to soften them up and promote the single. In Britain the single stayed on the charts for twelve weeks, giving Lizzy ample time to milk the promotional possibilities set up by their management.

Lizzy's first gig of the New Year was held in Dublin at the National Stadium on 10 January, perfectly timed to exploit their current chart status. In fact, the tour dates for the opening six months of the year were actually quite sporadic due to the number of promotional appearances for "Whiskey". In order to sustain the band's high profile, the management contacted Tony Brainsby, a publicity agent based in London. Brainsby's customer list

41

included some of the most prestigious names in rock 'n' roll. Paul McCartney and Wings, Mott the Hoople, the Small Faces and Queen.

"There was an unusual quality to both Queen and Lizzy because with all the groups I've handled, I'd say only two made an instant impression on me and that was the both of them," Brainsby recounted to Laura Jackson, author of *Mercury, King Of Queen*. "They knew what they wanted and knew they'd be big – it was just a question of finding the way. In my experience that's not normal, but it's a huge advantage for a PR consultant when a group has that depth of belief in themselves. It's also that edge that was going to make them stars."[28]

When the much-coveted spot on *Top Of The Pops* arose, Lynott and Lizzy went for it hook, line and sinker. Lynott tackled the mimed performance with a look of youthful arrogance – although it may have been sheer nerves upon the face of a new kid on the block.

Although "Whiskey" blew out the cobwebs and helped the Lizzy coffers, it had an adverse reaction on lead guitar player Eric Bell. He was soon harbouring doubts about the internal politics of the music business. His concerns were further exacerbated when the tribute to Deep Purple eventually surfaced in January of 1973.

"There's a live photo which is apparently us on the front cover while the back cover is plastered with all this blurb enthusing about the band Funky Junction," complained Bell. "But it didn't even exist. That really showed me what the music business was all about. It's a joke but it's still part of a hidden Lizzy history."[29]

In a strange twist of fate, Lynott and Lizzy also performed "Whiskey" on the children's TV show *CrackerJack* which was presented by the late Leslie Crowther – Lynott's future father in law.

As opposed to touring in support of a new album, Lizzy found themselves being whisked across Europe to mime to playbacks as well as being interviewed about the most mundane topics over and over again. Though they did some gigs during February and March, it was the pressure from Decca to produce a suitable follow up to "Whiskey" that began to sit heavily on Lynott's shoulders. The *Shades* album was now almost a year old and they had yet to lay down any tracks for their forthcoming album.

Having been satisfied with the production job Nick Tauber did on *Shades*, the band recruited him once more and headed for A.I.R. studios in London to record their latest material. This session included 'Randolph's Tango' – a Lynott composition intended to be the ideal follow up to "Whiskey". The single has a delightful Mexican feel, emphasising Bell's carefree and distinctive Jose Feliciano-style guitar playing. Backed with a band composition called "Broken Dreams" featuring a coarse Lynott vocal, the bluesy overtone directly contrasted with the romantically playful and heartfelt love scenes portrayed in "Randolph's Tango".

Released on May 4 to little or no public acclaim, despite its charm, it was hardly the right track to follow up the success of "Whiskey". It was also released as a single in the States, but without the necessary promotion quickly disappeared without trace.

Around this time the band sat down with Peter Harvey of the *Record Mirror* at Tony Brainsby's office to share their thoughts about their current predicament and Lynott confided Lizzy's shortcomings in a frank conversation with Harvey:

"Well with 'Randolph's Tango' a lot of people simply didn't know it was us. Perhaps the song was too classy and that was its downfall. It was so subtle and easy on the ear that only people who listened to it as a special record managed to get off on it."[30]

On the other hand Bell simply stated… "I thought the record was a mistake, like Slade, every number has the same basic sound," while Lynott added, "Yeah, that's maybe the best way to do it for singles. Stick to the same sound with each record, then change when people are used to you and when you want to, do album tracks."[31]

The basic tone of the interview suggests the band were in as much as a quandary as the management and record label when it came to finding a suitable single.

The seeming reluctance of the public to fork out for this new original track was a kick in the teeth for the band, and Lynott in particular. The blow was softened slightly when the single reached No 14 in the Irish charts. It was possibly its failure to secure a spot in the British top forty that dictated that "Randolph's Tango" was not included on the band's forthcoming album.

However, before returning to the studios to record a new album they hopped over to Germany to play a short tour. Back at Decca studios in Tollington Park at the beginning of July, they commenced recording tracks that Lynott had written. These sessions clearly demonstrated a band enjoying a period of transition, with Lynott's songwriting showing maturity and and a newfound confidence.

The sessions for *Vagabonds of the Western World* provided plenty of material of which just eight songs made the final album cut. Intense pressure from Decca to include their top ten hit on the album was brushed aside as the band aimed to make a complete break from an image they considered somewhat cringe-worthy.

Aside of Nick Tauber taking control of production, the album was engineered by no less than four different people. Alan Harris, Alan Leaming,

Dave Baker and Pete Sweetenham all lent a hand, while Lynott once more picked up an associate producer credit. During the mixing Lizzy took time out to record another BBC session on the 31 July putting down "Gonna Creep Up On You", "Little Girl In Bloom" and the title track of their forthcoming album "Vagabonds Of The Western World".

The start of August found the band publicising their upcoming album, but still with no sign of a single to break it. The marketing men at Decca were seemingly stumped. The forthcoming album fulfilled their contractual obligation to Decca, so the pressure was building to turn in another hit single, if the contract was to be renewed. Rogers handled the talks:

"When they were coming to the end of their contract, we started negotiations and came up with the idea of producing a single. So I went to the Decca financial director, but to be honest we just couldn't afford them. In the end we managed to get Ted Carroll and Chris Morrison to agree a meeting and went out to lunch. We wanted to extend the deal, so during the meal there was a few bottles of plonk taken, which was quite potent. By the time we got back to the management offices Ted and Chris were willing to extend the contract for a six-month option. Now in the offices Morrison kept, if the weather was good the sun used to beat in through the window and on this day it was just the case. Ted Carroll denies this to this day, but right in the middle of negotiations he fell asleep after the wine and the sun coming in the window got the better of him. I remember Morrison nudging him trying to get him to wake without making it obvious. Anyway we did the deal and Lizzy came up with 'The Rocker'."

With their strongest album to date tucked neatly into the Lizzy holster, the band were particularly proud and felt that with a serious push the album could do extremely well commercially. After embarking on a six-week English tour, the band was once more turning a corner according to their management. With the Carroll/Morrison team leading the way, they were still trying to pick a track deemed suitable for radio. With help from Chris O'Donnell – whose foot became an increasingly familiar feature at the Lizzy door – it was decided that "The Rocker" fitted the bill.

Released on 21 September to favourable reviews, the album once again failed to make an impact on the British charts. An edited version of "The Rocker" was released in November 1973 and charted in Ireland reaching a respectable No 11, but failed to dent any of the charts in England. Once again the track had to be edited, omitting Bell's blitzing solo but leaving the band with a catchy biker anthem.

"Decca paid Lizzy £11,000 for the extension to their contract around Easter '74," says Rogers, "during which time they recorded 'The Rocker' and released it as a single. The option was for six months but during that time we just couldn't agree a deal with Morrison and time just ran out and both parties went their own way."

These disappointments were made all the more poignant as the album is Thin Lizzy's tour-de-force of the Decca years. There is an upbeat maturity not apparent on the first two albums. Whereas *Shades* seemed a tad sleepy, the arrangements were more focused and hence the material was a lot more accessible.

Lynott re-affirmed his belief in the album leading up to the start of the English *Vagabonds* tour when speaking with Peter Harvey of *Record Mirror*:

"We spent a lot of time recording it, so consequently it's a better production. We hope it will level out the band, and that people will listen to it to know what we are about."[32]

The album opener, "Mama Nature Said", is reminiscent of Rory Gallagher. Though lacking Gallagher's rawness, this pumping salute to ecological causes established a rather more traditional heavy rock flavour to the Thin Lizzy sound.

By way of a special thank you to Kid Jensen, he features on a spoken passage on the next track, "The Hero And The Madman". The album soon returns to familiar and far more subtle territory with "Slow Blues", a Lynott/Downey composition on which Lynott bellows out "My baby don't love me, My baby don't make me sad."

"The Rocker" picks up the pace and highlights an improvement in Lynott's descriptive powers when it came to detailing his adventures with the ladies.

The title track was one of the more ambitious the band had attempted thus far. Lynott, though a baritone, had the ability to reach very high notes and the title track belongs to Lynott for his outstanding vocal display. As a singer, he had taken on board the possibilities of vocal overdubs, notably building up the vocal track through harmonies. Added to that they were starting to layer various guitar leads – something that was to beome a real Lizzy trademark.

"Little Girl In Bloom" is Lynott's most re-assuring track of the period. His creative pitch has never seemed so focused, while the guitar solo blends and is bent to perfection. Lynott, now 24 years of age, once again pays biographical tribute to his mother Philomena. "Little girl in bloom/ Carries a secret, A child she carries in her womb/ When your daddy comes home/ Don't tell him 'til alone/ When daddy comes back/ Go tell him the facts, just relax/ And see how he's gonna react"

A return to rumbling rock comes via the track "Gonna Creep Up On You." A showcase for Downey's precise percussion and Bell's scratching guitar, while Lynott's threatening delivery highlights the song's themes.

The mood is brought back down by a casual note of sweetness, "A Song For While I'm Away". Lynott once again uses Ireland as a background to more private themes. Ireland in a way became a canvas for him to throw his ideas against. The canvas also became his weapon, and protector, a melody to hide behind, a lyric to confess. Lynott went on record about the track:

"It's an old fashioned love song. A fella never turned to his friend and said 'I love you', so I tried to write a song that took care of that."

The cover of *Vagabonds of the Western World* features the work of Irish artist Jim Fitzpatrick, possibly due to the disappointing reaction to the previous two album releases. Jim Fitzpatrick recalls the beginning of his working and social relationship with the band and in particular Lynott:

"Like myself he was an only child and we were both raised by strong independent women. We were both determined to be different and therefore to make a difference. I as an artist and he as a musician. At our first meeting Philip announced, 'We have to work together, we'd be a deadly combination.' It was decided there and then that I would do the album covers for his band. Over the next couple of years we became as close as brothers, we had a similar outlook on life and we shared the same sense of humour and sense of the absurd. I produced what I regard as my best graphic work for Thin Lizzy. I did everything from flashing logos to some cool cover sleeves, for albums and singles, T-Shirts and tour jackets."[32]

The sleeve dept at Decca were more than happy to let them get on with it as John Slater confirms:

"Yeah, Jim was a good pal of the band. Philip was the main guy we had input from and when they were at Tollington, ideas would either be accepted or rejected but his vision of what they should look like was really the main focus we worked on. Plus Jim was sympathetic to Celtic styles so that fitted well with Phil. Since they had had their first hit they would have that little bit more freedom for things like sleeve design, so in the end they just ended up using their own people. When we came up with a compilation album at the height of their commercial success in the late seventies it was Jim's designs once more that were used and we were happy to go along with that."[33]

During the latter part of '73, an agent by the name of Chris O' Donnell starting hanging round the Lizzy offices. Although it would be another six months before he came fully on board, he started getting gigs for the band. During November and December Lizzy played an Irish tour culminating in a gig at the Queen's Hall in Eric Bell's hometown of Belfast on New Year's Eve. It would be Bell's last as an official as a member of Lizzy, as he recalls:

"The media machine took over and it was if we were losing control. We had great pressure to produce a follow up in the same vein as 'Whiskey...' I mean people would come to concerts expecting to hear electric folk music. However I don't ever regret leaving Thin Lizzy because the band that went on to have the success were a totally different band to when I was with them."[34]

Eric Bell had been tiring of the scene for some time, but he had thus far managed to conceal his contempt for the music business. Now, wary of the hidden agenda, Eric Bell packed his bags, starting a trend of "departing guitarists" that would plague Lizzy in the years to come.

In fact, Eric Bell's trouble began with the lifestyle that the band was leading – notably too many after-gig sessions combined with the drugs of choice of the day. His health had been deteriorating for some time and Bell found himself in a position where he decided to look after number one instead of suffering for an art he felt increasingly detached from.

"I really had to leave because of ill-health," Bell confirmed. "It was exhaustion, and the majority of things that were available to me. But then again I was quite naïve at the time. The pressure of people telling you to do things that way and this way really got to me and I couldn't really handle it. I had the chance to make a lot of money and enjoy the fame or leave and get myself back to full health. I chose the latter which I felt was most important to me and left the day after the gig in Belfast."[35]

At the gig, Lizzy's roadies Frank Murray, Big Charlie and Peter Eustace struggled to convince Bell to get back onstage after he sensationally lofted his guitar into the air, kicked over his amps and walked off. With Lynott and Downey left on stage and Bell near-comatose from over-indulgence, the duo worked through the song as best they could before retreating to try and get Bell back on to finish the set. After a little bribery the band finished the gig only for arguments to blaze in the dressing room. Bell stormed off and left, as Lynott and Downey retreated to their hotel to review their options. Bell wanted out, but without a guitarist Lizzy was in trouble. Luckily, Gary Moore, was recruited as a temporary member to finish off the tour.

"Basically I got a call from Chris Morrison," Moore recalled. "He actually called round one day. He walked in and said, 'Gary, I need your help'. I just said, 'Get me the plane ticket'. I knew what had happened. Eric had thrown a wobbler in the middle of this Irish tour, threw his guitar in the air and walked off the stage. So they needed someone to finish the tour and I flew over the next day. We had six hours rehearsal and then we did the rest of the tour and that was that. After though, they asked me to join full-time but I had already committed myself to Jon Hiseman's Coliseum II, so we parted ways."[36]

Bell's departure wasn't the only incident of an eventful tour. A blister on Brian Downey's hand turned septic, forcing the band to recruit Gary Moore's drummer Pierce Kelly to fill in.

Before commencing another English tour, Lizzy played a few more Irish dates, including Ulster Hall on the 12 January and the National Stadium on 16 January. It was a chaotic experience, but the band had slowly begun to gel in preparation for the upcoming English dates in February. With Gary Moore came some new material, songs such as "Crawling" and "I Love Everything About You" on which Moore would take vocal duties. These were added to the set list which was drawn from the first three Lizzy albums, along with new songs like 'Suicide" and "Little Darlin'" as tasters from their next album.

Throughout the tour, the band's role varied between headliners and support slots. On their opening date they were supported by Shearwater, whilst at the Roundhouse they supported the Heavy Metal Kids. Gary Moore incorporated Irish jigs during his guitar solos, and the band also decided to feature "Sitamoia" in the set, which was then used as a springboard for Downey's drum solo. J. Geils' "Hard Drivin' Man" would also feature prominently.

Up until now a lot of Lizzy's material was written on the road. New songs such as "It's Only Money", "Showdown" and "Still In Love With You" appeared on set lists and the band considered it the perfect time to get back into the studio and put them down on tape. As yet, they still had to deliver one more single for Decca before fresh talks began about renewing their contract. "Little Darlin'" was going down particularly well on the recent tour and it was decided that this would be the next release.

On the 1st of February at the Central London Polytechnic, Richard Williams, head of A&R for Island Records, saw the band and wanted to sign them. After negotiations between David Betteridge, Island's managing director, Ted Carroll and Chris Morrison, Island decided against the proposal, as some of the senior staff members didn't feel that they were right for the label.

In mid-March after finishing the majority of their gigs, Lizzy returned to Tollington Park to record a number of tracks for their next album. Firstly though, the new single had to be finished, and in two days in studio 4 "Little Darlin'" was hammered out as well as "Sitamoia". In the end it was decided to put "Buffalo Gal" on the B-side instead. Though the marketing campaign for the single was described as "healthy" with some delightful promo giveaway badges, it still couldn't make an impression on the British charts and threw the band into further worries over their contract.

When Lizzy resumed their touring schedule in April, they returned to the familiar clubs, although Moore had begun to tire of the hectic social pleasures on the road. His need for satisfaction on a performance level was lacking within the Lizzy framework, and after completion of these dates, he decided to bail out and concentrate on his own career. This left Lizzy with another headache for their upcoming tour of Germany.

The circumstances surrounding the German tour in early summer of 1974 aren't remembered fondly by the band as it very nearly led to their demise. With Moore out of the picture, the band and management recruited two replacements in an attempt to salvage the tour. Near panic ensued as Chris O'Donnell (who was now a full-time member of the management team) boarded a flight to Hamburg to collect the deposit (rumoured to be around £1,500) from the German promoter knowing full well at the time that Lizzy were still down to a duo. At first it looked like the series of gigs would have to be cancelled, but in the nick of time two guitarists John Cann and Andy Gee were drafted in. Both rehearsed intensely with the band with only a matter of days to go before they were due to fly out. Downey thought the shows were below par and the whole experience left him with doubts about the future of the band. He eventually quit and returned to England where he started auditioning for other bands, leaving Lizzy missing an important wheel.

Andy Gee's initial introduction came as the band were in hot pursuit of yet another guitarist to fill the gaping wound left by Moore's departure:

"I first met Phil and Brian at a party in Bayswater and Phil mentioned they were looking for a guitarist. We did a couple of rehearsals and I met John Cann. I think Phil wanted to solve the problem of the difference between the 'live' sound and the 'recorded' double-tracked guitar solos. Solving the live sound problem was easily remedied by the 'two guitarist' line up, and before I knew what was happening, we were on the overnight ferry to Hamburg. I introduced the boys to German Schnapps and lagers, but I came off worst and promptly made our cabin uninhabitable for the night. We looked pretty rough the next morning when we got off the boat and had to meet the President of Polygram (Germany). Someone laid on a decent breakfast, which for some reason nobody was interested in," Gee recalls grinning.

"We pretty quickly knew John Cann wouldn't fit in after we arrived at a hotel in the evening and Frank Murray, our personal road manager, unloaded all the cases out of the car and John promptly asked Frank to carry his case to the hotel. We all just looked at John, laughed and picked up our cases and left him standing there. He was probably missing his girl and the good session money he was making in London. Instead he was travelling up and down Germany on the autobahn and stuck with us in the car. No 'superstar' treatment, just a bunch of guys getting on with it."[37]

Many years later, Robin Edmondson who runs a Yahoo Group for John Cann, met Lynott at a gig in Manchester, and broached the subject:

"I did speak with Phil about John who had suffered a car crash in Belgium whilst he was a member of 'Bullet/Hard Stuff', and that it had left him with severe and eventually chronic back problems. So, lifting and carrying were extremely painful. Phil said that John hadn't said a word about it. Hence John wasn't able to do too much moving gear, so the story of him leaving his stuff by the tour vehicle does have another side to it."[38]

On the whole, the year had begun disastrously, but things were about to get worse. Prompted by the failure of the latest single, Lizzy would be in dire straits when news filtered through of their current position with Decca.

3

A NEW BEGINNING

After much cajoling Lynott finally managed to convince Downey to return, and the pair embarked on rejuvenating the Lizzy set-up. This time there would be no half measures, so they set about trying to recruit those who they deemed ideally suited to the direction they wanted to take the band. Extensive auditions began at the Iroquo Country Club in Hampstead. Both Gee and Cann, along with another guitarist, Mick Cox, agreed to hang around to help the pair in their search for a new line up. With three albums under their belt and ties with Decca unravelling, Lynott and Downey now felt a renewed pressure to mould the band into a viable vehicle.

Desperate to find the right man, Lynott finally gave in to his roadie Big Charlie's repeated pleas that they try a young whizz-kid guitar player from Scotland. His name was Brian Robertson.

Brian 'Robbo' Robertson, as he came to be known, was born on the 12 February, 1956 in Glasgow. He grew up in Scotland, playing piano and cello as a child. His mother insisted he learned the piano, but Robertson wanted to play the Hammond organ. When the young Robertson saw his brother Glen playing a guitar, his immediate reaction was, "I'll have that."

Robertson turned out to be hot-tempered with a penchant for fast living, but he would become the all-important catalyst, pushing the naïve Lizzy into the era of raunchy Lizzy. Although the tendency for his lead playing to meander could cause ructions, he was undoubtedly a virtuoso guitarist, providing Lizzy with an instant star.

Since his pre-teens Robertson had been in bands in Scotland. Many of them never set foot outside their rehearsal garages, though he did occasionally get to play live as he recalls:

"Rue Morgue was the first band I was in with my brother. He played bass at the time. The majority of it was just rehearsing with a few gigs here and there in local venues. Heidi, my next band was probably the first serious gigging band I was in, and I was only about eleven or twelve at the time. To be honest though, there wasn't anything really substantial behind Heidi. Half the time it was a case of paying to play instead of getting paid to play. We played covers because that was the trend at the time. Ireland and Scotland were similar in that you had to play the chart music. We used to play a few chart numbers and then throw in a few Who numbers. If we didn't play that other stuff we wouldn't be satisfied with our playing, and if we didn't play the chart music we wouldn't get booked. It was certainly a Catch 22 situation when we were starting out, but we just hung in there and got through it."[1]

It was while playing with Heidi that Robbo demonstrated his highly competitive nature when his band were due to play at a local venue. The Bay City Rollers were also on the bill until a dispute arose as to who would headline the gig. Arguments ensued until Robertson had a crafty notion…

"It was a double headliner, but we arrived there first. I ended up nailing my gear to the floor so they couldn't put theirs down first, which pissed them right off. I never had much time for them and when they started acting like assholes, well I just said, 'Hang on a minute mate…' and went ahead and pulled a stroke over them."[2]

Of Robertson's many ventures in the early seventies, most notable was the time he toured with David Bowie as a guitar technician. His school pal, Charlie McLennan was also on the road with Bowie, but Robertson in particular wasn't too happy when the tour hit Scotland:

"Yeah it was pretty good for a while, with Big Charlie there as well, but by the time we hit home I'd just had enough. I loved playing too much to get caught up in this. My argument was that I'd have the guitar tuned and the band would do a soundcheck and de-tune the lot of them. I knew I could do better, so I left the tour, headed home, collected my bags, got my few quid together and after a period of time I was in London."[3]

It was this decision to leave Scotland that set Robbo off into finding new avenues. At the same time, over the other side of the Atlantic, similar possibilities were being explored by a young Californian called Scott Gorham.

By the summer of 1974 Gorham had been in England for about four months. With only a six-month visa, time was running out in trying to hook up with a band. Born on the 17 March 1951, Gorham suffered from the apparent luxury of his upbringing, though he himself recalls it as normal:

"I had a really happy childhood. I grew up in an upper middle class family. It was by no means a poor family, neither a very rich family. My dad was a builder and my mom was more or less like any other mom. It was a good upbringing and for me California was a great place to grow up in. As a kid you had the beaches and the great weather, I'd have to be honest and say you really couldn't ask for more. My dad bought my first guitar for me when I was about nine, a cheap little department store guitar with nylon strings. I didn't even really know why he bought it for me. It was just one of those things really. I opened up the gift and was kind of thinking, 'Wow what the hell is this?' He had gone to the trouble of getting someone to come over and teach me two chords so he could show me what it was all about. I remember being amazed that my dad could actually pick up this guitar and make this thing work. As a kid I was always bouncing around with a beat up tennis racket or a broom pretending they were guitars anyway, so a little stretch of imagination in this direction might be the thing for me, turns out I was right."[4]

The youthful Gorham had taken a keen interest in Surf music and by his early teens had begun testing the water with a few makeshift covers bands.

"Yeah, I listened to a lot of surf music when I was growing up – Dick Dale and all that sort of thing. After that it was probably the Beatles, when they hit town, that caught my interest. The first time I heard them I was thinking who the hell are these guys? That really started the ball rolling, though I was in a band before the Beatles hit. We were called the Jesters and we played a load of three-chord surf music. The first band that I ever saw play was at a school dance called the Original Continentals. Five guys in the band and I didn't dance once cause I was at the side of the stage mesmerised, wondering how these guys were making this sound. They were probably really shit, but to my twelve or thirteen year old ears they were just nirvana. That probably more than anything got me going, because we started a band the very next day. One of the guys played drums in the school band and another played guitar, the only thing left was the bass guitar and I didn't even know what that was, but hell if it gets me in a band, I'll play it."[5]

Gorham then began playing in "tons of local bands playing in Hollywood clubs". The Jesters usually ended up playing at huge parties, anywhere and everywhere. In time, though there came a point where his circle of friends became bored with playing the same thing, and he decided it was time to take a leap. As a means to an end Gorham took on a number of menial jobs in order to earn the money to buy a ticket to get to England.

"It was really just to get out of LA and see what's on the other side of the world. England was where the great music was coming from, so I thought why not. I got a six-month visa and took a chance. If something happens in six months great, if it doesn't, too bad. I took the step and that was it."[6]

Robertson had his Lizzy audition in early June, having previously auditioned as drummer:

"It's a common misconception that when I got to London I just walked into the Lizzy job straight away, that's simply not true. Firstly, I auditioned as a drummer for a group called Slack Alice and got it. I brought down the drummer that was playing with me and we both auditioned for the gig. I got it and he got shafted which pissed him right off. It wasn't until about a week or so later that I got the gig with Lizzy."[7]

"I was actually into Lizzy dating back as far as the *Vagabonds* album, so I knew the material. I walked into the auditions and saw those guitarists lined up. Andy Gee and Mick Cox were there, but to be honest they were only filling in. They had already helped Lizzy out of a tight spot and toured with the band for a short time. I thought they were both pretty lame to be honest. Now you could call me arrogant but you have to have a little extra to get there. You had to have the confidence and belief that you can handle the job. Looking back now, Andy Gee wasn't too bad but the other guy was smoking dope and using a Stratocaster: By the end of it, it was Downey who gave me the nod and that was how we started. We started talking about the group set-up and it turned out that Phil didn't want to get somebody else in. He wanted to get back to a three-piece. Three pieces were dead, and I said it straight out to him. It wasn't a case of me not having the confidence to play as a three-piece it just wasn't the time. I felt that if I was going to have some input then we needed to change it. What Phil was writing at that point didn't really suit a three-piece. In the studio it would've been fine, but touring would've been impossible. By this stage we didn't have a record deal, so we had to hit the road to prove our worth. Downey couldn't see it as a three-piece either, so that put paid to Phil's thoughts on what route the band should be taking."[8]

Meanwhile, Scott Gorham was still playing around the pub circuit with his newly formed outfit Fast Buck.

"I originally had the intention once I arrived in England of auditioning for Supertramp whose drummer happened to be my brother-in-law, Bob Siebenberg. The guitar/keyboard player Roger Hodgson hadn't quite decided to play either instrument. Bob kept on at me to come over and give it a go with them and finally I made it over after working up my plane ticket but that took forever and by the time I got there the gig was gone. I went out hanging around all the pubs because that was the big scene back then the pub circuit, did a few auditions, got to know a few people, poached a few guys from different bands. The basic play was, if you liked the playing of a guy in another band, to try and convince him that the band he was in was shit and basically he should come on board to Fast Buck and conquer the world. It was a covers band with a few originals as I was writing material with a guy named Peter Bennett (singer/keyboard in Fast Buck). We were together for about three months before I auditioned for Lizzy."[9]

It was while playing with Fast Buck that Gorham got noticed when Siebenberg brought along a saxophonist pal, Ruan O'Lochlaun from a group called Bees Make Honey, to watch him play.

"Ruan knew a good bit about Lizzy and it was him who put my name forward alright, but I think he knew Ted Carroll as well, so there were varied connections. Lizzy were being managed by three guys, Chris Morrison, Chris O'Donnell and Ted Carroll. Ted mentioned it to him that Lizzy were looking for another guitar player. Ruan used to come to our gigs a lot and jam because we never had enough songs for a full set, so we'd have this crowd of people up on stage having a blow. Ruan dragged me to the side of the stage after a gig one night and mentioned that there was this Irish band called Thin Lizzy looking for a guitar player. I never heard of them by this point because they hadn't really had much success outside of 'Whiskey' and I don't think that was even released in America, so my knowledge of them was quite limited."[10]

After agreeing to the audition, Gorham set off to Hampstead where the band was still in residence at the Iroquo Country Club, then owned and run by African drummer, Ginger Johnson. With the trio jamming around Vagabonds material, Robertson, Lynott and Downey were once more losing momentum after a succession of misfit auditions. Thankfully the American arrived just in time on a cold dark rainy night:

"I headed down to this place in Hampstead for the audition, which was an African club with African paintings all over the place, and all these black guys who were working there. As I was walking down the hallway, one of the first guys that came into view was Phil and I thought he was one of the waiters. It was only when I got closer to the stage and he bounced over and introduced himself and said that he was the singer/bass player that I realised he was actually in the band. I'd have to say my first impressions weren't all that great... I thought Brian Robertson was an arrogant prick, Brian Downey a complete antisocial who wouldn't say anything to anybody, and Phil just seemed like a really colourful character who was really upbeat and approachable – but I was still wary."[11]

Whatever the first impressions, Scott's guitar playing turned out to be exactly what they were looking for. The band ploughed through some of the new numbers including "The Rocker" and "Suicide", plus two other numbers that Gorham recalls, "were never actually played again." Gorham's choice of guitar, however, caused some consternation.

"I hadn't much money at this point so all I had was this really cheap black Japanese Les Paul copy that didn't even have a name on it, it was that cheap. So Phil says, 'Whip the guitar out and lets get going', and so I did and everyone's jaw just dropped as if to say what the fuck is that piece of shit? And it really was a complete heap of shit but it was the only thing I had but it did get the job done."

Robertson asserts...

"At the time that Scott came to do the audition I was playing an SG Junior. Scott waltzed in with a black Les Paul copy, and we nearly died. We were recording everything in the back room and when the audition finished we headed back to the house to listen to the takes. Up to the time that Scott came through the door everything was taking a pear shape, so consequently Phil wouldn't stop talking about the three-piece scenario again. We convinced him to give it more time looking for the right player and then Scott happened along. He liked playing chords and rhythm and once we had a jam I thought, 'Hey I like this.' I hated playing chords, still do, but the way Scott and I sounded in unison, he was the ideal guy that I could play off. It didn't matter that his guitar was shit, it was what he could do with it and what he did do with it at the time."[12]

With Lynott, Downey and Robertson happy to offer the job to Gorham, the band set about trying to get a record deal. Having parted ways with Decca, the band's financial position was hardly the envy of others. To make matters worse they were £20,000 in debt.

During the latter part of June, the new four-piece was road-tested in England with a short stint in Britain before the official unveiling of the band in Ireland. In the meantime they secured the precious support of an A&R man at Phonogram. His name was Nigel Grainge.

"I signed Lizzy on the basis of one song, but with them that's all it took. They were part managed by Ted Carroll who ran Rock On records and I was down there on a Saturday buying records and Ted mentioned that he was managing this band called Thin Lizzy. So jokingly I said, 'Why don't you come to a real record company', and he surprised me by saying, 'Okay make us an offer'- as it happened, they had just changed the line-up with Robbo and Scott coming in. Ted sent me on a tape, which had only one track on it. It was called 'Still In Love With You' with Gary Moore on guitar and it just blew me away. It was a great blues ballad and I'd been expecting some no-nonsense hard rock because Ted told me they were rockers. Later I went to see them at the Marquee but we'd already started negotiations with them by then on the basis of 'Still In Love With You'. When I saw that they could genuinely rock as well, it sealed it for me. I knew they were a band of serious quality."[13]

Though the saga over remaining a three-piece had been solved, Lynott had decided that he wanted to change the name of the band in order to get away as much as possible from the "Whiskey" image. But the management insisted that they hold onto the name for fear of losing bookings.

"It was a little after the time that Scott joined when Phil decided that he didn't want to call the band Thin Lizzy anymore," Robertson remembers. "It was a new band but the management insisted that we keep the name. I wasn't too bothered about it but I could see their angle. They had had the hit previously with 'Whiskey' and a certain amount of success with *Vagabonds* but it was hard to ignore Phil's angle. This line-up had nothing to do with the previous incarnation of Lizzy, but it could well have been the success of 'Whiskey' why Phil wanted to get away from it. Phil would've been a lot happier if 'The Rocker' single had been a bigger hit. At the time it was a case of turning the page – the fact remains that the name stayed intact and the four-piece Lizzy was a new entity. Phil's writing was completely different because of it. It was a conscious thing in that he didn't want it to be the way it had been. We needed a new direction, it took us a while to sort it out but we did in the end."[14]

Lynott's dedication to the new line-up was total and the band worked extremely hard to get in shape for the upcoming gigs.

"When I look back now I realise that Thin Lizzy was my first real experience of what rehearsal was all about," recalls Gorham. "Any of the other bands I had been involved with, usually rehearsed for about an hour and after that it was, 'fuck this!' Enough of that and we'd head off. It was my first look at what being a professional musician was all about. We were rehearsing for about eight or nine hours a day just going at it until we got all the material correct. We were all flattened at the end of each day but it was the right thing to do because by the fourth show we ended up with a record deal."[15]

Nonetheless, the new four piece would have an inauspicious start. Despite Robbo's description of how they, 'were jumping around like idiots' to make an impression, when the band debuted in England at the Lafayette Club in Wolverhampton there was a turnout of just six people. In all there were more employees at the club than punters. The band was still trying hard to lose the folk-rock tag that the previous line-up had acquired. In fact, doubts regarding the public's perception of him would be something that haunted Lynott throughout his career.

After seeing the continuous tensions reach their limit on far too many occasions, and seeing his own interests outside of the band start to flourish, Ted Carroll finally decided to relinquish his interest in Thin Lizzy. However, things were not all bad. After a show at the Marquee on July 9th where a Phonogram representative was in attendance, the label expressed an interest.

With Lizzy disassociating themselves from their previous three albums, they went on to preview some of their harder material during the Irish tour, and at the end of August they eventually signed their contract with Phonogram's rock outlet, Vertigo. Through much of September the band were in the studio recording material for what was to become the *Nightlife* album. With Ron Nevison at the production helm, the band initially thought they had the right man to bring their music into focus.

With some material in the can, Lynott took time out on his birthday to record a song titled "Philomena" – a heartfelt tribute to his mother. It would become Lizzy's first official release for Vertigo. Because the band had been constantly on the road over the previous year, it hadn't left time for any ensemble writing, hence Brian Robertson's torrid memories of these sessions.

"On *Nightlife* we were short on songs, which explains the dichotomy of the material. We hadn't any time to write much, so all this Barry White-type stuff started rearing its head. It was the record company that fixed up the ill-fated Nevison partnership. On the other hand we did have Keith Harwood on board and he worked with the Rolling Stones. Overall though *Nightlife* was a weird album. I liked it and still like it – primarily because it was the first album I recorded. There's a real sense of innocence about the whole thing. There was Barry White in there, Little Feat, hard rock. To be honest I don't think anybody knew where we were going at that point. As well as that though, I don't really hold with a lot of journalistic opinion on this one. They said we didn't know what we were doing. What it was, was that there was four different people with a lot of different influences, who didn't know each other that well and we were learning each other's thing at the time. We were getting through that and having to record an album at the same time, that's a pretty heavy load no matter who you are. Aside of that we had to deal with Nevison.[16]

Unfortunately, all involved vouch mercilessly that Nevison proved to be detrimental to their progress as a rock 'n' roll outfit.

"Ron Nevison would drive up to the studio in his Rolls Royce at the height of summer and he'd be wearing this huge fur coat," Robertson continues. "He was an American twat shouting 'eh hey eh'. In the studio he gave me a pig nose fender twin to play through and I just said 'fuck you'. I wanted to get the Marshalls in there but he said no, they'd be too loud. Even at that age I knew that was bullshit. I can safely say that Ron and myself didn't get on too well while making that record. Back then I didn't know about mixing desks or how I should be focusing a microphone. I was literally running on empty there and half way through the album I realised that most of the time Nevison was talking through his ass hole."

Gorham agrees with Robertson about Nevison, but is less keen on the music on *Nightlife*.

"I was really disillusioned by the end of the *Nightlife* project. I wasn't real big on Ron Nevison after we finished. It was my first album, as it was Brian's and we were two young guys trying to find our way in this situation. When you're in this situation you look to guys like Nevison to help you through the rough spots and it seemed that it was just a gig for him and something that he wanted to get through and get done with it. He wasn't that enthusiastic about the music and probably rightly so because it wasn't a great album. We hadn't found our feet yet, so it really was a bad experience for all involved. *Nightlife* to me is more like fucking elevator music to be honest with you."[17]

In a later interview with Harry Doherty from *Melody Maker* Lynott himself, who was credited as co-producer on the album, took a sententious tone when asked about the *Nightlife* album:

"Ron Nevison had no inkling of what I was trying to do. He had just come from working on the *Bad Company* album, and it was Brian and Scott's first time as such in a studio situation so he had no idea what I was trying to do with Irish songs. I remember that at that time I'd been trying more and more to sing with an Irish accent. I was really starting to get hung up singing lyrics in an Irish accent. Shortly after that I did 'Philomena' where I took it a stage further and tried the Irish accent but got slammed to death because of it. And where did I get slammed to death about it, in Ireland, I got taken apart. Admittedly, the song does sound really empty, the way it ended up."

The album sleeve was once again the product of Lynott's close association with Jim Fitzpatrick. Though according to Chris O'Donnell, nobody clicked with the reference to Lynott on the cover. The image of the black panther getting ready to prowl the night seems to have been a little too subtle for some.

What emerged from *Nightlife* was too much light and shade and not enough balance. There are highlights and it remains an under-rated effort, but just like previous albums, Lizzy failed to establish an identity with the wider public. It opens with the sultry-cum-slinky "Showdown", incorporating some superb guitar playing along with a re-visiting of the lyrics to "Johnny". It seems The Fox had created his lair and it was here that Lynott would constantly return for inspiration.

The title track "Nightlife" unravels and swells to produce a lilting little piece that reflected the hectic pace of the band's lifestyle. However, the opening pair of songs, although demonstrating the material had improved, still failed to harness the band's aggression to its maximum potential. "Its Only Money" on the other hand much better cemented the direction in which the band was heading. The lyrics are piercing and helped along with the powerhouse playing of Robertson and Gorham who are gelling well.

"Still In Love With You" sweeps in with such emotion that some argue that this may well be *the* high point of Philip Lynott's creative energies. This version contains the original lead solo played by Gary Moore – (the track was actually recorded at Saturn Sound studios earlier in the year when Moore was still with the band. In fact, it is rumoured that "Still In Love With You" began life with Gary Moore as early as 1969). Robertson apparently refused to re-record the solo, stating that it couldn't be improved upon. The track also features a friend of Robertson's, the multi-talented and criminally under-rated Frankie Miller. His vocal is etched with pain and vigour, while Lynott plays a somewhat understated role.

'Frankie Carroll' is a broad reference to two Lizzy personnel, Frank Murray and Ted Carroll. It is a moist-eyed and heartfelt little number, but very unlike Thin Lizzy, with an arrangement that neither belonged near, next to, or on a Lizzy release.

"She Knows" brings the band back up to pace with another confident display from the two dual lead players while Lynott growls his contempt for the subject of the song. The following instrumental "Banshee" probably needed more than a catchy groove to sway listeners, an alternative vocal version with Lynott lyrics was discarded. It is "Philomena" that takes the album to another plain. If only Lynott had lost the old "Oirish" tone in his vocal maybe the song might have made more of an impact. But as it stands the soulful intentions are lost amid muddling paddy overtones which are too overbearing.

"Sha La La" finds the band back in heavy terrain, and is noteworthy for a savage display from Downey whose co-writing credit comes as no surprise. On the LP this drum-driven number reeks of filler, but it obviously found its way into their live set for showcasing the exquisite ability of Downey to beat his skins beyond all recognition. "Dear Heart" closes the album on a melacholy note, but it remains one of the most under-rated in Lynott's repertoire of ballads. It may be soft-focus material but the string arrangements by Jimmy Horrowitz and keyboards from Jean Russell succeed in a producing a tear, if not two.

Nightlife certainly has its faults, but it marked a significant progression from the previous Decca releases. With the album due out in November and a new tour to back it up, "Philomena" was released as a taster. The poetic, maternal tribute was hardly a suitable single for Lizzy, who were selling themselves as a rock 'n' roll band, and it failed to chart.

The advance from Phonogram was for two albums and would help clear their debts, as well as fund the cost of a putting a band on the road. It was also time once again for a management reshuffle.

"We were 20,000 quid in debt," Lynott told Niall Stokes of *Hot Press,* "which was a lot of money at the time. As soon as we got the new record deal with Phonogram, and got the advance to clear off the debt, Ted left. His heart went out of it when Gary [Moore] split plus he had other interests he felt were worth pursuing."[18]

Carroll in fact maintained that he left because of the increasing clashes of personality between Lynott the visionary and his new lead guitar player, Robertson. After selling his share in the company, Carroll went on to found Ace records and still runs a highly successful business today.

Robertson meanwhile reckons that the same friction that caused Carroll's departure was also the catalyst for some of the band's best material.

"Lizzy like most other bands at the time had their tempers, all of us did, maybe me more than most, in fact me more than everybody. Phil was mean when he wanted to be, Downey was passive and Scott was your archetypal rocker. The tension in the band was always between Phil and I. Phil needed the aggravation and in my opinion thrived upon it, and what came out of this aggravation were some of the classic Lizzy songs."[19]

Lizzy took time out on 27 November to record a session for John Peel at the Paris Theatre in London before returning for yet another series of homecoming gigs in Ireland in December.

As the band gigged mercilessly throughout the country, once more there was a feeling of dejection as news filtered through of *Nightlife*'s failure to dent the charts. The gigs were going well, but the lack of chart success only heaped the pressure back on for their follow-up Vertigo release.

The slimmed down management team of Chris Morrison with Chris O'Donnell publicly claimed that the album sold around 10,000 copies on release, but pressure from Phonogram dictated a massive improvement for their follow-up.

In the lead up to Christmas, plans were set for Lizzy's first visit Stateside early in the new year. The proposal was to tour supporting Bob Seger, ZZ Top and Bachman-Turner-Overdrive. It was a short three-week tour, but long enough to bring on the usual excesses and obscenities, raging drinking sessions, groupies and general good-natured mayhem.

During the tour which started on 16 March, they became friendly with Bob Seger. Lynott and Co were amazed at the fact that he would often refuse to include his liquid rocker "Rosalie" in the set. It was sometime later upon their return to Britain that the band started rehearsing the number and as Lynott was often heard to say, "Let's Lizzy-ate it". It would later became a favourite in the Lizzy live set and was often the band's opening number.

The budget for the US tour was minuscule, with the band sleeping in Holiday Inns, sometimes with two to a bed. Two members were also involved in a fracas with a groupie named Star. The incident involved Gorham, though primarily Robertson.

"Phil and I ended up at the Holiday Inn with Star and her friend. I was actually sharing a room with Downey at the time, who was trying to watch the boxing match between Ali and Frazier but he kept on at me because I was blocking the view while trying to get it on with Star. All of a sudden she started biting into my tongue and wouldn't let go there was blood everywhere, then she went for my forehead. It was the only time I've ever hit a woman…"

Gorham confirms that, "She left his room and arrived at mine, Christ she ended up biting me too."

Robertson continues: "Around six in the morning and the local sheriff is at the door claiming that a woman fitting Star's description reported to him that she had been assaulted. It turned out O'Donnell calmed him down, explained our side of the story and he buggered off."[20]

Lizzy's hard living reputation and 'tough as nails' attitude meant that the band was likely to clash with the the more restrained BTO. Robertson recalls the days.

"Those fat Mormon shit-heads. We were slim, fairly good looking and kicked their ass. We had a lot of angry episodes with them, Brian Downey especially. But they were Mormons for Christ sake – no sex, no drugs, no drink – and then Thin Lizzy happened along. They were convinced we were off our tits, which we were, but at the end of it when it came to playing we kicked their ass night after night. We did get the drummer fucked up on one occasion, I think his name was Robbie. Basically he was being told what to do, who to be and where to be by Randy Bachman. So we hired four hookers and stuck them in his room just for the hell of it."[21]

Lynott too had reservations about touring with BTO.

"I've nothing against the Mormon religion," he later recalled to *Record Mirror,* "but I think they used it as an excuse to be horrible to other people. They didn't drink, they didn't go with women and they didn't smoke. They didn't even allow people who do into their dressing room. You can imagine what they were like with us. They also had a bad attitude with the press. People would come out to give them a big welcome but if they smoked, they got thrown out of the room."

In spite of this, Randy Bachman remembered Phil and Lizzy with real affection.

"I remember reading a British music paper and seeing the name of a band called Thin Lizzy. The first person I noticed when I saw the picture was Phil Lynott who had this cool Hendrixian-gypsy-vagabond look about him. Later when we toured with them Lizzy was our opening act. I loved his accent and he had a very cool persona about him. Together we rocked many fans."[23]

By the time both groups returned to their respective homes after the US tour, it was decided that they would pair up again for a European leg due to begin in May. Lizzy's confidence was growing immeasurably and they had every right to look forward to another bout of gigs with BTO, this time on their own turf. Before that, Lizzy were committed to headlining the Hammersmith Odeon on the 5th of April and another homecoming to Eire at the National Stadium on the 25th of April.

It was after this short English tour that BTO apparently started getting anxious at the way Lizzy were going down and the way they were being shown up. BTO had just recently had a huge hit with "You Ain't Seen Nothing Yet", but that was a Stateside number 1 – in Britain their status was pretty minimal. It was totally disregarded by Lizzy who went out there every night with the intention of annihilating them both physically and musically as Robertson remembers:

"The biggest stroke Lynott ever pulled was to get on the European tour with them. Somehow Phil managed to get the support slot with BTO when they came over to Europe with a red hot hit in their hands. You've got to remember as well that we hadn't put anything in the charts in our present standing. We went out on that tour with none of our own back line, hired gear and we still kicked their ass. After a few dates they asked us to headline and Phil politely declined the offer with a wry smile. They hated the fact that we were going down so well and they ended up hating us much more. They didn't understand Phil on that wavelength. The one thing about being a support group is that you have nothing to lose. If you're the headliner and you don't deliver the goods you're fucked. Phil realised that pretty early on and of course if the support band gave the headliners a run for their money all the reviews would be in our favour, Phil was very astute like that. If that wasn't enough there was even more hassle with them another time when Downey was found in Bachman's room with some bird in the middle of the night. Bachman arrived in with his two managers with Downey sprawled out on the bed in his Y-fronts, I don't think he was after knobbing her yet or anything. So, apparently Bachman is going crazy and picks up an ice bucket and chucks it over Downey. Downey started screaming 'Mormons, you're all a bunch of fucking morons.' The upshot of this was at the next gig when they put limiters on our PA and cut all our lights. They tried everything to reverse the trend of us kicking their ass night after night, but we won out in the end."[24]

After the dismal efforts of Nevison with *Nightlife,* the band decided to produce their next album themselves. A tough move, considering they had only been together a short while, and made all the more difficult when Lynott maintained he alone was the man for the job. Keith Harwood who had helped out with *Nightlife* also came back into the fold.

"It was basically Harwood that produced the *Fighting* album," Robertson claims. It wasn't really Phil as such it was Keith."[25]

The sessions took place throughout summer 1975 at Olympic studios in Barnes. Preceding it was a single of the Lizzy-ated version of Bob Seger's "Rosalie", backed with a new number written by Lynott dealing with racial prejudice called "Half Caste". Like the majority of their early single releases, it failed to crack any markets. It also opened up a can of worms for the band when it came to meeting with their management and the record company.

Like any band they constantly tried to defend their corner when it came to the choice of singles. But it was uphill task at the time to break into the British charts with hard rock epics, when songs like David Essex's "I'm Gonna Make You A Star" were riding high. Lizzy had yet to attain that sort of commercial appeal, and in an age of swirling harmonies and bubble gum pop, they were only just emerging as the new punks.

Fighting had already started to take shape. With a larger selection of songs, the band set about choosing the material suited to the album's title. Clearly Lynott was keen to go for an aggressive feel. In this he had been boosted by Chris Morrison who had witnessed their Roundhouse gig in London on 22nd June. Morrison suggested that Lynott focus his aggression onstage, using it as a weapon as opposed to concentrating on the more mellow aspects of his stage persona. In the end, some tracks were more raunchy and explicit than others, some as tame as anything they had produced.

For all its flaws, *Fighting* is a shade better than some of Lizzy's later albums. The opening power chord of "Rosalie" heralds hand claps and vocal harmonies. Although a boisterous beginning, for some reason the lead guitar sound sounds blunted.

"Rosalie" is followed by the somewhat corny, but melodic, tribute to George Best, 'For Those Who Love To Live". The renowned footballer had become quite friendly with Lynott after spending many a night at Philomena's hotel in Manchester. Best and Lynott would also frequent the same clubs and gradually a solid friendship developed. It was perhaps an ode to the sometimes overzealous and frenetic lifestyle that both men enjoyed, though mostly aimed at a warning. Clearly, neither man was taking any heed whatsoever of the advice. "Oh the boy he could boogie/ Oh the boy could kick a ball/ But the boy he got hung up/ Making love against the wall."

The next track "Suicide" has lyrics cradled by a pumping and riveting bass line and an over anxious guitar riff. The guitar solos on "Suicide" are a relentless chase along the fret board, in search of the killer note that would solve the crime. Frank Rogers maintains there is more than one version in existence:

"I have a tape somewhere in my collection that I took with me after leaving Decca, but haven't listen to it in years. It's a 15" reel to reel of Lizzy that's packed with songs including a seven- minute version of 'Suicide' with Gary Moore playing lead guitar."

"Wild One" is Lynott once again cast as a Romeo figure, the lonesome hero as writer. The twin guitar harmonies work splendidly to convey the sad sense of departure in the song. It was intended as a tribute to all those who had fled Ireland during the struggle to maintain independence. Lynott incorporated his own pleas and carefully wove the historical facts into a love story...

The song remains one of Lynott's best tributes to Ireland and the influence it had on his early years.

On "Fighting My Way Back", a defiant Lynott prowls through a vocal that warns the foe that a white flag will never be seen from his gang. Lyrically, Lynott was now constantly using the language of over-indulgence, be it describing the use of alcohol or drugs. Musically, the song was another step forward – the start-stop lead guitar gap would become a useful tool in Lynott's increasing arsenal of tricks. Closing side one, Lizzy were on the up.

Side two brings another startling discovery in "King's Vengeance". Credited to Gorham and Lynott, it proved their collaborative attempts were now gaining credibility. Lynott's sizzling lyrical prowess finds him commenting on social standings, judge and jury, whilst once again incorporating snatches of romanticism.

Though credited solely to Lynott, "Spirit Slips Away" owes much to Robertson's blues influence. Its mood has Robertson all over it like a rash. However, a heartfelt vocal from Lynott brings it to another dimension. There's almost a medieval poignancy to the song, which lingers on well into the next track "Silver Dollar". Credited to Robertson, it's nothing more than a throwaway piece and the album starts to slide towards suffocation because of it. Why "Try a Little Harder", a joint composition by Robertson and Lynott, didn't make the cut is unknown, but it is much more worthy of inclusion than the limp "Silver Dollar".

"Freedom Song" brings the band back up a notch and Gorham's influence is easily apparent with one of the catchiest guitar licks on the album. Surrounded as it is by harder edged tracks, the commercial opportunities of this song were annoyingly overlooked. The album closes with "Ballad Of A Thin Man" – another track that would have been better left as an out-take.

Some of *Fighting* sounds craggy and constipated, and in places falls foul of fickleness and folly, but undoubtedly its bright spots shine as bright as any Lizzy flame. Gorham remains less sure of its appeal.

"By the time it came to *Fighting* we were getting there," Gorham maintains, "but it was still a poor album. The pair of them, *Nightlife* and *Fighting* didn't sell shit because the confidence wasn't there in the studio. We'd spent more time on the road then anywhere else and the studio was still this unexplored place so we got caught slightly in no man's land."[26]

The band was assisted in its final choice of material by Nigel Grainge. Having taken the original tracks to him, he felt their direction was somewhat off course, so he rallied the band into making a more co-ordinated effort.

"Around the time that they handed in the masters of the *Fighting* album was when I started to worry about the direction they were taking. After listening to it I knew that four or five tracks weren't right for Lizzy. They were forced, almost mindlessly hard, and I didn't like them. So I faced the band with this and told them what I thought, which was pretty hard-nosed of me really. Because I was only a jumped up salesman who's come in as a junior A&R man and was promoted to head of A&R, simply because the company didn't have anyone else. So here was this untrained youngster telling these seasoned tough guys that he didn't like their album. I expected them to tell me to fuck off, but they didn't. They didn't over-react at all, they just said, 'What don't you like about it,' and we sat down and talked it out. Phil was good like that, he could act the tough guy and he could be a maniac at times but he could also take advice. Anyway, they had run out of budget at this stage so I gave them about ten grand – and they came back in a couple of weeks with the best four songs on the album, one of which was "King's Vengeance" which is still one of my favorite Lizzy tracks."[27]

With the album set for a late September release, the band began the task of picking which tracks would work well on stage and which should be dropped from the set-list. In the end most of them found their way in.

Another tour had been booked to take them across Britain, so it was back to the daily grind of rehearsals. With five albums under their belts, both Lynott and Downey acknowledged the continued need for a hit. They agreed on "Wild One" as the next single, though the rest of the band claimed little responsibility for it and it sank without trace.

"It was mainly Phil and the record company who were involved in the issuing of singles. The rest of the band simply didn't get into it. I'm not saying the final decisions were wrong or right, in fact maybe I shouldn't say anything at all," says Robertson laughing.[28]

The sleeve for the album was another matter entirely, it is generally acknowledged as one of the worst in rock. Featuring a thugged-up Lizzy, the band posed in a London alley brandishing a shotgun, knife and iron bar whilst intimating they were ready to take on anyone. It was an image that would later be adopted by the punk movement, but hasn't stood the test of time.

"Phil had a vision that he wanted for the band," Robertson recalls. "I was too young and too intent on learning what the studio had to offer. Phil was pretty cool with the image and he had ideas on how he wanted Lizzy to be seen by the public. I was never too interested in how the band should've presented their look in a photo shoot. *Fighting*, I have to say is a very underrated album. Maybe it's the cover, the worst cover ever to grace an album sleeve."[29]

But with yet another tour lined up and an album in the shops, Thin Lizzy's sheer persistence was beginning to pay off. They had started to build on what was now an incredibly loyal following.

The tour was known as the 'Rocktober Tour' and officially began at the end of September with dates in Bristol on the 29th and Cardiff on the 30th. Lizzy shared the bill with a variety of acts including the talented String Driven Thing and City Boy. As Robertson recalls, "Phil was never afraid of having a good band supporting us because he knew we were good enough to nail it."[30]

Upon its release *Fighting* was the first Thin Lizzy album to chart in Britain, hitting No 60 and selling a reported 20,000 copies. Though still well short of the band's expectations, it got their foot in the door and enabled them to manoeuvre that little bit more easily. By the end of 1975 Thin Lizzy had the reputation of being one of the hardest working bands in the business, a mantle and throne they would maintain up until their demise in the latter stages of 1983.

4

THE BOYS

By the New Year, certain people were speaking in hushed tones about the big time being just around the corner for Thin Lizzy. In typical fashion they had stolen the show at a three-day festival dubbed 'The Great British Music Festival' on New Year's Eve at Olympia. Steve Marriott was there, as was Steve Gibbons, along with one of Lizzy's toughest hard-rocking opponents Status Quo. As headliners, Quo completely underestimated the support acts and suffered accordingly. Lizzy blew Quo right off the stage.

During the majority of January and February, Thin Lizzy found themselves holed up at Ramport Studios in Battersea recording their new album with new producer John Alcock at the helm.

After the unpleasant experiences in the studio with Ron Nevison on *Nightlife* and the diasspointment with the self-produced *Fighting* project, it was decided to bring in a calming and encouraging new face as producer. Having already worked with John Entwistle, John Alcock went on to claim the role as guiding producer. Chris O'Donnell and Chris Morrison approached John Alcock to see if he would be interested in producing the new album.

"They asked me to go and see Lizzy performing in some remote corner of the country during a college tour," Alcock remembers. "My recollections are still clear in that I'll never forget the weather on this typically foul night that is infamous in England during January, it was so bad I nearly didn't go to the gig. I went and by the time I got there Lizzy was about half way through their set though I was already familiar with some of their material like 'The Rocker' and 'Whiskey in the Jar'. Anyway after the show we all had one of those uncomfortable backstage meetings where everyone is polite and everyone agrees that a new direction is needed. I agreed to meet Phil a few days later to explore the possibilities of working together. That meeting went well and I liked Phil plus some of demos the band was after coming up with were great. I couldn't help but not be impressed with Phil's enthusiasm and conviction that Lizzy could create a great record."[1]

However, it soon became aware to Alcock that there was trouble brewing under the surface veneer. "Rehearsals did not go well," says Alcock, "as long arguments raged over trivial issues such as guitar tuning. By the time we arrived at Ramport in the first place almost all of the material lacked proper arrangement."

Under increasing strain to come up with new material, the two-year old Lizzy line-up of Lynott/Downey/Gorham and Robertson was in grave danger of losing the support of their record company Phonogram. Under the guidance of their co-managers Chris O'Donnell and Chris Morrison, Lizzy had exhausted all resources and the pressure to produce a hit single and album was becoming unbearable. It was clear that Lynott was coming up with some of his strongest material yet, all that was required was for the band to polish his initial ideas, in what was in essence their last shot at the big time.

"By the time we got to the *Jailbreak* album that's when we thought we'll start doing demos so we went out to a farm in the middle of fucking nowhere and spent three weeks out there by ourselves knowing that this was probably our third and final shot." Gorham recalls. "We pretty much knew that we had to hunker down and really work at this thing. I don't remember any pressure on us because we were a lot younger at that point and you don't feel that sort of thing until much later in life. We ended up writing fifteen songs and we had to whittle it down to ten and we didn't know what songs were right for the album. One of the songs we were going to leave out was 'The Boys Are Back In Town'. It was Chris O'Donnell who looked at the list and listened to the songs and it was Chris who said he rather liked that one and then we put that back on the list and it went out on the record. We just thought, 'well that's one person who likes it' so back in it went."[2]

John Alcock had the unenviable task of trying to harness Lizzy's strengths in the studio.

"I had insisted on recording at The Who's already completed Ramport studios as I loved the studio and it had very much a family atmosphere for me," Alcock recalls. "But to begin with the rehearsals did not go smoothly. As a band Lizzy seemed to thrive on conflict with long arguments raging. Whereas Robbo was brilliant at times he was always pretty angry at everything and everyone. On the other hand Brian Downey was always a calming influence, alongside the inveterate worrier which was Phil. Now I was right in the middle of all this trying not to lose sight of what I believed were Lizzy's strengths that needed to be captured on record. As I saw it, these strengths were Lizzy's dual guitar parts and harmonies, Phil's vocal style and lyrics and Brian's drumming power."[3]

Despite the need for discipline, it was clear that Lizzy were not going to let go of their usual excesses.

"During sessions with John Alcock we continuously got pissed in the studio," says Gorham, "and really he was the guy who was meant to be keeping this type of thing down to a dull roar but it didn't really work out like that."

Despite the heavy drinking the band were making progress.

"The pressure from Lizzy's management was considerable at this point as Lizzy really had to deliver the goods," Alcock remembers. "Lizzy normally arrived late in the afternoon and after about a week or so everything clicked. Despite the occasional problems, the record's basic backing tracks were coming together. A sound was developing, and it was heavier and denser than Lizzy had ever accomplished before. Phil had a great ear for tuning and when it came to guitar overdubs it grated him if there was even the slightest discrepancy."

As a producer, Alcock was finding out what was necessary to get the best out of the band.

"After much discussion regarding the overdubs I discovered that Scott was much more so the technician and invariably got his parts right fairly quickly," Alcock continues. "Robbo on the other hand was a totally different type of player. He was an emotional player and his mood and sound had to be caught at the time. If you didn't get the performance down when Robbo was hot, days could go by before he hit that emotional peak again. Phil's vocals went smoothly enough, whilst criticisms from the band and I were accepted and he generally had a knack for changing parts in light of the input he received. Apart from Phil the rest of the band were usually not present during the vocals and when we were all satisfied with the outcome, the band would come back in and make their comments."

As the band put the finishing touches to the record, their thoughts once again returned to what might be the best track to release as a single.

"After nearly five weeks of working fifteen to eighteen hour days," Alcock recalls, "we got around to mixing the record and we had to come up with suggestions for a single from the album and we stuck 'Running Back' out to be slated as the first single. Although the choice of 'Boys Are Back' was suggested as a single it was met with some scepticism as it was felt that the lyrics might not appeal to Auntie BBC. It turns out we were wrong."[4]

With a single release in mind some guest musicians were wheeled in to juice up and commercialise a couple of the tracks. It was at this point that Robertson's arguments with Lynott finally came to a head

"'Running Back' for example, what a piece of shit," snorts Robertson. "I like the song as it originally stood when Phil brought it to me before the rest of the band. I wanted to do it in a blues format but he insisted it be poppy. I said fuck that and walked away. On the demo I played piano and bottleneck guitar and it sounded great but Phil and Alcock really pissed me off when they tried to make a single out of it at the record company's insistence. In the end the song didn't come to fruition the way they wanted it, so they got Timmy Hinkley in to play keyboards – which I took enormous offence to. I couldn't understand why they'd pay this guy a fortune of money just for playing what he did. I mean listen to it and tell me its not bollocks. It was a very big stumbling block on that album. In fact I didn't end up playing on the final version that made the album. That can happen when you try to hard to make a hit out of something. I think if we had gone my way, the song may have done something in the charts."[5]

Lynott's opinion was typically somewhat different:

"'Running Back' is very much influenced by Van Morrison. I really like that song. I used to go to Van's gigs in Ireland. He was the only one who was happening in England, he was with Them at the time."[6]

After finishing the album in the latter part of February, Lizzy were back on the road warming up for their next American tour. With the album now titled *Jailbreak*, Lizzy played throughout England with Graham Parker and the Rumour as support act. The reaction to the new material was good, though a single had yet to be chosen. In fact the band nearly conceded to recording a cover version to promote the album, in an attempt to guarantee hit single they so desperately needed.

The album opens with the cracking title track. The innocent imagery of the past has now been replaced with Lynott's refined lyricism. The band too have moved up a gear in virtuosity. The impact that America had upon Lynott's writing began to become even more apparent. "Angel From The Coast", jointly credited to Lynott and Robertson, reveals the band in brisk and confident form, though the esoteric nature of the lyrics perhaps reveal a lot more about Lynott than he would have liked. Occasionally lacking subtlety, Lynott's words here have the tendency of allowing people to glance behind the façade a little too much.

The LP version of "Running Back" proved Robertson's misgivings and is nothing more than light hearted fluff, a timid piece of romantic rumbling. "Romeo and The Lonely Girl" followed the same theme, though superior on all fronts. "Warriors" closes side one in thunderous fashion. It has been said that the theme of this track is drug-related with its warnings and ultimatums. Everything within it suggests death.

Side two opens with an all out rock and roll attack. "The Boys Are Back In Town" provided Lizzy with their anthem in much the same way that "Light My Fire" did for The Doors and "Bohemian Rhapsody" did for Queen. Simply it's a classic in all senses of the word and to think that it very nearly didn't make the album is quite a frightening thought.

"Fight Or Fall" is simply a regurgitation of "Half Caste", dealing with the colour issue, but not at all on the same level. "Cowboy Song" remains a little under-rated and proved Lynott was really at home singing prairie tales. It might well have pushed the album into the top ten in Britain had it been released as a single instead of "Jailbreak".

The next track was a return to Ireland as Lynott revealed one of his most tormented of lyrics with the excellent "Emerald". Lyrically, it was all about men storming down from the hills, taking up arms and merging bravery with honour. Lynott's words are superbly punctuated by Gorham and Robertson's guitar playing. Robertson is keen to stress the contribution that all the musicans made to the strength of the album.

"It's not the only band composition on the album, everyone put something into all the songs, another Lizzy myth destroyed I guess. With Lizzy it was never down to just the names on the paper, there were contributions from all angles on all aspects by all the personnel at the given time."[7]

The Irish launch party for the album took place in Dublin, an event which is still firmly in the memory of Marcus Connaughton who was working as label manager around this time.

"The launch took place at the Tara Hotel in Booterstown and back in those days the record companies spared no expense whatsoever concerning food and drink but that's where it ended. After making the best of what was on offer at the reception and having a great time we headed off into town, Neary's (just off Grafton Street) to be precise.

"Now at this stage the last thing any of us needed was to extend the free flowing mood of the reception. The notion of continuing was fraught with danger as one could well end up getting very, very jarred. Back then the day was structured around two receptions every night of every week of every year when promoting an album by any group back in the seventies. There was an amazing amount of energy required to keep your head above the water.

"As the night wore on we headed for a club, the name of which I can't recall for reasons familiar of the situation and condition we were in. When we got to the club I realised things were not as they should have been, as did a few of the others, Phil in particular. The evening culminated with our drinks being spiked and the end result was that my briefcase arrived back into work two days before I did."[8]

As the band were flying to America, all the stops were pulled out for what was being described as the album on which Thin Lizzy had finally delivered. The following statement was circulated to promotional managers at the record company in the US by Mike Bone:

"You got it here first! Here it is. The new Thin Lizzy album is called *Jailbreak*. Learn this album backwards and forwards. We will not miss out on this one. In my time at Phonogram I have never asked for much from staff. I am now asking for everything for Thin Lizzy. Call in favours and debts, threaten, promise, do whatever it takes, "Jailbreak" on. Sounds heavy, huh? You're damn right it is! What we have here is a monster that is ready to pounce on America like ugly on a gorilla."

It was a fine reflection of the confidence their American company Mercury had in the band. The company clearly believed the big time was now looming and an opportunity to sell this album could mean a major financial success for all involved.

With the decision still up in the air over the choice of the debut single release from *Jailbreak*, Lizzy flew to the States for an intended six week tour where they were due to support a variety of stadium rockers such as Aerosmith, ZZ Top, REO Speedwagon, Rush and Styx. In the event, the sojourn in the States lasted for nearly three months. When media reports were more than generous, their American record company chose to put out "The Boys Are Back In Town" as their new single. It was a shrewd move. The cut gradually got more and more airplay and eventually peaked at No 12 on the Billboard charts while the *Jailbreak* album reached the enviable position of No 18. Even though the band had toured mercilessly throughout the UK over the previous six years, it was to be Scott Gorham's homeland that handed the band international recognition. During the time that Lizzy spent over in the States their asking price per gig apparently jumped tenfold from a paltry $500 a show to $5,000.

During June the band were booked to return to America to support Richie Blackmore's Rainbow but various sources claim that with the increased stature came increased indulgence. Whatever happened on the night before the start of the tour, Lynott took ill in Ohio and under strict medical advice was hospitalised. Without letting on to his band mates or management, Lynott struggled to continue, but after a few more dates his condition had deteriorated so much that he started to turn yellow. It was the consequence of infectious hepatitis. Robertson remembers the fiasco surrounding the situation.

"It was a huge kick in the balls for us. We were going to tour with Rainbow. My pal at the time, Jimmy Bain was the bass player and I was basically looking forward to seeing my mate and going on tour with him. I got to the hotel and the power went as there was a storm brewing outside. Shortly after the manager came up to my room saying Phil was in hospital and that the tour was off. Then one of the Rainbow guys came up and said they'd prefer if none of us came to the gig, the road crew, management, nobody connected with Lizzy. Later when Phil came back I headed for his room to see if he was all right and the doctor wouldn't let me in. The place was cordoned off, no entry for anyone. The effect on the band was immense as we were really cooking at this point and had we done the tour I think it would have finally elevated the group to Division One success. Richie was going nuts at the whole thing. In my opinion this was just as big a fuck up as me fucking up my hand. Nobody knows where he got the hepititis from but he nearly died, it was a real black hole for the band."[9]

After flying back for a period of recuperation at his mother's hotel in Manchester, Lynott started to compose material for 'Son Of Jailbreak'. It was an unenviable task for anybody struggling to recover from serious illness, let alone maintain their place on the unreliable ladder of rock and roll. For the meantime Lizzy were in the public eye with another crack at the Top Ten, this time in Britain. After the success of the "The Boys Are Back In Town" in the States, Phonogram decided to issue the single in Britain. Released on 29 May, the single entered the UK Top ten peaking at No 8. A promotional video was filmed in early May with a budget of around £2,500.

On the back of the single's success, the album too began to take off and, as a final thank you to the fans, Lynott left his hospital bed against doctors advice to perform a one-off gig at the Hammersmith Odeon on 11 July with Graham Parker and the Rumour in support once more. With *Jailbreak* finally hitting the upper echelons of the charts, Lizzy had made the jump into the next division. Success both at home and abroad brought greater incentives, although it also moved the band onto a new plain of indulgence. For now, they chose to ride the wave, and ultimately build on their success.

"It was really when we got back to Britain when we went from playing to about five or six hundred people at The Marquee to playing to three and four thousand at places like the Hammersmith Odeon," Gorham recalls.

"Lizzy mania was up and down the country, it was great. Then when we got back to America we felt the impact there but bad luck always seemed to be lurking in the shadows when it came to Lizzy."[10]

A week later Lynott was back in hospital for more check ups and was finally given the all clear with strict stipulations regarding limits on his social life. Meanwhile, the band prepared for the launch of the title track from the album as a single. On 30 July, "Jailbreak" stalled at No 31, even with the benefit of a slot on *Top of the Pops*. Their performance was staggeringly out of sync with Robbo and Gorham seemingly about to fall off the stage at any moment. Laughing at the preposterousness of it all, Robertson comments:

"The BBC are fucked up, everything to do with them is a joke. The first ever session we did for the BBC we walked in this particular day which also happened to be the day Phil's Dad turned up. The mixing desk was backwards and the faders were the same. It is so institutionalised, they're horrendously crap."[11]

One of the astonishing aspects of the album is that there were only two songs culled and issued as singles when in fact the band could have chosen a number of others. "Romeo And The Lonely Girl" would have been ideal for the seven-inch format showing the public that Lizzy wasn't just about hard rock. It seems the gentler side of the band was passed over in favour of more raunchy choices of singles.

By and large the American experience had been an eye opener for the band as it gave them the chance to see the slick operation of the headlining acts. However bland and sometimes annoying the others acts were, the fact that Lizzy were technically more proficient than some of their counterparts really began to gall some of the members. They played with a variety of people throughout the tour including Styx, Rush and REO Speedwagon. Brian Robertson recalls the experiences.

"REO, Jesus they were so shit they were thrown off the tour. We were also playing with Rush at the time who were a great bunch of guys. We were well down the bill on that one and REO were second. The gigs were massive, some twenty or thirty thousand and they were arguing constantly and pissing Rush off no end with their performances, so they threw them off and we were put up to second on the bill, what a great bunch of guys!"[12]

The American tour lasted through the month of May 1976 and after gigs in Detroit, Illinois, Chicago and Cleveland, the band returned home to embark on an English tour to promote the *Jailbreak* album. It proved to be substantially successful, especially as the support act was the up-and-coming Graham Parker and the Rumour. Parker recalls his first tour with Lizzy.

"Even though Lizzy's music was quite different from ours, I think we went down well with their UK audience. I don't recall anything specific, but no outbreaks of mass booing come to mind. I did buy a guitar from Phil at that time, though. A Martin acoustic. I ended up paying him a hundred and fifty quid for it. I've written a few songs on it and always think of him when I play it. I've still got it somewhere, too."[13]

5

BEYOND THE BORDERLINE

By the middle of August, Lizzy and John Alcock were in Munich preparing to record their next album at the infamous and now defunct Musicland studios, but once more disaster was about to strike.

"The making of what turned out to be the *Johnny The Fox* album was fraught with more problems than *Jailbreak*," John Alcock rmembers. "A management decision was taken due to tax purposes to record the album outside of the UK and they suggested Germany. My engineer Will Reid-Dick hated the place. He clashed with the chief engineer of the studio and heated arguments ensued. The early sessions were plagued with technical problems and I hated the monitors and the mixing console. Lizzy as a unit weren't happy with anything – even the hotel they were staying at. Phil was trying to write as we were short of material and we had constant disagreements over the direction of the new material. I felt we were rushing into it too soon after *Jailbreak* because they had been touring and promoting and the time to compose material wasn't available.

"Phil seemed more interested in songs that moved into a direction he had in mind, which was difficult to identify, but was less like the heavier rock impetus of *Jailbreak*. By the end of the second week in Munich we called it quits and returned to the comfort and familiarity of Ramport once more.

More problems ensued on our return when we discovered a problem with the tape on which we had recorded the German sessions. The oxide on the tape was falling off! We transferred the material on to a different type of tape at Ramport and tried as best we could to proceed. After reviewing the tape we decided to abandon all of recordings and start anew once again.

"I still feel to this day that the greatest problem with *Johnny The Fox* was the lack of material. Phil and I were not getting on especially well and I think he was unhappy about my general lack of enthusiasm over the new material, and viewed my comments as generally non-supportive. He was probably right and I should have lobbied the management and the record company to postpone the release date until the following year, giving Phil more time to write."[1]

But the new album wasn't just about problems in the studio, there was the inevitable personality clashes within the band. Lynott the control freak, at times tried to nurture Robertson, but was also on the receiving end of a barrage of abuse from the axe-man. The fervent Robertson could be his own worst enemy but out of this adversity came a strange union. The success of *Jailbreak* brought another dimension of pressure, Lynott was desperately trying to recover in time for the sessions and the producer was questioning the material. The Christmas market wasn't too far away when Lizzy re-emerged from the studio in late September and rather than risk a seasonal burial, the band quickly released the album a mere seven months after *Jailbreak*.

Johnny The Fox contained some of Lizzy's most rousing material to date. Though the sessions were fraught, and there were the usual claims of lack of good songs, this has been refuted, especially by Brian Robertson:

"There wasn't a lack of material for the *Johnny The Fox* album, in fact there was more than there was for *Jailbreak*. There was probably eight or nine on top of what appeared on the album. It's actually one of my favourite albums from a playing point of view. We used Olympic for this one as well as Ramport. It was a kind of a continuation of the *Jailbreak* idea in that the same studios were used, the same producer, which I have to say was not how I felt about doing it. With that album I would've gone with someone else like Tony Visconti. I thought, because he was a musician himself, he could pull stuff out of you that another guy couldn't. I didn't agree with bringing in John Alcock at all. Having said that he did deliver the goods not once but twice, so it is hard to argue a point when the man does that."[2]

John Alcock has never forgotten the hard slog that the *Johnny* album represented:

"In my view, Lizzy basically really should have taken more time off to write before we started recording the second record, but the record company was pushing for a new album… my blood pressure still hasn't recovered, mainly because they screwed up the promotion of *Jailbreak* so badly. This led to what I think was "filler" being included on *Johnny The Fox*, such as "Boogie Woogie Dance" which I thought had no business being on the album, but possibly could have been an OK live song. Add the stress of recording sessions, and very quickly you discover how people react to pressure, and how they deal with the other people they are working with. It pulls out the best, and worst, of personalities. There was much more pressure during *Johnny the Fox*, as it became clear that the recording would be a struggle. I would say though that the "rock" was Brian Downey. He was very much in control of himself all the time, and my impressions of Brian didn't change much as time passed…he was always the reliable one."[3]

The responsibility for the album sleeve again fell to Jim Fitzpatrick and he came up with arguably his most impressive Lizzy cover. The oft-overbearing Celtic motifs were at once in line with album content. The resemblance to the *Nightlife* sleeve was hard to ignore.

Kim Beacon (String Driven Thing) and Phil Collins of Genesis appear as guest musicians on *Johnny The Fox.* The LP unashamedly contained some of the filler that Lizzy were beginning to produce a little too often. Tracks such as "Boogie Woogie Dance" neatly fouled up the theme of the album, whilst "Old Flame" and "Sweet Marie" were sweet, syrupy and lacked grit and determination and would have been better left for some future solo project. On the other hand, they did stay true to form with the classic "Don't Believe A Word", although Brian Robertson even now questions the writing credits.

"Phil disappeared during recording 'Don't Believe A Word'. We were in the farmhouse that we used for the *Jailbreak* sessions. We had booked in for four weeks and Phil came in one morning with a couple of songs, one of which was 'Word'. I don't think it was even called that at the time. It was a slow, minor 12-bar blues number and the first thing I said to him was that it was shite and he ran off. We didn't see him for the next few days. I mean we were in the middle of nowhere with no where to run off to. We thought he might have run off to the local pub to try and hook up with the landlord's daughter, it was known to happen. But he wasn't there either so we just got on with it.

The next morning after that episode I was thinking about the song and I said to Downey that we may as well do something with it. So Downey and myself knew Phil would be really pissed off if we hadn't done anything by the time he came back. I can still remember Downey putting his hand on his head rattling through some ways of getting this song to work in a Lizzy fashion. He put in a ¾ shuffle and I came up with the riff. Not long after

Phil appeared and we played him the revised edition, which he liked. On the other hand it took us about two hours to convince him to play it. This track is a perfect example of Thin Lizzy, it wouldn't have gone anywhere if it hadn't been for Downey putting in the shuffle and if I hadn't re-wrote the riff. As far as I'm concerned that song should have been credited to the three of us. It did after all give us one of our biggest hits."[4]

It would prove to be a sore point for all involved and perhaps provided a prelude for bust ups in the future. The incessant argumentative nature of Robertson and Lynott would boil over on a continuous basis, so sooner or later something had to give.

Johnny The Fox is without a doubt up there in the top three Lizzy albums, opening with the ballsy "Johnny". A gruesome take on life, it once more showcased Lynott's ability to see life through the laden eyes of a bum. Due to constant touring the band itself was also continually on the run just like 'Johnny' – in fact so close was the comparison that it was becoming increasingly hard to distinguish Philip Lynott from the characters in some of his songs. Lynott rather liked the notion of acting out the part of the desperado, and for the moment he could always write to fight another day.

"Rocky" is another thrilling affair, based heavily on the personality and panache of Robertson. Ever the man with his fists sky-rocketing, it is easy to see the resemblance between the two.

Of the characters that Lynott's imagination continually brought into his songs, he could never quite leave the name of 'Johnny' alone. Lynott was 'Johnny The Fox' in every sense – the cool cat, the level-headed guy under pressure. If he was in over his head, he could always play his way out. One of Lynott's biggest challenges was keeping his own persona intact, as opposed to acting 'The Fox'.

"Johnny The Fox Meets Jimmy The Weed" is another uncensored attempt by Lynott to relate his experiences, albeit wrapped in the gentler restraints of a funky rock and roll number. Marcus Connaughton confirms.

"When I look back at the songs that he recorded, one in particular tends to bring a lot home for me when I think of Phil and that's 'Johnny The Fox Meets Jimmy The Weed' which is very emblematic of who Phil was. He wore his heart on his sleeve and when you do that you can get hurt and that's exactly what happened to Phil. He was a fragile personality but never let it show preferring to let the bravado smother it."[5]

"Borderline", written by Robertson and Lynott is another Thin Lizzy gem that should have been a single. A blend of the trembling emotion of "Still In Love With You" and the anxiously drawn breath of "Wild One", it is one of the highlights of the album. Robertson confirms its origins.

"'Borderline' was written about a girlfriend I was really in love with, she hated me. I was extremely down when I wrote it but the thing is an emotional experience can have that effect and 'Borderline' is what came out of it."[6]

In "Fool's Gold" Lynott returns to the subject of Eire as he recalls the famine and the ravaging effect it had upon the population, while "Massacre" is another gem drawn from Lynott's rich imagination. It was rather surprisingly a number written in the studio, according to producer John Alcock. Lynott never feared a dependant melody and promptly came up with the most suitable and most adroitly crafted lyric.

The band undertook a European tour before gearing up for the all-important tour of England during October and November. Dates in Germany, Holland and Sweden provided the initial soundboard for the new material from *Johnny The Fox*. The support band for the English tour was an American group called Clover whose singer was Huey Lewis. Lewis recalls the help and advice that Lynott kindly heaped upon him and his band:

"Initially Phonogram flew us over to make a record and while we were there they put us on tour. Philip was a gem really, from day one he came into the dressing room and said, 'man this is going to be a great tour.' He gave us hints right off the bat as to what audiences were going to be like and from that day on we got on just great. The dates in Glasgow, Manchester and Liverpool were great. The thing is the venues were really neat, all with a thousand or so people, which is a perfect number because it means you've got the big stage to play on. Yet the venue is the right kind of size, not too big, so as you can get a really good atmosphere going and communicate to the people the sort of music that you're into. Sometimes I would come onstage during their set and Phil would give me a solo and the audience would go nuts, and I'd just look back at him asking for another one. It was all they could do to tear me off the stage sometimes, I was just was so into the whole thing it was incredible."[7]

The English dates in October and November were promoted by Adrian Hopkins who had recently been recruited as tour organiser by the band. Hot on the trails of a worldwide blitz, Lizzy found themselves promoting material from two albums instead of previewing material primarily from *Johnny The Fox*. The tour was also being recorded for a possible live album. Hopkins claimed in the biography *The Rocker* that it was a pleasure to be involved with promoting them at their peak.

A Christmas tour had been planned for the United States for late November and December with Graham Parker in support. Following the successful jaunt earlier in the year it was felt that the band could capitalise on their new-found fame. It was simply not to be. Dates in New York, Pittsburgh, Detroit, Cleveland and Chicago all had to be cancelled after an incident at the Speakeasy club in London on the night of the 26 November. As opposed to repeating conjecture, Brian Robertson tells the tale and sets the record straight about the fracas.

"I went down to the Speakeasy for a steak, I wasn't drunk or in any other form of intoxication. I had a whisky and settled down to a meal. After the meal I headed up on stage to jam with Frankie Miller, who was off his tits after a boozing session. Next thing I knew was Frankie was just about to get a bottle over his face and I pushed my hand out to stop it, but the glass just tore through my hand. We were going to be going on tour the next day. I know I probably shouldn't have been in there but I was hungry. The papers of course said 'Oh Robbo was drunk again and started a fight.' The truth is I was jamming with Blackmore and Jeff Beck, having a laugh until my friend got into trouble. The band was pissed off big time. I had a really rough time with that incident. With everything that happened before none of the band would listen to me, the management wouldn't listen and it got to the stage, well if you're not going to talk, fuck you! Me neither."[8]

Because it was too late to wheel in a replacement for Robertson the whole tour had to be cancelled. It was another example of the bad luck that dogged the band's assaults on America and foiled their carefully conceived plan for Stateside domination. It marked the end of their short-lived affair with American audiences. Though they would return several times, they never rode the crest of the wave again. To make matters worse, "Cowboy Song", which was released as a follow up to "The Boys Are Back In Town" fumbled to No 77 during October.

6

REPUTATIONS

"Don't Believe A Word" was officially released on 15 January and started an immensely successful year for Thin Lizzy in the UK, giving them another top twenty hit in the charts. It peaked at No 12 in Britain and No 2 in Ireland. The video was filmed the previous November at Hammersmith Odeon with a minute budget of $4000, and was nothing more than an 'in-concert' performance intercut with crowd participation shots.

The previous November, Phil and Scott had attended the preview party for Queen's *A Day At The Races* at Advision Studios. Conversation led to the bands discussing the possibility of collaborating on a tour. The idea was once again on the table. Chris O'Donnell headed to the Queen offices to negotiate terms on the bands' behalf.

"Basically we couldn't believe our luck," O'Donnell recalls. "I was a young manager then in partnership with Chris Morrison. I heard myself saying we can't do this, or yes, we will do that, but at first it was very strange, I could hardly contain my delight. Because I didn't agree with the practice, Lizzy did not pay to support Queen. It was a personal thing. In this business it's called tour support money, and basically a band sells the slot to help defray the cost of light and sound, with the payback for the support band suppos-edly being the exposure which could lead to them being big."[1]

The only problem with the upcoming US dates was that Robertson's relationship with both band and management had become increasingly strained and he was still in no condition whatsoever to work. After the Speakeasy incident he was more-or-less incapable. He couldn't pick up a guitar, yet alone consider the upcoming possibility of a US jaunt with Queen. Robertson:

"In the aftermath of the Speakeasy I couldn't do anything, I couldn't play, I was on painkillers for about six months until I did a tour with Graham Parker and got back on track."[2]

Parker confirms...

"Yeah, Brian Robertson played with us for a European tour while Lizzy were Stateside with Queen and played guitar on both studio tracks on my EP *The Pink Parker*. Brinsley, one of our guitarists, was ill and could not come on the tour and as Brian was free for the period he decided to join us. We recorded *Pink* in Germany, I think it was, at some time during that tour when we had some down time on our hands."[3]

As a result Gary Moore was promptly wheeled out as Robbo's replacement, though according to the guitarist it was a situation that had come to a climax over recent months.

"I think Phil was having trouble with Robbo for some time and he wanted me back in the band. When they were originally going to be going to the States Phil mentioned that we ought to have a chat when they got back. Then the Speakeasy incident arose and fate intervened, before I knew what was going on I was heading for the States on one of the biggest Lizzy tours ever, from a profile point of view at the very least."[4]

Whilst rehearsing in America, Lizzy managed to re-arrange their set appropriately enough to accommodate the lightning and thunderous guitar playing of Gary Moore. With Brian May of Queen the contest was wide open when it came to guitar virtuosity. Of the many reviews Lizzy managed to outshine Queen on a number of occasions with one in particular commenting, "Lizzy is not going to be a second bill band for long, in fact I've seldom seen a band get more out of what it has than this one. Lizzy's set was a showcase for a band that does very little wrong."

There were times on the tour that Lizzy played them off the stage," O'Donnell remembers, "and I think that was because Queen was now so stylized. The slightest thing going wrong threw the whole balance right off. Whereas Lizzy were so hungry and raw by contrast they had this unpredictable energy on stage, and it showed. Having said that they were a great package."[5]

With the tour underway, Lizzy and Queen frequently had run-ins, mainly concerning the more professional restrictions of playing with one of the most successful bands on the planet. In general the relationship between the two crews remained cordial as Peter Hince, roadie for Freddie Mercury, recalls:

"In certain cities Lizzy went down very well – mid-west rock heartlands for example. In others they were received poorly – in all honesty the audience were there just for Queen. This is not unusual, particularly in the States where being an opening act is very difficult. Lizzy were well-rehearsed and the short set they played was good. In fact the crew all enjoyed Lizzy and got on well with them and their personnel – believe me this is quite rare. I think they were impressed by Queen's professionalism and discipline and after the tour Lizzy incorporated a few 'ideas' they had picked up from Queen into their own set."[6]

Brian May, for one, enjoyed the experience: "I have great memories of working with Phil and the Lizzies in the rock and roll decade of the seventies. We used to affectionately call them 'Tin Lizzy'. To me Phil was a kind of Jimi Hendrix of the bass guitar. It wasn't necessarily through virtuosity, but through presence and command. Phil wrote and played from an honest heart, directly to the people."

On more than one occasion Scott Gorham had reason to ponder the reality of supporting Queen...

"We played this one gig at the massive Winterland Arena in Frisco. So, we were first up and I'm blasting away and rushing about the left-hand side of the stage, thinking I'll go and mess with the audience on the right. The spotlight is chasing me, and I get over there and look up and there's like 500 of the gayest guys I've ever seen, man. They were wearing sequin hot pants, satin jump suits, huge floppy hats with waving ostrich feathers, and they're jumping off their seats throwing feather boas in the air. As soon as I arrived at their side, they all started lunging at me shouting, "Yeah! Shake it boy!" Geez man! I'm thinking, 'Whoa there, buddy. I'm not really ready for that kind of contact!' And I'm making a beeline to the farthest right I can find!"

"Freddie was a real kind of different guy for me. Thin Lizzy were 100 per cent a politically incorrect band. For a start, we were all completely homophobic, we didn't know how to treat this Mr. Mercury character, until we met him of course. Freddie had a real strong personality, strong enough to win anybody over, and that's what he did with Thin Lizzy."[7]

Whilst the Queen/Lizzy tour was in full swing in America, Robbo decided to lick his wounds and get back to writing with Jimmy Bain, the bass player with Rainbow. Soon it was announced that he was going to form a four-piece rock outfit with Bain. The pair had been sharing a flat and writing material with the hope of securing a record deal for their new band called Wild Horses. One of the first songs they wrote together was a track called "Girls", a song which went through a significant changes before it finally surfaced on Lynott's debut solo release, *Solo In Soho*.

"The basic idea for Wild Horses was to use all the songs that I'd written that never suited Lizzy," Robertson recalls, "and I suppose the songs that Jimmy had written but never got to see the light of day when he was with Ritchie Blackmore. We felt that we had really strong material and that we could do a killer album. I shouldn't have let Jimmy persuade me to agree to him singing though. We were actually looking around for a singer in the first place and maybe things would have been different had we found someone."[8]

When Lizzy returned to Britain after the US tour with Queen they were dealt another blow. Gary Moore decided to give Jon Hiseman's Coliseum II the nod instead of another dalliance with Lizzy. Having recorded an album with Hiseman's outfit, rather than abandon ship he decided to return to the ranks of Coliseum.

After recuperating from the US tour Lizzy were due to hit the studios once more to record the follow up to the *Johnny The Fox* album. As a result, in May Lizzy headed to Toronto to record as a three piece with a new producer, Tony Visconti. Visconti was noted for his work with Bowie and Marc Bolan amongst others. He had first met the band in the autumn of 1975 when Lizzy were still trying to find that breakthrough record. It would be the next meeting however that would hang in Visconti's memory.

"Back then I felt that I could make better records in the more relaxed atmosphere of my own home. I had mixed *Young Americans* for Bowie there and also recorded and mixed *Indiscreet* by Sparks. Being a father and studio owner brought a certain air of sobriety. I didn't expect a stretch limousine to pull up outside my modest home and two inebriated rock stars to get out waving large cans of Fosters Lager. The rockers were of course Phil Lynott and Scott Gorham. They were pretty drunk, but at the same time very friendly and full of enthusiasm. As we started talking about the possibility of working together I showed them around the studio but it quickly became apparent that Lizzy's gear couldn't be afforded much space in my project studio. Another issue they had was income tax. It had been decided to record outside the borders of Britain, Canada was chosen. They ran through a few ideas of what they wanted to work on, I liked the new material and accepted the job."[9]

Visconti had trouble with immigration getting into Canada. The upshot was a very tired Visconti arriving to join the band at the Royal II Hotel in Toronto. At the first sessions for the *Bad Reputation* album, Visconti met the laconic Brian Downey for the first time. At Lynott's insistence it was

Gorham who handled all the guitar work. Bereft of Robertson's emotion-ally charged playing, Gorham managed to acquit himself in a satisfactorily professional manner, but there was clearly something missing.

"I kept saying to Phil that this was a two-guitar band," Gorham explains, "but he said, 'No you can do it, not a problem.' Phil kept saying it would be fine and I then spoke to Tony and he was the same saying that I'd be able to take care of the rhythm and harmonies and there wouldn't be a problem. On my part it was a confidence thing but Tony was the sort of producer you looked to and got the direction and stability in order to make a ses-sion a success in the studio. In the end he was right. Finally though Phil relented because the time was approaching when we had to go out on the road and play this shit so he agreed to have Brian come back to overdub a few tracks."[10]

As the summer drew on, Robertson maintained his contact with the band and management. He hadn't been formally fired so there was little surprise when, a month into the sessions, he joined Downey, Gorham and Lynott for the sojourn in Toronto. There have been many theories concern-ing the events that led to Robertson regaining his place with Lizzy, though the man himself claims that the band wanted him back as much as he wanted it himself.

"After some serious discussions I agreed to go out and record the album. The mood of it was obviously different in that it wasn't all the guys together type of thing. I went out to Toronto and stayed in my room. I wouldn't socialise with them in any capacity, Christ I wouldn't even have a drink with them. I was there as a session player as far as I was concerned. Having said that I desperately wanted to be back in the band. Lizzy was my life at the time but I couldn't let them know that. Scott wanted me back in the band, as did Downey, Phil probably did as well but under no circumstances would he say it. It was strange time. On the way to Toronto I got stopped going through customs, they ripped through my luggage, my clothes and stuck a glove up my ass looking for drugs because I'd been a mate of Keith Richards. He had been busted recently in Canada. Don't ask me why they linked us up but they did, so once more things didn't start off particularly well."[11]

To make matters worse upon Robertson's arrival he was given a room right next door to Visconti. Visconti recalls…

"He seemed to want to let the whole hotel be aware of the fact that he had a new boombox, I didn't know it was Brian in the next room, so I banged on the wall and phoned the desk and finally the noise stopped."[12]

The album according to Visconti was "recorded quite speedily", and one thing which surprised the man behind the desk was the fact that Phil handled all the vocals on the album. Visconti quickly found out just what a vast range Lynott had…

"He was a baritone but could sing really high parts, just listen to him on the 'turn yourself around' sections on the title track. Those are all Phil's backing vocals."[13]

It would be several months before the results of the sessions were heard by the public. In July came the official announcement of the re-appointment of Robertson, thus re-uniting the duelling guitarists. The previous month the band adjourned to the Hammersmith Odeon to cut the promotional videos for the upcoming double A-sided "Dancing In the Moonlight" and "Bad Reputation" single. Both were filmed on a stripped stage to enhance the moody effect. "Dancing In The Moonlight"'s video attempts to extend beyond the realms of a straight-forward 'in concert' performance by incorporating snatches of the finger-clicking introduction and Lynott slow dancing with a model. The exclusion of a saxophone player is questionable considering the classic solo on the track – John Helliwell who played on the studio version is nowhere to be seen. The shoot lasted one full day and was offset by a budget of a $10,000. Once again a Phonogram aide handled the direction with assured tenacity guaranteeing the optimum effect. It was also decided to shoot an alternative video for "That Woman's Gonna Break Your Heart", possibly for use in another territory or even as the follow-up to the debut single. It was never released and though the video was completed has yet to become commercially available in any form.

Whilst the band were in extensive rehearsals for the upcoming tour of European festivals Phonogram decided to release the "Dancing In The Moonlight" single on 13 August. It peaked in the British charts at No 14, whilst settling comfortably at No 4 in the Irish listings, staying on both charts for two months. Tony Visconti would later go on record as saying that this single "was one of the sexiest he had ever produced."

The advent of punk inspired Lynott to pen some of his most boisterous material over the coming months. But with two major festivals in sight and the prospect of playing with his latest rival, Bob Geldof, who was fronting the Boomtown Rats, Lynott's demeanour was tense to say the very least.

At the Reading Festival, Lizzy topped a bill that included Aerosmith, Ultravox and Little River Band amongst a host of others, whilst at Dalymount support came from the Boomtown Rats and Graham Parker. Geldof later admitted the day was won by Lizzy and he announced that, "We didn't go down an eighth as well as Lizzy." The previous night Lynott held a birthday party at the West Wing, Castletown House, Celbridge, Co. Kildare. The night ended rather abrasively with an impromptu visit by the drug squad.

"The police arrived at the venue," Brian Robertson recalls. "They sprung out of thin air and of course there was a mad panic so everyone threw their stash in an open fire. The police happened along to the overwhelming funk of weed in the place. We all tried to tear away in various directions to avoid any sensationalism. I managed to slip away and eventually I got a lift from some truck driver back to the hotel, that was one close shave I can tell you."[14]

Graham Parker is another who can confirm the rather audacious behaviour of the band after the Dalymount gig.

"All I remember of Dalymount was being in this huge place that seemed like a castle after the show and getting stoned as usual and hanging out with the Rats and the Lizzy's. Someone kept taking photographs and Phil ended up sticking a toothbrush under his nose, which made him look like Hitler while on the other hand half of the Rats were running around wearing pyjamas, just another crazy night really."[15]

Also at the Dalymount Park gig were the Radiators From Space, a local band specifically recruited by Lynott as a support act. Phil Chevron, lead vocalist and guitarist recalls his first meeting with Lynott...

"The first time I actually met Phil was at a press conference in Dublin to launch the Dalymount gig that September. I found him charming but at that point we did not speak for long. I can say that The Radiators were on that show because of Philip: he quietly insisted on us being on the show, despite unspecified resistance from the promoter."

Bad Reputation finally emerged in early September and immediately made all the correct noises in the charts. It would go on to give Lizzy their highest chart position thus far.

It opens with the blazing "Soldier Of Fortune" which included the latest in synth technology, while Downey bangs away on a gong. The arrangement echoes a Celtic motif, but it soon becomes buried beneath an array of carefully constructed riffs on Gorham's part. In the age of Punk and New Wave it was a pretty bombastic opener, but the band pull it off. "Bad Reputation" and "Opium Trail" are on an altogether different plain to any other tracks on the album. Featuring destructive lyrics, their content would ultimately mirror Lynott's helplessness. The first side closes on a soothing note with "Southbound". As Visconti recalls... "Quite a lazy rocker that one, almost American sounding with the signature lead guitar of Lizzy easily apparent for all the right reasons."

The hit single "Dancing In The Moonlight" opens side two with gusto. The mood is modified by the piercing guitar virtuosity combined with Lynott's acute lyrical awareness on "Killer Without A Cause". His continuous romantic take on the darker and sinister edge of life is approximated by seedy and sordid calculation and swayed solely by the lyrical content, as we are told about his cutting ways outside of the law. This is consistent with Lynott's romanticism of the old Hollywood heroes and their sometimes barbaric endeavours.

"Downtown Sundown" on the other hand is a regurgitation of "South-bound", though not on the same level either musically or lyrically. John Helliwell re-appears, playing the clarinet alongside Lynott's soulful vocal, and complimented by Gorham's lead solo. Side two closes on more or less the same note as it began, this time with the help of Visconti's former wife.

"'Dear Lord' closes an astonishingly spiritual album, with my then wife Mary Hopkin providing a 16-voice women's choir whilst on a flying visit to me. Mary has the voice of an angel. Her cumulative voices here sound divinely unreal. Phil (Mr. Rock and Roll) couldn't believe Mary was singing on a Lizzy track."

The album was received remarkably well considering the timing. *Sounds* exploded with, "This is their finest hour, a proverbial gem, a beaut." But Brian Robertson had other thoughts.

"It was a good album though a tad weird because I hadn't written any of it. I thought it was going down the road of heavy riff shit. Why? Simply because Scott was writing riff upon riff upon riff. You can see where the actual songwriting ends on that album."[16]

Robertson's criticisms aside, the album was a tour-de-force and the perfect remedy for the ill-timed *Fox* debacle. Lizzy were now in complete control of their own destiny, with an album riding high in the charts, a hit single to promote it, the magic foursome back together and headlining a two month UK tour to prove any critics wrong.

The album sleeve was another issue altogether. For the first time since the *Fighting* album, Jim Fitzpatrick wasn't involved. The rather bland result was the creation of Linda Sutton and Roger Cooper who would also later contribute to the artwork for Lynott's first solo release.

Fitzpatrick recalls the events leading to the confusion about the sleeve...

"I was living in America at the time and I got a call from Philip to say that he was coming over to see me. He was doing a gig in the mid-west or something and he asked me where I was and I said that I was in Madison. He said, 'Okay I'll ring you when I get there.' Next thing I get a call from him saying, 'We're here Jim but we can't find you, you said that you lived near the sea, a wharf road'. I said, 'Philip, I'm in Madison, it's east Wharf road, you can't miss it, it's a small town.' So I hear him asking Frankie Murray in the background, 'Is there a sea around here?' After a long silence Philip said, 'Jim, you're in Madison. But there's no sea in Madison. We've just been talking to a policeman and he said there's no sea here. Of course then I realised that he was in a different Madison entirely. They were in Madison, Wisconsin and I was in Madison, Connecticut. Those kind of hiccups aside, working with Philip was great because he had a great visual imagination."[17]

Due to time limitations Lynott and Lizzy went along with the Sutton/Cooper take, which featured Lizzy as a threesome. Claims that Robertson was omitted because of his destructive nature are a shade wide of the mark. It could just as well have been the circus-like goings on that proceeded the Fitzpatrick debacle. Or was the band being smart and trying to put Robertson in his place? Perhaps it could have been avoided by editing in Robertson, but it became a rather bleak premonition of Robertson's status in the band.

Overall, Lynott was impressed with his working relationship with Visconti.

"Canada was a great place to record. Tony Visconti was dynamite, he was really good to work with. Great vibe, it was really nice and sunny. It was nice being in a different environment, the only thing was the air-conditioning got me after a while. And of course you missed everybody, you missed what was going on, that was the worst part."[18]

As September swung around, Lizzy were gearing up for the replacement US tour with Graham Parker and The Rumour in support. With a stronger album in their artillery they had the material, also Robertson was back in the line-up, so it seemed that all the elements were in place. The only hiccup was when Frank Murray decided to call it a day after the tour. His relationship harked back to the days of when Philip was playing in the local clubs in Dublin, but now his need to distance himself from the Lizzy organisation became paramount.

By the end of 1977 Philip Lynott and Lizzy were enjoying the excesses that fame brought them. In the early days everyone was doing the same thing, but from this point on, things would start to get extremely dangerous. Attempting to trace the events that would eventually end Lynott's life may seem pointless to a degree, but the problems which now ailed the band took on a greater significance for him as the primary creative focus. They had been enjoying enormous success throughout Europe, but inconsistent records and woeful bad luck had dominated their romance with the American *Billboard* charts. Poor marketing, poor material, poor management, poor promotion – it could have been any of a million reasons for the indifference of American audiences.

Lizzy arrived in America with a week to rehearse before the tour began, and the mission to break the Stateside market. Though there are wild claims of unfair behaviour by Lizzy towards their support players, one in particular thinks the judgement is slightly wide of the mark. Graham Parker…

"Opening sucks, there's no getting around it, but Phil and the band respected us mightily, as we did them, and whenever possible we always got a fair shake with soundchecks etc. Lizzy were professionals and good guys to boot. Lizzy were a really sharp, hard working outfit when we toured the States with them. They were good every night. It was not easy for us to go out in front of them in the States, largely because our music, with its swing and soul music element, plus the brass section, were almost entirely alien to an American audience at that time. It wasn't as bad as opening for Journey, Skynyrd or Blue Oyster Cult, something we also did, if only for brief periods, but it was still like playing to people who were hopelessly narrow-minded and hopelessly out of date. People have to realise that new wave and punk were really just scary rumours to rock audiences in America. Even into the late '70s, and an audience that went to see Lizzy was not aware that Lizzy in fact had something in common with us due to the underlying soul in their music. Most of the crowd could only hear the big-ass rock element of the band. As for us, we were like something from Mars to them. Just having short hair and straight-leg trousers confused them. The only time we really scored on the 1977 tour was when we played New York. After our set, at least half the audience left as Lizzy were doing their opening songs. In New York, the crowd couldn't believe that we were the opening act. But that's just one gig. On the rest of the tour we seemed to be merely tolerated, at best."[19]

By the time the band got back to Britain it was imperative to have them on the road for the build up to Christmas to push the album even more. A tour was booked to take them right through until Christmas week, not leaving any time to write material, be it for a new Lizzy opus or for a proposed Lynott solo album.

The punk era had exploded. Over the course of the next two years Lynott would take on board its ingredients and instil elements into his own music. Brian Robertson's old publicist Mick Rock, the renowned photographer responsible for the classic Queen "Bohemian Rhapsody" image, has previously gone on record as calling punk, "nothing more than a media event." Robertson too thinks that Lizzy were not really affected by this new trend.

"Thin Lizzy were the original punks – the punks to be honest just tagged onto us. All the hard rock bands around at the time were more punky than any of the so-called punk artists. Even down to Downey, he could swing a few in his day. One time at an after show party I arrived with my German dog and the Sex Pistols were there, I really hated them. Roger Chapman came over to me and said, 'Kick their ass Robbo' so I went over with a bottle of Johnny Walker in one hand and eventually had Johnny Rotten in the other. I said, 'Punk, you're no fucking punk' – thing is we've been the best of friends ever since. On the other hand Phil embraced the punk thing, I wasn't particularly interested in it to be honest because the notion of punk was bollocks. They called it punk because they said 'fuck this' and 'fuck that' over and over. They've been doing that in rock and roll for years and the thing is Lizzy did it a lot better than anyone else, I believe. The punk movement was looking to Lizzy and saying, 'You're cool.' To be honest if they had come up to us with the 'fuck everything' attitude we'd have just nutted them and they knew it."[20]

Lynott no doubt took a calculated risk in inviting the Radiators to do the *Bad Reputation* tour in November and December. Lizzy's previous three guests had been Clover, Graham Parker and The Rumour and the Boomtown Rats, all of whom would be a little more audience friendly to Lizzy punters than the more provocative Radiators From Space. Phil Chevron recalls the tour...

"Well during the tour Philip told me about his own experience supporting Slade. He claimed it was one of the most difficult experiences of his professional life: the audience yelled for Slade throughout Lizzy's set. Philip said they could have collapsed under the pressure or else rise to the challenge. He said that that tour taught him about professionalism, about getting an audience over to your side, about presentation... everything. The implication of course was that the Radiators and myself could equally turn this tour to our advantage. Only age and experience has taught me just what a great thing Philip did for us. We never quite won over the audience to the point where we got an encore, but they definitely paid attention. When we complained once that we weren't getting enough attention from the crew at the soundcheck, Philip personally supervised that soundcheck, making sure we had everything we wanted. He did not upbraid his own crew but, in leading by example, I think he embarrassed them. We were never given short shrift again on that tour."

On another occasion however, one of his fellow Radiators was not so sure, although Chevron himself believes there was no foundation to the rumour:

"Well, one of the Radiators holds to this day that the Lizzy crew deliberately set out to sabotage our show another night. He claims to be certain of this and also says that the sabotage order came 'from the top' after he made a nuisance of himself in Manchester at an after show party in Philomena's hotel. But I have absolutely no evidence that this is true, nor can I see why anyone would have wanted to mess us up. Philip and I had our differences later, maybe, but that was not the atmosphere on this tour. Such are the complex and contradictory rock and roll dynamics in such a pressure cooker atmosphere of a major tour."

7

ALIVE AND DANGEROUS

1978 began with Lizzy discussing the possibility of releasing a live album of recordings undertaken over the previous twelve months. Their reputation as a live act had garnered them unparalleled status across Europe and a live album seemed like a perfect foundation on which to build further success. First up though Decca, Lizzy's old label decided to re-issue a maxi-single of "Whiskey In The Jar", coupled with "Vagabond Of The Western World" and "Sitamoia". Even with Lizzy's star burning brightly, Decca's ploy to cash in backfired and it didn't break a sweat in the charts and went more or less went unnoticed.

Away from the band, Lynott took the opportunity to work with a variety of rock and rollers, and it seemed to be the perfect antidote for Lizzy. His dalliances were satisfying and musically rewarding as is audible on Johnny Thunders' *So Alone* album, where he played on a cover of "Daddy Rollin' Stone" and the Thunders' composition "London Boys". He also carried out production work with his old pal Brush Shiels on "Fight Your Heart Out". But, in truth it was the *War Of The Worlds* soundtrack on which he exceeded all previous expectations. Produced by Jeff Wayne, Lynott would take the part of Parson Nathaniel for the "Spirit Of Man" track:

"It was difficult trying to do an English accent, especially as I had had too much elderberry wine. But I did find it interesting." Lynott later commented about the possibility of branching out into acting…'Oh I don't think there are many roles for black Irishmen."

Robertson was also moonlighting:

"I hit the studio with Bowie in the middle of touring," Robertson recalls, "but I was the only one. Phil wasn't pleased about that one at all. It could have been that he wanted to play with Bowie, maybe it was jealousy. With instances like that it showed how close we could be, I mean I was pissed off when he did that album with Jeff Wayne, *War Of The Worlds*. Why didn't he get me involved in it? It was the kind of situation whereby we'd say to each other, how come you went off for a gig without me. Downey didn't do any sessions back then, one of the great mysteries of rock and roll that one, one of the best rock and roll drummers provides quite a puzzle for me, always did and always will."[1]

Robertson's misgivings aside, *The War of the Worlds* was a serious step for Lynott to take, especially as he was a rock star not an actor. Nor was he particularly capable of pulling off an accent outside of his own thick Dublin brogue. Whether it was this, or something else, Lynott was soon prompted to start thinking about committing ideas to tape for a solo venture.

In amongst all this, record company pressure dictated another new studio record from Lizzy even though time was not on their side. Lizzy had managed to convince Visconti to remain as producer and, swayed by the success of the previous album, he agreed. However, the plan came to a halt when it was realised that he was already committed to producing a Bowie album, as well as being involved with projects by the Steve Gibbons Band, Radiators From Space and Rick Wakeman. Phil suggested a compromise of doing something with the live tapes they had. A live album appeared to be feasible and with a couple of weeks in hand, Visconti sat down with the band and set about choosing the right versions for the record. Visconti continues the story.

"We listened and we listened and listened to at least thirty hours of tape, recorded during many gigs from Toronto to Philadelphia to London. We knew we had something, but the task of choosing the right takes was awesome. When we did, Phil asked if he could touch up some vocals. No harm in that, this is commonly done for live albums because of technical faults, like microphone wire buzz and other gremlins. So we spent a few days re-recording vocals until we got it right, the trick to getting the studio vocals to sound like a convincing live vocal is to sing it the same way. After that we noticed that Gorham and Robertson were not on microphone for backing vocals half the time. Listen carefully and you'll notice Phil doubling the backing vocals at the same time as he was singing lead. Phil then asked

about his bass parts as he had missed notes while singing and then it was
decided to replace all his bass parts. Next job was the lead guitars, could
they re-do theirs? 'Of course!' but it was now obvious that this was not completely live anymore. Downey's drums and the audience participation were
left, fortunately Downey liked his playing so we kept all the drums."[2]

This confession has done nothing to diminish sales of the record, though
there are a number of people bitterly disappointed by Visconti's claims.
Brian Robertson in particular.

"Visconti reckons there was loads of overdubs done, but that's just not true.
We recorded for about a year around Europe and USA. The only reason we
said that it was recorded all over, was obviously for tax reasons. There was
backing vocals done by the band and guitar overdubs done by Scott. The
thing was, I had a huge argument with Phil about it. He asked me to re-do a
guitar solo and I refused. On the basis of it being a live recording I thought
it should remain untouched. So everything that Visconti claims is bollocks.
I'm not quite sure why he came out and said that stuff about it being 70 or
80 per cent overdubs, but I do seem to recall a bottle of brandy in the control room which may be the cause of lapsed memory on his part."[3]

The only song not to have been taken from any particular concert was
"Southbound". According to Visconti, "there weren't any good takes before a
live audience, so we used the recording made during a soundcheck onstage
in Philadelphia and dubbed in the introduction and fade out audience reaction from that night's show."

With the early stages of 1978 taken up with the mixing the *Live And
Dangerous* album, Lizzy were booked to play at the Rainbow on 29 March.
The gig was filmed to coincide with the release of the new album. Though
planned and used for TV, it was later issued as the *Live And Dangerous* tour
video, albeit a mere sixty minutes in length. Somewhere a mass of extra
footage exists from this concert. Robertson confirms:

"The whole show was recorded and so were the rehearsals the day before,
but I haven't got a clue who's got the original tapes, perhaps Chris Morrison
or Chris O'Donnell."[4]

From the opening power chord of "Jailbreak" through to the thunderous version of "The Rocker", Thin Lizzy had finally found their feet. With
Lynott at the height of his creative pitch, another tour of the States had been
booked for later in the year. The honeymoon in the British press continued
as Nick Kent held hands aloft at their achievements.

"A near perfect statement of intent by what is right now the best hard
rock band in the world. This band should be huge, not just big but huge
– because they have more power in one bass pedal than all of the other geriat-

ric behemoths who are currently shifting platinum like we shit beans. Lizzy have always played like warriors and this is an album made by heroes."[5]

In April they re-released "Rosalie", albeit in a somewhat different format to that which originally appeared on the *Fighting* album. Firstly the band had embellished their take on the Bob Seger number by adding snatches of "Cowboy Song". Also as it was a live cut, it was the perfect taster for the forthcoming double live album from the band. It went on to reach a respectable No 20 on the UK chart, staying there for thirteen weeks whilst it fared slightly better on the Irish listings by reaching No 14, though only for three weeks. The official promo video was shot at the Rainbow Theatre the previous month, though it is clear that this was cut with alternative material shot in the afternoon prior to the evening concert.

Also released in April was the 'Parisenne Walkways' single which would provide Lynott with one of his biggest hits outside of Lizzy when it made number 8 on the charts. This collaboration with Gary Moore would later be successfully resurrected after Lizzy had disbanded, when it hit the charts again. A promo was made featuring a cheesy Parisian backdrop though this is unavailable in any commercial format. The coded message in the song has Lynott tracing his own origins when he sings… "I remember Parris in '49". Parris being his middle name and '49 his birth year.

Next up was a European tour in preparation for the release of the new live album. By the time the band returned to Britain after the German and French excursions the record company was preparing to push the boat out for *Live and Dangerous*. Released on the 2 June 1978 it shot straight up the chart to No 2, kept off the top spot by *Grease* featuring John Travolta and Olivia Newton-John. *Live and Dangerous* eventually stayed on the UK chart for an almost unbelievable sixty-two weeks.

By now, the fisticuffs which had started the previous year between Robertson and Lynott had become an issue. As Brian Downey put it, "He [Robertson] always seemed to be in the wars – broken bones, cuts, bruises, you never knew if he was going to turn up for the next gig in one piece."[6]

Although extreme behaviour was no stranger to Lizzy, Robertson had overstepped the mark once too often. With little on the agenda for July, Lizzy left for a one-off gig in Ibiza at a bullring festival on July 6. Unfortunately, it would turn out to be Robertson's swansong. The magic circle broken once more, Lizzy were again reduced to a three-piece. Scott Gorham recalls…

"Phil and Brian just bumped heads again and that was it, Brian was out. I said 'fine, fuck it! It's over and that was it'."[7]

"Lizzy, like most other bands at the time, had their tempers," says Robertson. "I've always said that Phil and I arguing tooth-and-nail was sometimes good for creativity. I mean, Scott wasn't going to argue the point out, Downey didn't want to know, which just left the two of us. I always looked at our arguments as constructive in that what came out of them would be tracks like 'Emerald' and 'Warriors'. I had told the boys that I was leaving after the Wembley gigs anyway and to be honest I was just being smart, as I knew that I was going to get kicked out sooner or later. I felt that Jimmy and I had written some really strong songs together and that Wild Horses could rise to the same level as Lizzy within a short period of time. Boy, was I wrong."

With an American tour lined up for the following month, the on-going saga of a replacement guitar player began again. Once more Lynott returned to old faithful Gary Moore. The previous US jaunt with Moore on board had been a positive experience, so he agreed.

As a favour to his old pal Frankie Murray, Lynott agreed to play at the opening of a new venue in London called the Electric Ballroom. The venue was an old Irish carousel ballroom and Lynott would take an ensemble group along in the guise of the Greedy Bastards who included a couple of Lizzies, a couple of Sex Pistols and a few others. The set list ranged from songs by Lizzy, the Boomtown Rats and Pistols to the usual rock and roll standards. If anything for Lynott, the Greedy Bastards was a way of getting away from the pressure of album-tour-album-tour.

By the time Lizzy was ready to tackle the American tour, Lynott had also made a few important connections through his photographer pal Chalkie Davies. Denis O'Regan was one such person, as he recalls his first introduction to the self-styled wild man of rock.

"My first impression, along with many other people probably, was how softly spoken, charming and amusing he was. I knew through Chalkie's dealings with him that he was very interested in photography and how his image and that of the band was presented to the public. Having been introduced by Chalkie, it later transpired that he and Philip were drifting apart professionally. I had been doing a lot of work for *NME*, again through Chalkie, who had balked at the punk movement, and suggested that since I had already photographed bands such as the Damned (at a school in Mill Hill), I should photograph those bands for the paper. My career with Lizzy began toward the end of the *Live and Dangerous* period, doing a few European and UK tours right up until the demise of the band. Philip played to the camera, and he knew, in his own words, how to 'throw a shape' on stage. He performed as opposed to simply playing, and that is often difficult for a guitarist to achieve. The input for image primarily came from Philip really. He knew how he wanted the band to look in photo shoots and made his point only if he really needed to."[8]

Robertson reaffirms that the rest of the band had little to do with it.

"I was never too interested in how the band should've presented their look in a photo shoot, and it was mainly Phil and the record company who were involved in the issuing of singles. The rest of the band simply didn't get into it, I'm not saying the final decisions were wrong or right, in fact maybe I shouldn't say anything at all… (laughing)."[9]

It was the day after the Camden affair that saw the official announcement of Gary Moore rejoining Lizzy. Through August and September Lizzy would support Kansas in the States.

The choice of guitar players wasn't the only worry for the band come the autumn of 1978. Brian Downey also threw in his hand, explaining his reasons as "exhaustion, and a lack of interest in seeing a stage again for a while." As Gary Moore recalls…

"Phil freaked when Brian said he wasn't going on tour but we had a few spare days in LA so we auditioned for a while and that's where we found Mark Nauseef."[10]

Mark Nauseef had previously played with the Ian Gillan band and was admired by Moore, so he slipped comfortably into the Lizzy organisation.

"I had just got back from England when I got a call from their road manager after a stint with Ian Gillan," Nauseef recalls. "I was in New York at the time while they were in LA rehearsing at a rehearsal room owned by Frank Zappa. They had got a few names together along with mine, Terry Bozzio was there too and he played well. Then after I finished my set with them we hung out for a while and had a chat. Outside the studio Tom Waits used to sleep in a car waiting for rehearsal time, it was crazy back then. Anyway Chris Morrison was there and after the band had a chat and asked if I'd be interested we discussed a few details and I was in. We rehearsed what was more or less the *Live And Dangerous* set where they kept throwing tunes at me to get the set as tight as possible. I was even using Brian Downey's drums kit at the time."[11]

"When I joined the band I wasn't a fan but when I left I loved those guys and the music. They were great people, energetic, committed, with a strong belief that wasn't arrogance as a lot of people have mistaken it for. Lizzy was their family, their baby, social club and that's why I take my hat off to them. Lizzy as a band worked their ass off to get where they were, with Phil's background, he was up against the odds and he wanted it so much that it took him all the way to Wembley, a true rock legend."[12]

With the *Live and Dangerous* tour in full swing in the States, the record itself had seemingly stalled on the charts in the US. Be it the failure to secure a headlining tour or just plain lack of interest, the album scraped into the top 100, settling at number 84. Lizzy were with a new record label, Phonogram's sister company in America, Mercury, who were primarily involved in promoting soul acts. Based in Chicago, Mercury Records was being run by two men, Charlie Fash and Irwin Steinberg. According to John Burnham, "They didn't have a clue how to promote a rock and roll band." Questions had to be asked as to why Lizzy failed to follow up the success of the "Boys Are Back in Town". The singles taken from *Johnny the Fox* and *Bad Reputation* didn't even make the *Billboard* charts, while the albums only made a mysterious top fifty spot. Events swiftly came to a head:

"As well as us, there was Graham Parker and The Rumour and the Boomtown Rats under the same umbrella. Lizzy would record an album and there'd be no back up, nothing at all. They wouldn't put on any tour support, the albums weren't getting into the shops. So, all three bands had a chat. The result of that chat led us to challenging Phonogram and demanding out of our contract. It wouldn't have mattered what material we came up with if we stayed with them, it wasn't going to make it to the shelves to increase sales. In the space of one day we all left the label."[13]

With Warners trying to lure them, Lizzy swiftly made the break, but even the benefit of a nationwide tour failed to push the album into the upper echelons of the US charts.

Towards the end of the tour, tension crept in, and bar fights began to outshine the playing. The dangerous behaviour peaked with a bandit-like car chase through Memphis that nearly ended Lynott's life.

"Phil decided to go out looking for Jerry Lee Lewis," Gary Moore recalls, "because he heard he didn't like black people. After searching a few clubs he eventually gave up and I went to call our limousine which was parked outside. He was parked on the other side of the road and had to cut through this gas station in order to turn around and come to pick us up. As he drove across the forecourt another car blocked him in, and much to my amazement he started to ram this other guys car with the limousine. He started smashing the shit out of it. Now the guy in the other car was a huge black man, like a Barry White clone and he went nuts. The next thing we knew was our driver has screeched up outside the club shouting, 'get in the car! The motherfucker's got a gun!' We sped off at a hundred miles an hour being chased by the Barry White clone. At one point he drove up right along side us waving the gun in the air. To make matters worse there was a police strike happening at the time, we were helpless. In the end we arrived at the Holiday Inn which, of course, turned out to be the wrong one and with the clone in pursuit we started the chase all over again until we finally shook him off."[14]

The band also took time out in Memphis to record some new material, as Mark Nauseef recalls…

"During the USA tour we cut some stuff in Memphis which was a big thrill for Phil, as Elvis had apparently recorded some stuff at that particular studio. Everyone knew how much of a fan Phil was of Elvis but none of it was released in any format to the best of my knowledge, which is a pity. Now it may not have all been polished up but those sessions are clear in my memory."[15]

By the beginning of October, Lizzy was back in the States playing a short tour supporting Styx before heading for New Zealand and Australia.

During this brief tour down under, the band was supported by a humble list of home-grown talent in the shape of Wha-koo, Jon English and Sport. The highlight of the tour came when they played a free concert on the steps of the Sydney Opera House watched by an estimated half a million people.

The band delivered an edited version of the *Live and Dangerous* set but also threw in a few new songs, some of which would emerge on the new album later the next year, albeit in a somewhat different format. Being a free gig, the audience numbers were large even by Lizzy's standards. From footage of the event Lynott looks to be in great shape physically, and though the band seem a little stretched in places, the crowd receives them enthusiastically. This concert footage lay in the vault for years, even though the overdubs were completed when the band got back to Britain. It finally emerged in the late 1990's with Lizzy's short set being disappointingly inter-cut with songs by Jon English and Sport, ruining the desired effect.

By the end of the tour it was evident that Brian Downey was ready to be accepted back into the group's ranks, so Mark Nauseef's services were no longer required.

Of the material that the band had worked up on the road over the past several months, much of it dated back to when Brian Robertson was still with the band.

"I remember playing some of the new songs written by this point," Robertson recalls, "songs like 'S&M', 'Waiting For An Alibi', 'Black Rose' and 'A Night In The Life Of A Blues Singer'. I didn't really like the songs and at that point neither did I care. On the short *Live and Dangerous* UK tour we did slip a couple of those tracks in as well, 'S&M' and 'Waiting for An Alibi' but mainly we kept to the object at hand."[16]

A short run of Christmas gigs coincided with Gary Moore's debut solo effort *Back On The Streets* being in the shops on 7 December. It received a rather cool reception. Nick Kent in the *NME* had this to say.

"Moore himself isn't really adequate solo material, a fact nailed home with a vengeance in the clumsy juxtaposition of styles from track to track. But saving graces are provided by Lynott, whose, three or so originals give Moore actual songs to work on. Inevitably, they sound like Lizzy out-takes."[17]

As the year wound down, the band once more were under pressure to get back in the studio to put on tape the songs that they had previewed at the Australian gigs such as "Waiting For An Alibi".

8

ROSES ARE RED!

Rumours abounded in various music publications about the first official album featuring Gary Moore as a full-time member of Thin Lizzy. It had in fact actually begun to take shape in December 1978 and continued throughout the initial months of 1979, primarily in Paris, again for tax reasons. Tony Visconti remained on board through the summer of 1978 for the recordings at the Pathe Marconi EMI Studios and Good Earth Studio in London. The album attempted to show the more commercial side of Lizzy and Visconti's attempts at bringing in a more accessible sound. It was thoroughly blatant, though much needed, as Lizzy wanted to capitalise on the success of *Live And Dangerous*.

The sessions evolved in a cagey and down beat manner as it became apparent that they coincided with Philip Lynott's immersion in heroin addiction. Though the material on the album is readily accessible, the tone and mood of the compositions are quite startling – drunks, drug addicts, death, love, sex, all rolled into a complete but unstable line-up. Yet few suspected it, in an almost boastful way it prophesied the downfall of Thin Lizzy. Even at this stage his creative energy was beginning to waver.

Nonetheless there was a pool of songs for the band to draw from, though many of these would fit in the context of the Lizzy format, many were discarded for future use as material for solo albums from Lynott, Robertson's Wild Horses or even latterly the group Moore and Mark Nauseef formed, G-Force.

Live And Dangerous had eased the pressure on Lynott and Lizzy writing to demand, and it gave them time to concentrate on perfecting the material they had recently written. At this point another studio album was not due to be delivered until early the next year, which gave them ample time to play around with as many ideas as they wanted. Taking into account that they had all been writing and playing with a wealth of different people, Lynott used the influences to his advantage when coming up with his post-punk material. As early as January 21st Lynott was busy at Ramport Studios putting down versions of "A Night In The Life Of A Blues Singer" with Gary Moore. During the same session he would also demo a song called "Rock Your Love". Though "A Night In The Life Of A Blues Singer" would surface as a B-side during Lynott's last days, 'Rock Your Love" has failed to find a commercial release.

The final week of January would prove to be one of the most fruitful for Lizzy. Leaving Visconti to take the responsibility for the *Live and Dangerous* editing, they returned to Ramport to demo tracks that would eventually surface on their upcoming studio release, which would in fact take another twelve months to reach the public. Songs such as "Ode To A Black Man", "Spanish Guitar", "Parisienne Walkways", "Are You Ready", "Black Mail", "Waiting For An Alibi", "Fanatical Fascists", "Hate", "With Love", "Black Rose", "Got To Give It Up", "Toughest Street In Town" were rehearsed. There was also a slow tempo version of "Don't Believe A Word" recorded. In all over fifty percent of what turned out to be the *Black Rose* album was finished by the time that the *Live And Dangerous* album appeared, but touring put paid to any further exploration of the material until the band re-entered the studios later.

Another track, "Cold Black Night" would also be recorded on the 1st of February, though again this has yet to be given an official release. There seem to have been many tracks left in the Lizzy vault, songs such as "Blues Boy", a Lynott/Robertson composition from the *Jailbreak* era, 'Jesse's Song', a Lynott song left over from the *Fighting* sessions, 'Leaving Town', another Lynott song from the *Jailbreak* era. Though perhaps not suitable for inclusion on the albums the band were recording at the time, surely there is another outlet for this material.

For the Ramport sessions Lynott had brought in Clover frontman Huey Lewis, with a view to lending some harmonica to the tracks. Lewis can be heard on songs such as "With Love" and "Black Rose" amongst others.

Another track recorded during the "Black Rose" sessions was a Lynott composition titled "Just The Two Of Us", it would surface as the B-Side for "Do Anything You Want To", the similarity between the two songs cannot be missed, though the lyrical content is completely different.

Although prolific musically, all of the material Lizzy put down during this weeklong spate of recording at Ramport suffered, as lack of time left Lynott's lyrical ability weak. Collaborations outside of Lizzy had provided him with an outlet to off-load an array of ideas, but latterly he was beginning to spread himself too thinly. Out of these collaborations, there is a lot of material that never came to light on any album, as Mark Nauseef confirms.

"The majority of it was recorded at Morgan Studios where Gary, Phil and myself worked on a lot of material. One of the songs that we finished, which has never come out is called 'When You Fall In Love With Love'. Other sessions were done with Paul Jones and Steve Cook from The Sex Pistols but again a lot of that never came out of the studio."[1]

The sessions quickly degenerated into an uncontrollable surge in substandard material. Various solo collaborations, Robertson's departure, drug and alcohol abuse had all left Lynott's penchant for catchy tunes in a wasteland. With a loss of focus added to the now constant blur of his habit, Lynott found himself attracting more press (most of it bad) for his socialising, than for his songwriting.

Though the majority of *Black Rose* was recorded in France, some of the tracks were completed elsewhere. For instance, "Sarah" was recorded at Morgan Studios with Mark Nauseef handling drums, Huey Lewis on harp and Gary Moore taking care of guitars. "With Love" was mastered at Good Earth with Jimmy Bain on bass, along with 'Flyaway', on which Lynott also laid down a lead vocal. Wild Horses released the song as a single, but the version with Lynott's vocal has never appeared officially. Another song produced during this period was the melancholy heartstring puller "A Night In The Life Of A Blues Singer" which featured some outstanding guitar work from Gary Moore, but mystifyingly was never included on any Lynott-related release until a few months before his untimely death.

On 3 March the first single to be taken from the new album, "Waiting For An Alibi" was released, peaking at No 9 in Britain and staying on the charts for eight weeks. The song was a masterstroke in terms of lyrical sensibility complimented with a monster melody. The video that accompanied the single was another straightforward performance directed by David Mallet. Staged at Molinear Studios in Soho with a budget of $10,000, the film has appeared in various guises, be it a black and white take featuring Lynott in character as a gambler, or the band, especially Gary Moore, over-acting as he feigns the lead solo along with Scott Gorham.

The band returned to Jim Fitzpatrick to provide them with a cover for the new album. With a title already agreed, Fitzpatrick set to work. Early drafts and ideas have since appeared on Jim Fitzpatrick's Official Web Site featuring a lady in an illicit pose with a tattooed black rose upon her naked thigh, though these were later discarded. Fitzpatrick's attempts to spray a red rose black failed as he saw it fade and wither. But once Fitzpatrick set his eyes upon the James Clarence Mangan poem *My Dark Rosaleen* his inspiration was complete as he graphically interpreted Lynott's compositions, with the title track obviously being the focal point, "I see the blood coming from the rose."

The title song also provided the band with an unrivalled closing track, as Tony Visconti recalls...

"'Black Rose' is certainly years ahead of its time. It is an unabashed tribute to Irish Celts, heroes past and present. This fabulous suite, with its Celtic pride, predates *Riverdance* by more than ten years. You just can't resist getting up and doing a little jig when this is playing. In fact this was one of the first tracks we recorded for the album, and let me add, the rest was easy compared to the complexity of this track."[2]

Though Visconti is credited with the main production, a lot of behind the scenes work must be accredited to Kit Woolven who was serving an apprenticeship under Visconti's watchful eye. Being in such heavy demand, Visconti was spending a lot of time abroad producing other artists. This benefited Woolven who went with Lizzy to Paris. Woolven ended up handling a lot of the demo material for both the Lizzy album and what would turn into Lynott's debut solo effort.

"I was working as Tony's engineer when we flew out," Woolven recalls, "and I can remember how the rooms were very big, live and extraordinarily high. It was around this time that Tony taught me a lot about studio techniques. One of the things is that he doesn't have set methods that he uses for everything he does. He's forever changing to adapt to the artist or the music."[3]

Recording sessions in Paris did not however pass without incident. As a portent of things to come, Visconti recalls the difficulty in trying to reason with Lynott.

"During recording, after a particularly long night at the disco, Phil collapsed in his hotel room. He told his personal assistant not to call a doctor, and said he just wanted chicken soup and juice. I was into holistic medicine at the time and was (still am) an advocate of the 'Bach Flower' remedies. I knew which questions to ask to determine which remedy would work best, and I wanted desperately to help Phil, but he refused to see anyone. Two days passed and Phil was still laid up so I told his personal assistant to put a few drops into Phil's juice. The P.A. was willing to try anything at this stage since he had never seen Phil look quite so bad. He was struggling to breathe and his eyes were glazed over and to be honest even at this point I think Phil had pneumonia and probably emphysema. All the same, the remedy seemed to work as Phil was back in the studio the very next day."[4]

Black Rose opens with the under-rated "Do Anything You Want To", featuring some wonderfully wicked snipes at society's self-important gentlemen. Lyrically Lynott is in venomous form and doesn't flinch in advising the listener to put their neck on the line, take the risk or throw the die as it were.

"Toughest Street In Town" is a rarity in itself, a collaboration between Lynott, Moore and Gorham. When Lizzy presented the record company with the final song list for the album, they were apparently taken aback at the content of some of the material, especially the lyrics. 'Toughest Street In Town', was deemed too risqué by the record company, and Lynott was forced into a quick re-write before the album was pressed. The original lyrics are shown below:

"Like a rat in the back, the junkie opens his packet of smack,
On his arm there's a track, that he can't take back,
On the corner is a man w/ a tattoo on his right arm,
It's there as a constant reminder of grievous bodily harm".

Hewn from an all-night jam session with waspish lyrics added by Lynott, it tells a story of street violence. People seem to be dropping left, right and centre with every verse ending. The tone is continued on the next track, "S&M", a Lynott/Downey composition that Visconti recalls with passion:

"The drums are played with incredible balls and the drum sound itself is something I finally got right on this album. Repeatedly through the track Phil is saying 'Yeah', with his voice put through an Eventide Harmoniser dropping in pitch in the re-circulation mode. It sounds like a talking tom-tom drum, I love this track and God is it far too funky for its own good."[5]

"Waiting for An Alibi" provides arguably Lynott's finest lyric. It concerns the down and out hopeless and helpless gambler Valentino – another character with whom Lynott seems to have a perfect understanding.

The prototype lyrics were written during the sessions of winter '78, but Lynott found time before the final recordings to polish them to perfection. Listening to those original sessions, the development of the song becomes apparent. Initially Lynott sang of characters such as 'Chilly Willy, Billy Jack and Billy Joe', substituting for 'Valentino' until he could come up with appropriate scenarios.

"Chilly Willy's got a bookie shop,
Everything he takes, he gives for what he's got, or

Billy Jack is back, keeps a gun in his haversack, or
Billy Joe has got nowhere to go, oh she's feeling low"

The chorus displayed a charm all of its own, not too dissimilar from the final take. It showed Lynott's willingness to play as much as he could with a lyric until he felt he couldn't better it.

"Sarah" closes side one on a romantic note with a fitting tribute to Lynott's recently born daughter. Named after the grandmother who raised Philip, his daughter would play an intricate part in the development of Lynott's songwriting guises. More personal, it was an example of how Lynott could let go of his stage persona if he wanted to.

Side two opens with a depressing admittance of over-indulgence and hopeless squalor with the anger ridden "Got To Give It Up". Lynott continued to flaunt the truth about his life, assuming the third person when writing. But it failed to convince as the next three or four years passed.

'Got To Give It Up' was another song worked on in the winter sessions, and the version recorded then is more or less as it appears on the album, though the arrangement is in its rawest of forms. Harmony guitar parts have yet to be worked out in full, and Lynott re-shapes the lyric to suit a junkie rather than a drunkard, though there are glimpses of both.

"Tell my mama and tell my Pa',
That, their fine young son didn't get far,
He made it to the end of the bottle,
Sitting in an easy chair".

Lynott, as always, draws from the worst possible storylines, expanding on the predicament of people who are no longer in control of their own destiny. As a prelude of what was to come it is without value in hindsight, but sifting back through reviews of the album suggests that certain people in media circles had already realised what was really happening to Lizzy personnel away from the stage.

"Get Out Of Here" on the other hand is an upbeat number written with Midge Ure, who at this point was playing with a band called Misfits, though he didn't participate in its actual recording. Ure had known Lynott since the latter Decca days when the three-piece Lizzy were playing club dates in Scotland. Around this time Ure was playing with pop band Slik, but after their break up, had decided to high roll it to London where he became enamoured with the new wave scene, later teaming up with Billy Currie in Ultravox.

"With Love", credited solely to Lynott, had been around for quite some time. Starting life during sessions for Gary Moore's *Back On the Streets* album where it appeared as 'Fanatical Fascists', it was also nearly spirited away for a Wild Horses album. It turned out to be one of Lizzy's strongest album tracks. Lyrically somewhat "optimistic and mournful" according to Visconti, it nevertheless gives Lynott another Romeo persona to play with. Aching and full of soul, Lynott once again toys with the notion of faltering love, on the very edge of losing it all over again.

"Roisin Dubh" puts Lynott into the shoes of many of his heroes. Made up of four separate scenes including, (1) Shenandoah, (2) Will You Go Lassy Go, (3) Danny Boy and (4) The Mason's Apron, it is a startling piece of musical discovery. Lynott's obsession with heroes past had peaked, he had nothing left to give them, nothing more to dedicate. Where he could go from here was a matter for some serious inner consideration. Phil Chevron agrees:

"When I later interviewed Phil and harked back to the recording of the 'Black Rose' track itself he got extraordinarily defensive about the lyrics. As he saw it he was 'celebrating' Ireland, unlike 'certain others' (he held my gaze here) who just wanted to 'slag Ireland off'. I don't think it can be denied that he later became a master of self- parody. The dire puns of 'Black Rose', the lyrics of a man no longer in command of his wit. He had, I believe, bought into 'The Rocker' to such an extent that he sometimes had trouble connecting with the poet."

April saw the release of the *Black Rose* album and it quickly made all the right noises with the buying public when it peaked at No 2 on the British charts. It would be the commercial high point for both Lynott and Lizzy. Various promotional performances were booked for the single "Waiting For An Alibi", most notably the *Kenny Everett Show* whose director just happened to be David Mallet. The band is in visibly gregarious form, though it was seven o' clock in the morning when filming began. Neither this nor the fact that they were flying out for a US tour the next morning seems to have taken any gloss whatsoever off their performance.

Lizzy undertook a short American tour playing second fiddle to Nazareth during February and March. This moderately successful jaunt served to tighten their set of new material. Gary Moore told Mark Putterford in his biography, *The Rocker*, that the members of Nazareth continuously tried to psyche Lizzy out, but all efforts failed.

Lizzy had precious little time on their hands after returning to Britain for the opening night of their British tour which commenced in Brighton. They had a set list sprinkled with material from the *Black Rose* album.

During the UK leg of the *Black Rose* tour, Lynott met a young photographer by the name of Antony John Barnes, known as Tony Johns.

"I actually first met Phil outside the LA Forum in California the previous year, and being from England Phil was more than happy to talk with me. Of course the usual football talk came into the conversation and he mentioned that the next time Lizzy were playing the UK that I should look him up. So began my relationship with him. We were taken backstage and met the rest of the band. Now at the time I was about twenty and my confidence far outweighed my ability as a photographer, but Phil didn't seem to mind. In fact when got backstage (myself and the girlfriend that is) Phil couldn't take his eyes off her. To say she was well stacked would be an understatement, but nevertheless we all got on quite well. After that I ended up travelling with the band through the *Chinatown, Renegade* and *Thunder And Lightning* tours.

The tour was also not without its brushes with the law. Two close encounters occurred in Sheffield and Bridlington Spa. In Sheffield the band noticed several undercover policemen prowling backstage, so quickly began to dispose of their illegal substances. This time they were lucky, as they would be in Bridlington, when once more policemen donned fans' garb in an attempt to outwit the band. Lizzy escaped by the skin of their teeth.

After the hectic onslaught of touring, Lynott returned to the studio to continue work on his debut solo album. It was to the Bahamas that Lynott went with the usual entourage hot in pursuit, as Mark Nauseef recalls.

"In the Bahamas, Scott, Gary, Phil, Huey and me lounged by the pool most days and then had dinner before heading for the studio where we worked until about four in the morning whereafter we would go to the casinos for a wind down. We spent less than a week out there working on some stuff. 'Spanish Guitar', Gary's song, has its origins there along with a few others, but most of the stuff didn't go near Lizzy, but did go into solo ventures be it Gary's, Phil's or later on even G-Force's."[6]

Lynott and co's time in the Bahamas coincided with a murder on the island. They had been recording until the early hours of the morning, and after finishing up and making their way to the casino, they were stopped and told to step out of the car at a police roadblock. Gus Curtis, who was driving, filed out as did Moore, Lewis and Nauseef. Nauseef takes up the story:

"Now whereas most of us just had hold-alls, Phil always has this thing that looked like a brief case. We were all dreading what might be in there, so after our bags were searched, Phil's was the only one left. When they opened it the only things that fell out were some girls' underwear along with a set of handcuffs. We all fell around the place laughing, man he didn't live that one down for a long time."[7]

Surviving the sardonic reactions of his friends, the sexual warrior continued on to the casino and rode out the merciless piss-taking.

Once again, history was beginning to repeat itself. In the same way that Lynott and Robertson's relationship was based on friction, so Phil's relationship with Moore was beginning to get heavy once more. Both Moore and Lynott were strong personalities and Moore's hunger to make it as a solo artist was starting to drive him out of the band.

For now, Sweden, Germany, Holland, France, Switzerland and Belgium provided the perfect remedy before taking the *Black Rose* tour back across America with the likes of Aerosmith, Journey, UFO and The J. Geils band.

Prior to leaving for the European tour, the band returned to the studios to film the video for their next single, "Do Anything You Want To". They recruited director David Mallet to shoot what was essentially their first foray into making a short film. Instead of the usual "in performance" technique favoured by the band, they opted to try a few new things. Of course with the song's theme being anti-establishment, situations featuring authority figures were thrown in to enhance the effect. Mallet confirms…

"That was shot at Molineir Studios and probably cost in the region of twelve or fifteen grand. Most of the shoots I did with Lizzy back then only lasted a day, again maybe eight or ten hours worth of footage. It was just leading up to the time when big budget videos started appearing."[8]

The single was released on 16 June, the band were back in the States on another promotional tour, often still as support. Suffering from underdog mentality, the tour quickly became a shambles with Gary Moore citing lack of commitment from Lynott. With the tension continuing to build, Moore soon made a somewhat spectacular exit from the Lizzy organisation.

As "Do Anything You Want To" strode up the chart to a respectable No 14 on the British listings, the band became a fragmented unit. Moore had had enough of Lynott's behaviour and wanted out. By the time they got to Reno, Nevada he disappeared. Lizzy were forced into the position of having to cancel their slot at The Coliseum to try to work out how to avoid abandoning the rest of the tour.

Downey had seen the writing on the wall for some time:

"It didn't surprise me in the least, which was the ironic thing. Nor did it surprise anyone else in the band. It seemed to surprise a lot of people outside of the band, the fans and especially journalists. I know Gary very well and anybody who had any illusions when Gary joined the band was crazy. He said himself when he joined the band that he wouldn't last too long and Gary's just like that – he never lasts long in a band. He seems to have these false illusions about how good we should've been. I think that's bullshit myself. We were playing fairly well, I don't see why Gary should have come back and say we're not fit to walk on stage. I can't see his point, saying that the band is musically bad. What I can see, actually, is that Gary was getting frustrated in the band and said a couple of things out of turn that he shouldn't have said."

In the meantime the press had a field day with the confrontational nature of the band, suggesting their unprofessional demeanour was a major cause for concern. Moore rightfully claimed that he was not sacked from the band for unreliability, but that he had wanted out purely for professional reasons.

Moore was interviewed by the *Record Mirror* regarding his departure:

"I can honestly say I wasn't fired, the conversation which was alleged to have taken place between myself and the management never even took place. With Lizzy and me, we always tended to go off in other directions, and it always comes to the point where something happens that makes it impossible for me to carry on. The first time with Lizzy took about four months. This time took a little longer. It's just something that always seems to happen between myself and Phil. It's nothing personal, though I did lose a lot of respect for him as a musician. In all honestly I just didn't think that he was making the best out of the opportunities available, with whatever he had been up to the previous night. I felt that there was too much raving and not enough good playing, which got embarrassing when we got up on stage. I mean we were playing to some of the biggest audiences with Journey, they let us use their lights, PA and effects. We just hadn't had enough rehearsals put in and our record company Warners didn't even seem to know we were in town, the tour itself wasn't handled all that well either."[9]

The next few US gigs were played as a three-piece, before Lynott brought in Midge Ure for the remaining dates. Ure had a long history with up-and-coming bands that disappeared as quickly as they made their mark. He had previously been part of Slik, Rich Kids, Visage and Misfits. Though hardly suited to the hard rock image portrayed in Lizzyland, James 'Midge' Ure slotted in comfortably to Lynott's gang:.

"Over the last seven or eight years I had got to know the Lizzies. I initially met them in Glasgow when they were just a three-piece. God they were broke then. They came back to my parent's house and had a meal. I just kept meeting them whether I was in Slik at the time or Rich Kids."

Ure flew out on Concorde to meet the Lizzy tour schedule as quickly as possible, and frantically rehearsed all he could, listening to *Live And Dangerous* incessantly all through the flight. Heading directly to the band's hotel he took direction from Gorham as the two decided who was going to play which harmony part in each of the songs. A short while later whilst sound checking at the Municipal Theatre in New Orleans, everything was perfected and Ure would take to the stage in a few short hours to do it for real. Gorham later remarked that, "Midge didn't drop a note."

Shortly before the American tour with Lizzy, Midge had already agreed to join yet another band, Ultravox. But from July of 1979 through until the early months of 1980 Midge would be a regular with Lizzy.

Decca meanwhile, were poised to milk the Lizzy back catalogue by putting out a compilation album. Lynott on the other hand was wary of the venture and suggested that a remix of several tracks might be in order, literally to clean up the sound and overdub some of the material. This presented another problem – contractually it was illegal for Phil to have any new input into how the mixes went, as Frank Rogers recalls.

"I spoke to Phil about a compilation when they were starting to make big waves in the mid-seventies. He didn't want the compilation going out the way it was, so we paid him to come in to re-do the bass parts and the drum segments, which he happily agreed to. Phonogram never knew this and it felt great, because he was back working with us, old pals, he was more than willing to help. The original version of 'Suicide' was going to be included, but he wanted that taken off and replaced with something else. While they were in the studio working, the publicity department guy came rushing down, to see various Lizzy members working. He was chased out of the studio for fear that this little session might be found out."[10]

Instead of bringing back Eric Bell to overdub some guitar, Lynott chose Ure who impressed him immensely with his wild rendition of 'Whisky'. "I just played guitar on the Decca gig to beef up some of the older tracks like, 'Things Ain't Working Out Down At The Farm'," Ure confirmed.

Chris P. Mansbridge, a trainee engineer at the time, was present at the re-recording of parts for the Decca compilation eventually released as *The Continuing Saga Of The Ageing Orphans*.

"I was the tape-op on this record, and also cut it in the cutting rooms at Decca, my first cut actually. I can recall the sessions very clearly. An engineer called Adrian Martins was training me. We did the overdubs at Decca West Hampstead, Studio 2. Gary Moore was there, as was Midge Ure. Phil arrived with a terrible cold and his mother even showed up to the session. Phil played us all the demos for what turned out to be the *Black Rose* album. It was certainly my most memorable time as an assistant 'engineer/tape op'. That's wasn't all the work I did with Phil though, he came in to do some demos with a songwriting friend whose name escapes me, but Brian Downey was there and a guy called Kirby Gregory, who was the guitarist with Stretch."

Rumours abounded about Lizzy's availability for the Reading Festival scheduled for 25 August. It was just two weeks away when they returned from their disappointing tour of the States, and neither the band's management nor their publicist would confirm Midge Ure's claim that there was a possibility of a no-show. Lizzy's support slots in America showcased a fifty-minute set, and the two-hour set required for Reading was simply not possible.

The turmoil had forced a number of key issues to the fore. The music press acknowledged a marked change in the personality of Thin Lizzy, and in particular Lynott. Thus far they had been able to disguise and discourage public interest in how they conducted their lives away from the stage. However, this façade was starting to crack, along with their hunger to become world-beaters. Thin Lizzy's trajectory was entering the first of many stages of decline.

Whilst rehearsing for the upcoming Japanese tour it was agreed to bring in another guitarist, allowing Midge Ure to provide additional keyboards when required. With Japan looming Lizzy settled on Dave Flett, formerly of Manfred Mann. Flett recalls his introduction to Lizzy and Lynott.

"I was playing with Manfred Mann at the time when we were both on *Top Of The Pops*. Lizzy was doing 'Rosalie' and during the course of recording I met Scott and we got on fairly well, so we agreed to meet up for a beer and a game of darts a few days later. Phil was just one of these guys, he had a tremendous charisma. Then when I got to play with Lizzy and Phil it was like, this guy's Mr. Rock And Roll. Music was his life. You got exactly what you saw with Phil, but he was also a very humble guy. Of course he had a healthy ego like anyone else would've had in his position but he was never shouting 'I'm a big shot', he was quite a humorous guy as well. I heard about the position going in the band and went away to this cottage to rehearse their stuff for a week. Now there were others who did audition but I guess that my effort put in gave me an edge. After I joined, Scott and I spent some time in his flat working out who was going to be playing which harmony part and stuff like that. We rehearsed for about a week in some tiny place in Camden. The stage space was nil in comparison to what you had to work on at a Lizzy concert. I used to end up running about five miles at every gig."[11]

Flett, a late bloomer as it were, had only taken to playing the guitar at seventeen years of age, and eventually succumbed to the appeal of London aged twenty-two, leaving his hometown of Aberdeen. Flett landed the precarious position of trying to fill the gap recently vacated by Gary Moore, and passed with flying colours for his short tenure with the band.

"On the Japanese tour we only did a handful of gigs over a two-week period," Flett recalls. "The gigs were held in modest concert halls perhaps the equivalent of Hammersmith Odeon back in London but, for me it was really exciting, and I felt pretty good being the new boy in the band. The beginning went a little haywire as I actually got food poisoning soon after we arrived, having stupidly eaten some curry, I ended up puking every-where."[12]

In his attempts to break Lizzy in Japan, Lynott had previously taken the trouble to plague their promoter, Massy Hayashi, with photos of the band. He had successfully predicted the impact that Lizzy might have on the Japanese media. The Japanese immediately took to the band and each of their shows was sold out. In fact, at the last show in Tokyo local journalists booked the entire two front rows to catch the band. The first date however didn't go quite to plan, as Dave Flett remembers.

"Basically what happened was Yamaha wanted Scott and me to use a couple of new guitars, cunningly trying to get us to endorse them. There was no chance that I was going near them, I mean being the new guy in the band and preparing for my first shows, hell I wasn't taking any chances. Scott on the other hand decided to try one and about half way through 'Jailbreak' it died. It came to his solo and he was still messing around with a roadie trying to get it going so I looked at Phil, took off down his catwalk and played the solo. Scott ended up missing half the song but Phil was really pleased I took the initiative and got out there to cover."[13]

Indeed Lynott would later comment in the British press how pleased he was with Flett's covering job:

"That was Dave's gig, that was the first gig to me where he came into his own. I could even see what he was thinking, 'I have nothing to lose now, I'm going for it'."[14]

Though still nowhere near settling on a permanent guitarist for Lizzy, Lynott returned to Good Earth studios to finish off the debut solo album he had been working on for the last eighteen months. He also found time to contribute to the charity single, "Sing Children Sing" along with other celebrities such as Kate Bush, Pete Townshend, Paddy Bush and Billy Nicholls.

With Lizzy settling down for some relaxing festive gigs, Dave Flett had still not been offered the job on a full-time basis. Also, Midge Ure was com-mitted to Ultravox still expressed his lack of interest in the job. "I'm just helping them out in the interim, besides I couldn't stay with Lizzy because it's not really my kind of music," he insisted.

Flett on the other hand was keen to secure the post, but unbeknownst to him, the band had already been keeping their eye on several other players by the time November swung into view. Dave Flett:

"It came down to Snowy White and myself as I later discovered. He had to fulfil contractual obligations with Pink Floyd before he could join. But I knew he wasn't right for them. Snowy is one of the most tasteful guitar play-ers to listen to, but he just wasn't suited to a band like Thin Lizzy."[15]

In the early part of October, Lynott took time out to shoot a promotional film for the new Lizzy single, "Sarah". Made at Hewitt studios, it was a personal acknowledgement to his family. The various actors in the film could have had slightly better direction, but director David Mallet provided a mildly amusing climax as Scott Gorham made his way from the wings and took the job of feigning lead vocals as it goes to fade.

"Sarah" was released on the 20 October and reached a moderately successful No 24 on the British charts, though it did enjoy thirteen week stay. At the same time Gary Moore's new single, "Spanish Guitar" was released by MCA though it failed to make any impact on the charts and was critically slated for regurgitating the previously successful "Parisienne Walkways". After the falling out over the earlier debacle in America, Lynott's original vocals had been removed and replaced with Moore's own.

The Lynott/Moore saga would rage on for several years to come, but for the meantime both men concentrated their energies on their solo projects. As Lynott continued to push the singles from *Black Rose*, Moore began to look at a new venture having recently signed up with Jet Records. His album, *Back On The Streets* sold moderately well, and just before Christmas of 1980 he put together G-Force with Lizzy sub Mark Nauseef on drums. Nauseef himself entered the venture with trepidation:

"When Gary left mid-tour we soon joined G-Force and it caused a lot of hassle with Phil. After I left I hadn't been in contact for a while and I began wondering if he was a little miffed at me as well. So I rang the management to see what he was up to and they were all very positive, so I got I touch with him and he was delighted to be talking. I ended up doing some stuff on his solo album and once more when the European solo tour came around."[16]

Whilst in the studios for the final stages of his debut solo release, Lynott re-activated the Greedy Bastards who had now rather disappointingly changed their name to the Greedies. A public backlash regarding the up-and-coming festive single "A Merry Jingle" is thought to have been the reason. A jumped-up Christmas mutant that combined "We Wish You A Merry Christmas" with "Jingle Bells", it was a dismal affair, though taken in the right context it remains as an amusing aside. The Greedies were booked to take in the majority of British television specials leading up to the Christmas period, though it would do little other than push it to a lacklustre No 28 in the charts after it was released on December 1. It was Lynott's last musical product of the seventies. The Greedies line-up consisted of Steve Jones, Paul Cook, Brian Downey, Scott Gorham and Lynott and featured on the closing sequence of Kenny Everett's Christmas special. Director of the show David Mallet confirms, "It was absolute mayhem". It was also the final appearance of the Greedies, much to the delight of the more serious-minded Lizzy fans.

Lizzy's show at the Bingley Hall in Stafford on 18 December was not only their swan-song performance of the seventies, but also the last gig for Dave Flett as a member of Lizzy, as he recalls:

"I suppose the way I look at it is, I wasn't bringing anything new into the band, there wasn't much difference to what I was playing as to when Brian Robertson was with them. Perhaps Phil and the band felt that by bringing in Snowy they might be able to open up new avenues and take them into the next decade. But at the end of the day I was pleased to have been part of it, no matter how long or short that time was."[17]

9

SNOWY TIMES

The eighties were meant to bring fresh triumphs to Philip Lynott and Thin Lizzy. On the face of it, the signs were positive. Lynott was preparing himself for marriage, his debut solo album was being readied for release and his band were on the top of their form. Their previous studio album *Black Rose* had been enormously successful both commercially and critically, giving them three hit singles and much positive publicity. However, the once trenchant Lynott would soon fall victim to a series of errors, his own and those of the marketing men at Phonogram. Having kept it from the press for two months, Lizzy had in fact found their new guitar hero, Terence Charles White, known to all as Snowy. The reason for the secrecy was in order to give him time to complete his commitments with Pink Floyd.

The official announcement of White's inclusion in Lizzy was made in February, just days before Lynott's planned wedding to Caroline, the daughter of TV host Leslie Crowther, on Valentine's Day, 1980. White had previously played with some of the world's finest musicians such as Peter Green and Al Stewart and was the first English musician to be recruited by Lizzy. His bluesy style of playing was intended to be the fresh ingredient that would give the band longevity into the 1980s.

In January, Lynott held his stag night at the Clarendon Hotel in Hammersmith. The famous faces included Billy Idol, his pal Tony James, Simon Kirke from Bad Company, Midge Ure, Jimmy Bain and Dire Straits along with everyone connected with Thin Lizzy of course. Paula Yates recalled vivid memories of both the stag night and the hen party:

"Lemmy from Motorhead was uncontrollably excited and could be found in various stages of alcoholic stupor around the hotel. Actually when the three strippers appeared (most guests had triple vision at this stage anyway) it was hard to tell who was still awake. Caroline's hen party was held at Legends and organised by the wife of Jimmy Bain, Sophie. The hen party was a far more decorous affair as about 14 or more young ladies played complete havoc on Legends for the night. Sophie had made sure that the wine, strawberries and anything else kept flowing for the night. Luckily for once no one swallowed their gold teeth or wet themselves."[1]

Lynott's stag night was an enjoyable spectacle and provided ex-Lizzy axeman Brian Robertson with some enjoyable memories:

"His stag night was great… in fact we all ended up having a jam. There were lots of musicians there and everyone was playing, singing… just having a good time basically. I remember Ozzy Osbourne getting up to sing a few numbers but God knows exactly who played with whom."[2]

And so it was that on Valentine's Day, 14th February, 1980 Philip Lynott married Caroline Crowther. The wedding was held in well below zero temperatures at the St. Elizabeth of Portugal Catholic Church in Richmond with the reception being held at the Kensington Hilton. Paula Yates continued:

"Lemmy certainly looked the worse for wear when we got to the reception. The romance of the whole situation obviously got to him as he rushed up to me with a polaroid of himself sitting in a pair of pale blue underpants on a stuffed ant eater. On the other hand Mark Knopfler refused to come to the gents lavatories for a quick photo session with me but did say he'd think deeply about it."[3] [Yates was preparing a book about Rock stars in their underpants.]

Philip's Aunt Betty Wray has her own thoughts on events.

"Philip and Caroline's wedding was a lovely day. After all the family met up in London we all stayed over at Philip's place. Philip had arranged a taxi to come for the next morning and pick my sister Marian, niece Monica and myself up and head over to where Caroline's parents were staying where upon we were introduced to her dad, Leslie as he came in swishing around the place. All preparations were in place as we were served champagne and orange juice at some unearthly hour whilst getting our hair tended to. The one shock that fell upon all of us was when the Lizzy roadies turned up for the service. Philip had obviously only ever seen the lads in their T-shirts and jeans and now here they were wearing grey morning suits and top hats. It was a lovely gesture and Philip was delighted with their sincerity."[4]

The reception afterwards turned out to be just as fascinating as the wedding ceremony, as the best food and drink was served to the array of guests. When it was all over, the family headed back to Kew to party on for the rest of the night. Betty continues:

"The wedding couple had to stay behind because it was understood that they were to head directly to the airport once the reception had ended. You can imagine our surprise to see them reappear at the house a little time later when Philip walked in with everyone having a great time. Like a gentle breeze he sauntered his way over to me and whispered, 'I knew where the best hooley would be, so I came back to join you for a while.' Sure enough, the time came for them to go again and all I can remember are the tears in his eyes as he and Caroline were waving goodbye to little Sarah for a couple of weeks to head off on their honeymoon."[5]

Various stories abounded concerning how and where Lynott actually met Caroline Crowther. The reality was that Caroline worked in the offices of PR man, Tony Brainsby. Brainsby unwittingly introduced Lynott to his future bride, who was then a tender eighteen years of age. Lynott, eleven years her senior would walk her down the aisle at the age of twenty. Caroline was no stranger to controversy. In 1977 she had posed naked for a popular men's magazine *Mayfair* under the alias Hilary Stevens, rather naively believing the photos were only going to be published in Holland. Various reports have come to light in recent years regarding Caroline's father's opinion on Lynott, a musician with a considerable reputation. It is these reports that his mother Philomena is keen to address.

"Nobody seems to ask Phyliss Lynott what she thought about Caroline Crowther as a suitable daughter-in-law and that really irked me a bit. Philip in my opinion got a raw deal where the press is concerned."[6]

The wedding itself didn't pass without incident as Leslie Crowther recalled in his speech how Lynott had asked for his daughter's hand in marriage. He announced that his reply was a resounding, "Why not? You've had everything else." This nearly caused a skirmish within the Lynott ranks, as Brian Robertson recalls:

"When he said that, I wouldn't say people were necessarily rolling down the aisles with laughter. All the Lizzy roadies wanted to race up to the stage and stick him out. It was a totally inappropriate thing to say, and I can tell you, we weren't the only people who were appalled at the remark."[7]

Scott Gorham who took to the stage after Crowther's less than appropriate speech, was the unlikely best man. He wasn't aware that the responsibility of being best man also meant making a speech. Gorham quickly toasted the new couple, wished them well and rather hastily made his exit.

Upon his return from honeymooning in Rio De Janerio, Lynott quickly entered the studios to appear in a promotional video for his debut single, "Dear Miss Lonely Hearts". It would be the beginning of what was expected to be a long, productive and commercially viable solo career. Also in the pipeline was the new Thin Lizzy project, the first to feature the playing of new boy Snowy White. The plan was for work to commence on the new Lizzy album in April with a late Autumn release date.

On 14 March 1980 "Dear Miss Lonely Hearts" was issued. Co-written with Wild Horses man Jimmy Bain, it showed all the trademarks of Philip's lyrical genius. The song told the story of two young fools in love, who both write to an agony aunt in desperation, only for the aunt to send out the replies to the wrong people. The video was shot with the band in playful mood and introduced the public to Snowy White. However, the main two things that stick out in the video are Philip's chin and the a freaky expression on a worn-out looking Scott Gorham's face. He recalls the shoot:

"Even though it was a Phil solo single, I didn't mind doing it because I loved the song. Phil asked me to do the same on 'Sarah'. It all kind of melded together back then. He'd bring certain songs to the band that he thought were great songs and I'd probably listen and carefully suggest that he might want to use that for his solo album. The solo material was full of good songs but were just not right for Thin Lizzy, so if he wanted any help with a solo project we were always willing, be it a recording or promo shoot. There was never any issue of weirdness about the solo Phil angle."[8]

"Dear Miss Lonely Hearts" is probably the closest that Phil ever got to playing Lizzy-type material on either of his solo albums. Even so, the charts remained undisturbed by its appearance and it peaked at a paltry No 32, staying for six weeks before disappearing. Irish fans welcomed Phil's solo debut warmly pushing the song up to a highly respectable No 6.

Lynott wisely sought the ratification of an Irish audience before taking the new Lizzy line-up to Europe to debut their new guitarist. The tour itself was unusual in that there was no new Lizzy album to promote, it was simply a case of weening in the new boy to gauge how the band gelled.

Lynott had also started to invest his money in property and one of his first purchases was the magnificant Glen Corr, a short drive away from the fishing village of Howth, perched on the North coast of Dublin. It was actually Caroline who attended the auction and rather naively paid £130,000 for the property. It later transpired that it could have been acquired for a modest £90,000 but needless to say it would prove to be a wise investment for Lynott. He already owned The Walled Cottage at 184 Kew Road near Richmond that was worth £250,000 at the time.

But after the purchase of Glen Corr he decided to try and persuade his mother Philomena to return to Ireland and set her up in some form of business venture with her partner Dennis Keely. Graham Cohen recalls:

"Philip sent Caroline over to Ireland with the children around 1980. He wanted them to be brought up here and raised as Irish citizens, though things definitely turned out somewhat differently. So over she came to look for a house and rather briskly acquired Glen Corr. Philip after much hassling convinced Philomena to come over to Ireland to look for a house for her fiftieth birthday. He figured it was time for her to settle down. Because the catering business is quite hectic, he felt she shouldn't be up until all hours entertaining her guests. Considerable amounts of alcohol exchanged hands in those days and it took its toll. He wanted to buy her a house, but there was another reason that he wanted her back in Ireland. The truth being, that he wanted her to keep a watchful eye on Caroline, who was young herself with two young kids in a foreign country. Philomena settled on White Horses, which was acquired in April of 1980. At the same time she didn't take kindly to Philip's accusations, she felt she was being, 'put out to pasture'. Philomena is a domineering personality and it caused friction between herself and Philip."[9]

The tour of Ireland showcased a five-piece Lizzy with Midge Ure still tucked away playing keyboards. On their return they had little over a week before setting off on a short Scandivavian jaunt designed to clean up a few teething problems with the stage set-up. Rehearsals were set aside as Lizzy had been booked to record material for their forthcoming release, with a number of songs swinging around such as "Chinatown", "Sweetheart" and "Sugar Blues" in the live set. The Irish tour would also prove to be the swansong for Midge Ure as Lynott finally accepted the idea of keyboards in the band and prepared to recruit a full time keyboardist to add texture to their live gigs.

The rumoured inspiration behind "Waiting For An Alibi" was an old friend of the band, Joe Leach. According to Philomena Lynott, Joe's wife continuously threw him out of his house after he ran up too many gambling debts, hence the title of the hit single from the *Black Rose* album. It was Joe Leach who suggested a young keyboard whizz kid from Manchester named Darren Wharton. At a mere seventeen years of age Wharton walked into a whirlwind of opportunities as he travelled down with Joe for the audition.

"When I think about it now, what I was getting myself into it almost seems surreal." Wharton recalls. "We had got the train down from Manchester and the band was working on the *Chinatown* album in Good Earth studios in Soho. The introductions were made and Phil settled me down with a few wisecracks and told me all about the album and what they were trying to achieve with it and so on. Phil then asked me to play a segment from the 'Chinatown' track that was quite basic, but because he didn't know how to play it himself he seemed to be hugely impressed by my standards. No sooner had the audition passed and I found myself running through the band's repertoire and once again Phil and the rest of the guys seemed to be pleased with what they saw. A couple of weeks later my apprenticeship began."[10]

Within those two weeks Lynott's debut solo album was released on April 18. It came as quite a shock to the British press who slated *Solo in Soho* when it first appeared. Saleswise it peaked at a somewhat disappointing No 28 in the UK charts. It was especially disappointing to the Phonogram executives who were expecting better. Recorded mainly at Good Earth studios in Soho, *Solo in Soho* also featured brief highlights recorded at Compass Point studios in Nassau – notably the quirky "Jamaican Rum" and a basic outline for the rumbling thunder which was "Ode To A Black Man" featuring Huey Lewis on harmonica. Overall, the album showed how versatile Phil could be, but it was a direction that put him at odds with hardcore Thin Lizzy fans.

"Phil and his solo material could've been huge," says Jerome Rimson who played bass on several tracks. "The main downfall was that there was never enough time. He just took it as an aside as opposed to sitting down and actually writing songs with these people. If he had sat down with me and said I want to write some real r'n'b and soul music, we could have come up with some great stuff. *Solo in Soho* wasn't bad for a first showing considering that most of the songs were probably written in a day or two. Over the last thirteen years Phil had thrown as many albums out and he was feeling really tired, confused and ultimately burnt out. You just can't keep writing hit record after hit record especially under the influence of things. I'm sure there were a lot of people around at the time who were too afraid of making an honest opinion.

"One time I came up with this riff in his home studio in Richmond, and he came rushing over and built this harmony piece around the fragmented chorus I had got together. The track was called 'Have You Heard Lately' and it was intended for inclusion on his first solo album but it didn't make the final cut which was such a pity because it sounded really great."[11]

The title track opened the album with the Lynott penned words of a clapped out whore. "King's Call" is a pure and unadulterated tribute. It had taken Lynott time to come up with a suitable song for his hero Elvis. Without even mentioning Elvis's name, everyone knew exactly what the track was about. *Sounds* made the ultimate comment on Philip's tribute.

"Since Elvis will not be recording any tributes to Phil Lynott you'll have to settle for the reverse. Grabby and a delightful 'up yours' to those who think Lynott and Lizzy have only one shape to throw. It doesn't sound like Springsteen either."

Issued as a single on June 14, all involved were brought back for the promotional video. Filmed at Hewitt studios in London, David Mallet directed with a budget of £10,000. Mark Knopfler's overbearing yet mournful guitar playing is easily recognisable and his ruffled appearance in the video highlighted how much he suited both the tone and mood of the song. However it stalled in the charts at a meagre 35 before slipping out again after four weeks. It seemed Lynott's solo career was faltering before it had even begun. Once again, it fared slightly better in the Irish charts, scraping in at No 20.

"A Child's Lullaby", another song about Philip's fatherhood, was not in the same league as "Sarah", but still evokes feelings of a father doting on a child. According to Graham Cohen, a close friend and confidante of Lynott's, "he absolutely idolised them. Because he spent so much time away, the time that he did have was all that more precious to him, and he made it even more precious for them."[12]

"Tattoo" showed how much Phil could lay off the gas and still produce a little slice of pop. It later turned up on a demo recorded by Huey Lewis and the News, securing them a recording contract in the process.

"Girls" on the other hand was a rare collaboration between Lynott, Bain and Robertson. Although the track has dated badly (as have one or two others on the album), it is catchy. One can't help but think about Lynott's parting line, "Don't leave me alone." It was a constant plea throughout his songs, especially the solo output, and in retrospect appears to be a cry for help. "Talk In '79" closed an ambitious LP with an attempt at rap, signalling Lynott's acknowledgement of ever-changing trends in music.

"'Talk In '79' was done in Morgan Studios the same night as 'Sarah'," says Mark Nauseef. "I was frantically providing a drum solo against Phil's bass. He just told me to go in there and play anything and he played off the rhythm I was giving him. He was rapping like crazy on it. I have the first take where there is a guitar solo leading to the fade out where Phil mutters, 'this is my contribution to the IRA', just having a laugh really."

A couple of years earlier it would have been hard to believe that an Irishman's music would be used as the signature tune for one of the longest running UK music programmes in television history. The rousing anthem "Yellow Pearl" was adopted as its theme by the BBC's *Top of the Pops* for five years, and stands out as one of the most nonsensical songs that Lynott ever collaborated on, on this occasion with Midge Ure.

During soundchecks on the Japanese tour, Midge Ure incessantly played around with the fluttering keyboard line. Lynott later admitted to storing it carefully in his memory until the time came when they could work the basic idea into a full-blown song. After the tour finished Lynott spent a lot of time with Ure, despite his commitment to Ultravox.

The inspiration for the song could have come from any number of sources, but the one that holds strongest is the twist revolving around Japan's impending global dominance of the technological aspects of our society. The promotional video reinforces this theory when it appeared later the following year.

TV producers were obviously impressed with Lynott's jingle-writing ability, when a demo of "Together" from his second solo album was also used for Irish Saturday morning show *Anything Goes*. The demo originally featured Paul Brady throwing in some lovely harmonies and making the song a sure fire hit. Disappointingly, this duet has yet to surface in any format.

Thin Lizzy kicked off their short Scandinavian tour toward the end of April, it was Wharton's first major Lizzy gigs replacing Midge Ure on keyboards. Upon their return, Lizzy settled in to Good Earth Studios to continue work on their forthcoming album. It was provisonally entitled *Chinatown*, after the area in Soho where they were recording. Much of the material was slightly downbeat with sinister twists. At this stage Kit Woolven had fully taken control of the production.

Before they could finish the album, Lizzy set off in May and June for a British tour. 'Dear Miss Lonely Hearts' had been issued as a single and Lynott slipped it into the set list. It proved to be an inspired choice, as the banter he shared with the audience midway through the song provided Lynott with an opportunity to prove that he still had it in him to play the showman.

The sporadic recording sessions were now in danger of compromising the quality of the album, and combined with a tour promoting nothing but a sprinkling of new material and an avalanche of old songs was doing little for the band's progress. Also, mid-way through the tour they had to cancel half a dozen dates due to Lynott succumbing to a heavy dose of the flu. The dates were re-scheduled, costing even more time away from the studio.

May 24 saw the release of the "Chinatown" single to precede the album. The video directed by David Mallet, shot on a budget of around £14,000, featured the sleazy surroundings of the red light district in Chinatown.

"I always liked that one," Mallet recalls, "though it wouldn't be my favourite. It was the sleazy aspect that I liked most about some of the Lizzy shoots. We got the atmosphere just right for it and it totally suited the mood of the song. Phil was always the gentleman in the group as were the others of course. There was always something about Phil that made you take notice.

Often after the shoots, which might last anything up to ten or twelve hours, we'd head back to his place and stay up all night chatting. He was a very humorous guy who was hip without trying to be in the slightest. He was never the outrageous rocker at all which a lot of people tend to believe. In fact quite the opposite, the image in the papers is far from the Philip the people who worked with him still remember. He was unique, in a way quite like U2, though I'm not sure if he'd like the comparison."[13]

The single stayed on the UK charts for nine weeks but just failed to secure another top twenty hit for the band by stalling at No 21, though a familiar pattern was repeated when it fared better in Ireland reaching No 12.

Snowy White and Darren Wharton had by this stage become recognised features of the new Lizzy line-up. It was to Lynott's credit that he tried to bring Lizzy into the eighties by introducing an additional man on keyboards, acknowledging the increasing number of new bands using synthesisers. Having weathered the media circus that was punk, there was now a new challenge to brush aside – prissy pop. But Lizzy really needed something like Robertson's or Moore's bite to bring them back to the commercial fairground. According to one person who wishes to remain anonymous, the new choice of guitar player wasn't quite the man for the job.

"Snowy wasn't the type of player that should have appeared in a Lizzy line-up. He wasn't a rocker and never came close to that mould of player. For a want of a better expression he was a musician's musician and never quite fit into the Lizzy category."[14]

"I didn't have any expectations, because I knew their history and I didn't know whether I was going to like it," Snowy himself recalls. "I didn't know how I was going to fit in with the guys but when I discussed the whole thing with Phil, he said there was going to be a lot more space for me to do my own thing in the band. It never really came anywhere near that, so after a while it got frustrating."

When the band played in Dublin's RDS they were heavily promoting the *Chinatown* album. Whilst in Dublin, Lynott met his old pal Brush Shiels.

"I remember him playing me the demos for what turned out to be the *Chinatown* album. He played me a rough-cut of the title track and he was saying that's your lick there, the introduction to the song. It was one of the first exercises I showed him, of course I took it as a lovely compliment."[15]

During the tour, it was rumoured that Lynott had been struck by a bottle at The Gaumont in Southampton. However the story was nothing other than a desperate measure by the publicity team to get Lynott back in the headlines. It was reports such as this that greatly peeved members of the Lynott family. Betty Wray continues:

"When Philip finally found success with Lizzy we were all very pleased for him and the boys. I was only around for a limited amount of time when he was growing up so I never saw the development of his talent. I don't really know how much he changed over certain years in his life though I have enough facts not to believe all the rubbish that was fed to the media to keep him and Lizzy in the public eye."[16]

On June 21, *Sounds* interviewed a 'frustrated at times' Philip regarding his thoughts on the unusual aspect of touring before a new album release:

"The other night during a gig we had this guy shouting his head off about us playing 'Soldier Of Fortune' but when we did play that they'd all shout for something else. At the same time audiences can be funny in that they provide me with things to say. Like at the end of a gig I'd say to them, 'What song would you like?' "Rosalie" or "Emerald".' Well one night this guy shouted back 'Emily'. That was great, I mean I used that one for ages."

A little while later, talk turned to the introduction of Snowy White:

"He gets better and feels more at home with every gig. I mean, considering that we've got two new guys in, Snowy and Darren, and considering that we've only been playing around for two months, it's working out really well. Hell, Snowy's a limey alright but no one's perfect."[17]

White was obligated to play some shows with Pink Floyd during the start of August, so the rest of the band had to delay album further. It had been over two months since the single, and by the middle of August there were still no signs of a release date for the album.

As autumn loomed, the band prepared for two vitally important tours, one which would take them to Japan and the other back down under to Australia. Before that, another single, "Killer On The Loose" was issued on 27 September, at a time the Yorkshire Ripper was still on the loose. The timing of the single was slated by a number of feminist groups provoking an angry Lynott into the following comment.

"There were two things that really annoyed me. They wrote to everyone except me and I didn't like the idea that they were setting themselves up as the censor for Thin Lizzy supporters, whereas up to this they'd probably never listened to a Thin Lizzy record at all. They didn't credit the supporters with enough intelligence. It was written as a warning song, but I knew I'd be criticised for it. I suppose with past image of the macho studded character then that's understandable to a point."

However, the track attracted so much adverse publicity that they were forced to drop it from their live set for a period of time. David Mallet who directed the video promo has his own thoughts.

"Out of all the work I did with the band this always remained my favourite. The promo turned out exactly the way Philip and myself had laid it down on the storyboards. His input was always worthy of inclusion and he had a strong sense of visuals when it came to producing a video promo. When it was issued it caused uproar, with the similarities to the Ripper case, but we didn't take much notice of that, a video for a song is all that it was. We were making state of the art videos at that time and that's as far as it went."[18]

Scott Gorham agrees: "We had some problems with this song. Bad timing on our account, I guess. Looking back it was somewhat tasteless, but no one in the band thought it would cause such a row. Phil admitted afterwards it was wrong to release it, but he thought it had a good guitar riff to it."

In the meantime, the single fared well, reaching number 10 in the UK charts and No 5 in the Irish charts. Strangely, after the commotion it caused, Lizzy would struggle to put a single in the UK top twenty again.

Snowy White recalls the time in the studio attempting to put the finishing touches to his heavily delayed debut release with Lizzy:

"A lot of the *Chinatown* album was made up in the studio, especially Phil's lyrics. He used to leave his lyrics until the very last minute and then light up a spliff and head for the vocal booth and sing off the top of his head. Because he was such a perfectionist he was always changing things and thus it was very time consuming, delaying the album release even more. That's the only reason the *Chinatown* album didn't surface until towards the end of the year."

Jerome Rimson goes a step further as he recalls the days when Lynott was at work on both his solo release and the new Lizzy album:

"Lynott was incredible in the sense that most people that wrote songs are sensitive about their material. Like if I write a song I don't want anybody around me. I watched him record most of the *Chinatown* and *Solo in Soho* albums standing at a microphone and making up the words as he went along, and while he was singing there was a full blown party going on in the control room. Just think of it fifteen or twenty people in the control room raging while he's in the vocal booth trying to rescue these albums."[19]

The band flew out to Japan in early September for a number of dates, most notably in Tokyo. On their arrival, the *Chinatown* album was released and entered the UK chart at No11 before peaking at No 7. The possibility of ever achieving that No 1 album now seemed to be slipping out of their grasp.

"We realised that at this point we weren't actually getting any bigger," Scott Gorham explains "That in itself was one of the things that really got me down, because I felt that at the time the material was good enough to achieve our goals. The drug situation was also playing a part, in that drugs are part of the music culture, there were a few of us doing different drugs at the time."[20]

Above: Moore, Downey, Lynott and Gorham touring the *Black Rose* album.
Below: Gorham in classic Lizzy pose. *Photos: Phil Birch*

Above: Eric Bell, Colin Clowes and Philomena Lynott at the Lizzy Convention 1998, *Photo: Phil Birch*
Below left: Lynott and fan. **Below right:** White Horses, the house Lynott gave his mum for her 50th birthday.
Photo: Alan Byrne. **Bottom:** Snowy White, Lynott, fan, Scott Gorham and Midge Ure. *Photo: Styx Management*

Above: Moore, Lynott and Gorham in the *Black Rose* era.
Below: The stalwart and dependable Brian Downey. *Photos: Phil Birch*

Left: Robertson in full flow. **Above**: Lynott arrives pre-show in the late seventies.
Below: Lynott courting the aggression that made Lizzy impossible to ignore. *Photos: Phil Birch*

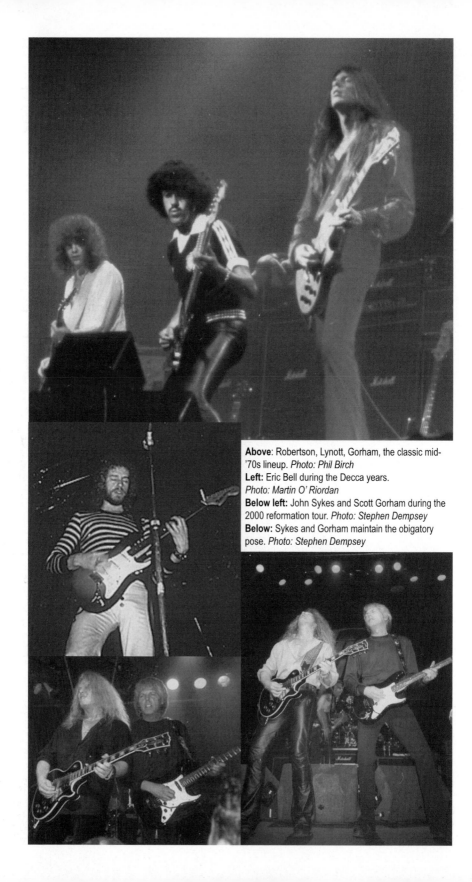

Above: Robertson, Lynott, Gorham, the classic mid-'70s lineup. *Photo: Phil Birch*
Left: Eric Bell during the Decca years.
Photo: Martin O' Riordan
Below left: John Sykes and Scott Gorham during the 2000 reformation tour. *Photo: Stephen Dempsey*
Below: Sykes and Gorham maintain the obigatory pose. *Photo: Stephen Dempsey*

Above left: Wharton, Sykes
and Lynott returning to the
stage for the first encore,
Birmingham,1983.
Photo: Kieron Loy

Above right: Lynott backstage before a Grand Slam
gig. *Photo: Kieron Loy*

Right: Lynott's grave in St.
Fintan's cemetery, with the
flat headstone bearing the
design by friend and one-time
neighbour, Jim Fitzpatrick.
Photo: Alan Byrne

Philip Parris Lynott (1949 -1986), the Emerald Cowboy. *Photo: Bruce and Chuck Drob*

No more singles were issued from *Chinatown*, despite the fact that the band could have released the courageously defiant "We Will Be Strong". It was classic Lizzy. The opening is reminiscent of "Do Anything You Want To" and finds Lynott in buoyant vocal form.

The title track from *Chinatown*, a group collaboration, has a rasping riff and off-centre lyrics that veer between the banal and the lunatic. However, it did little to deliver any of the oriental history or mystery suggested by the title – nor did the remainder of the album. Like *Jailbreak*, Lynott could have followed a continuous thread. *Chinatown* had nothing like that.

"Sweetheart", another Lynott penned ballad, suffers from sub-standard lyrics though the twin guitar harmony dutring the chorus cannot easily be ignored. It is perhaps the most significantly accessible commercial offering on the album.

"Sugar Blues" is a showcase for Snowy White, whose incisive playing reels across the number. Lyrically the song revisits a number of previous themes – drugs in particular – "sugar" being slang for cocaine. It is evident that Lynott was throwing his addictions straight into the face of anyone who dared to challenge what he was doing in private.

Side one closes in riotous fashion with the heavily criticised "Killer On The Loose", arguably the best track on the album. The song contains another powerful guitar riff emblazoned with a litany of hard core Lynott lyrics.

The little time available for its recording meant that the album has its fair share of filler, of which "Having A Good Time", a collaborative effort between Lynott and White, is adequate proof.

So far on *Chinatown* Lynott had failed to deliver lyrically, but then he rolls out "Genocide", his empathy for the American Indian and buffalo mirroring his own experiences. In much the same way that he was ridiculed, Lynott uses his early suffering as a springboard for other suffering, repeatedly asking questions and demanding answers, and finally retribution.

The understated "Didn't I" finds a tearful Lynott singing a sickly sweet dedication to lost love. Lynott's opening vocals tear deep within. However, it is clear that Lynott was either running thin on ideas, or lacking time to create new couplets. "Didn't I" staggeringly contains more or less the same verse as "Ode To A Blackman" and "Toughest Street In Town". One of the final verses before "Didn't I" breaks back into the chorus begins …

"There are people in this town that say I don't give a damn,
But the people in this town they never could understand".
Whilst on the *Black Rose* track, "Toughest Street In Town" it is …
"All across the city, no one gives a damn,
All across the city, no seems to understand".

"Hey You", the final cut, is one of the few real highlights on the album, a sordid story of hectic city life. It seems like a coded message about the never-ending destructive temptations laid before Lynott wherever he went.

Chinatown proved to be a marketing nightmare, and in truth it stands as one of Thin Lizzy's most half-hearted efforts. Primarily timing was an issue, being so close to Lynott's first solo release it may have confused audiences, although the two albums were quite different. Without the full support of the record company, the album quickly made its way out of the chart and into Lizzy folklore as the beginning of the end.

The *Chinatown* sleeve was another story entirely. As the band had settled on the album title early into the sessions, Lizzy stalwart Jim Fitzpatrick was brought back to design the cover. It portrays the feared secret society of The Triad. The middle claw representing evil, whilst the others represent power and money. Ultimately, it was to the detriment of the album that its contents did little to reflect the sleeve.

Kit Woolven recalls the confusion of working on both the *Chinatown* and *Solo In Soho* albums…

"Well, I started work on the *Solo In Soho* album as engineer, with Tony Visconti producing. But the way Phil works meant that he would often get an idea, and want to come in immediately to put it down on tape. Again because Tony was so busy, he often wasn't available and so we'd do it on our own. During the recording of the solo album, the other members of Lizzy would often turn up, and want to put some ideas down for what became the *Chinatown* album. So I'd find myself working on both albums at the same time and because the two projects were so different, I found it hard to switch back and forth between them, and maintain the right feel for each one."

Of course, having the band on the other side of the world at the time of the album's release did not help its promotion in Europe. After the spell in Japan, Lizzy made their way to Australia, arriving in Sydney on 7 October. Phil talked to Steve Gett of *Melody Maker* in a telephone interview on the night of the first gig, October 9.

"We're in the middle of grooving at the moment and everything has been going down very well. We went down a storm in Japan and tonight has been great too. It's great also because this is the first time we've been here with Brian and Darren, who only joined recently, and I have to say that all the Lizzies are looking forward to meeting some Australian colleens."

Just six shows made up the short Australian jaunt, before the band were due to hit the road in America for what would be the very last time in their career.

Sydney, the first date on the tour, turned out to be a bit of a *Spinal*

Tap-like disaster. For security reasons the band could not bring many of their stage props through customs. All the pyrotechnics were left behind in favour of hiring a local firm. Upon being informed by the firm that the material they were using was going to be pretty powerful, the band sauntered onto the stage to launch into "Are You Ready". Once they hit the first power chord the explosions went off, firing holes through the roof, one hitting Snowy White in the chest and blowing the PA. The gig came to an abrupt halt whilst repairs were made, the band coming back for the rest of the set over an hour later.

Back in Britain by the beginning of November, the band started rehearsals for the upcoming tour of America and preparations for Lynott's second solo album release. It would follow the same pattern as his previous solo effort – a "wherever, whenever" recording scenario.

Thin Lizzy and the USA had only seen eye to eye for a relatively short period. Things had never really gone as they should have – hit singles didn't appear, appropriate managerial supervision was lacking, and the lifestyle the band had become accustomed to began to prove detrimental to their stage performances. Many within their circle felt this was to be a last attempt to grasp at American success. Unfortunately, with their weakest album in several years, it would prove to be a futile effort. *Chinatown* simply didn't provide enough accessible material to grab any attention. Unbeknownest to them it was all over before it even began.

Problems mounted when during the course of the tour, Scott Gorham accidently slipped and dislocated his knee forcing him to complete the remainder of the gigs seated. The accident occurred in Washington whilst the band were playing at the Ontario Theatre and it was once again indicative of Lizzy's luck – or lack of it – whilst touring in the States. Any guitarist in a rock 'n' roll band would feel restricted whilst playing on a stool, especially when the latest recruit to the band didn't have the showmanship qualities to cover for him. This no doubt proved to be another nail in the Lizzy/American coffin.

10

RENEGADES ON THE RUN

By the beginning of 1981 a visibly tired Lynott and Lizzy retired to the studios once more to commence preparations for their next studio project. The somewhat lacklustre response by the public to the *Chinatown* tour necessitated a re-think, and with another Lynott solo project in the pipeline, important decisions were required. It was acknowledged that the release of Lynott's first solo album *Solo In Soho* had affected the possibilities for *Chinatown*, and such errors were supposedly taken into account when planning the upcoming release schedule.

For the first two weeks of January, Lynott gathered the usual entourage and headed for Compass Point Studios in the Bahamas where he attempted to complete his second solo album provisionally entitled 'Fatalistic Attitude'. Perhaps, the slating "Killer On The Loose" had received had put Lynott in a somewhat sinister state of mind. The bulk of the material for the second solo effort was eventually recorded at Good Earth with Kit Woolven over-seeing production, though some recordings were made at Windmill Lane in Dublin as Jerome Rimson remembers:

"While we were working on the early stages of the second solo album he asked me, 'What ya think?' And I said, 'It's a load of crap.' He grabbed me and snatched me out in the hall and said, 'Look man don't ever say that in front of anybody.' That's the kind of guy he was."

Lynott would barely have time to breathe as Lizzy were once again out on the road by the middle of January, an unenviable task considering his recording commitments. The European tour would be the only major public activity for Lizzy until later in the year when they would once again attempt to reclaim their British audience.

Again much of the confusion in the Lizzy camp in early 1981 stemmed from the uncertainty that no-one was sure whether they were working on Thin Lizzy material or songs for Lynott's next solo release. Up until the end of March, Kit Woolven had been producing while doubling as engineer. After reviewing the material during playback, it was decided to bring in a helping hand, Chris Tsangarides, who had previously worked with hard rockers the Tygers Of Pan Tang.

"When the time came to do the *Renegade* album I was actually meant to be getting ready to produce the new Wild Horses album," remembers Tsangarides. "I got a call not long before we were due in the studio from Chris O'Donnell and he told me that the Horses sessions were being called off and would I consider the option of producing the new Lizzy album. I was only about 22 or 23 at the time and of course more than happy to oblige. I had been a fan of Lizzy and was delighted by the prospect of working with them. They had most of the tracks by the time I came to the studios. The feeling of confusion was in the air in that sometimes nobody knew if they were working on a Phil solo record or a Lizzy album. For the *Renegade* album I worked on tracks at Morgan, Battery and Odyssey studios. While at Morgan I worked on the title track, "Angel Of Death" and "The Pressure Will Blow". At these sessions it was really down to whatever you made it. The confusion would continue because there was so much to be done, I had been working on the studio sessions, live recordings and the rest of it, it was madness."[1]

Sessions continued throughout April and May with the band desperately trying to rescue the album. In much the same way as *Chinatown,*, the *Renegade* album was left discarded at the studios waiting for a decision to be made as to when to run with it. In the mean time there were various festival dates to fulfill. Lynott also returned home several times during this period and on one occasion teamed up with his pal Smiley Bolger to take part in a piss-take of the Eurovision Song Contest. It had been won the previous year by Johnny Logan with "What's Another Year", coincidently written by Shay Healy, who eventually produced the documentary *The Rocker,* released some ten years after Lynott's death.

"That was in McGonagles, basically a bunch of middle aged guys having a laugh at the expense of a naff event," Bolger recalls. "Anybody and everybody came to play whatever song they had come up with, be it a cover or not. Phil and me did 'Mountains Of Mourne', well an x-rated version actually, but that's beside the point. We won by a mile, but that night will always hang in my memory as a great time."[2]

On 11 April Lizzy released their first greatest hits package, the aptly titled, *Adventures Of Thin Lizzy* with the cover featuring the band riding away into the sunset. It reached No 6 on the British charts and stayed there for thirteen weeks, whilst rather briskly notching up 100,000 sales and earning the band yet another gold disc. In preparation for shows at Milton Keynes and Slane Castle, Lizzy used relatively low key gigs to get the band into shape in time for the two colossal outdoor events.

The summer festivals were effective as they re-established Lizzy as a force to be reckoned with. Snowy White's playing and stage style seemed remarkably fresh in comparison to the previous tour. Privately, however, he was starting to regret his decision to continue to work with the band as their behavioral patterns were often at the opposite ends of the spectrum to his. For the time being White remained quiet, though not content, and anxiously waited for the outcome of their next album release.

Temporary man Dave Flett met up with his old buddies once they hit Aberdeen. Flett recalls the scene:

"Yeah…do I remember…after I left, Lizzy played my hometown a few years later, perhaps on the *Renegade* tour. I got a call from Scott asking if I'd be around and it just happened that a family member had passed away, so I was back in town for the gig which took place in a tiny club. So I did guest on a few numbers with them and we had a laugh. It was great to get back in contact with them for the gig and showed there were no hard feelings."[3]

On the day that the band played the Milton Keynes festival, a track called "Trouble Boys" was released as a single. Written by Billy Bremner from Rockpile, it also featured another non-Lizzy penned track on the B-side in the form of "Memory Pain". Probably the only attractive feature of the single was the Jim Fitzpatrick-designed sleeve. It only managed No 53 in the UK charts where it remained for four weeks. Even though it reached No 30 in the Irish charts, it proved to be a disappointment for the band. Snowy White recalls:

"I always liked the B-side "Memory Pain" and it was me who suggested we record it, but "Trouble Boys" was another story. Nobody wanted to put that out except Phil. Scott was dead against putting it out. I can't even remember how it goes to this day."

The reviews were once again nothing to write home about, *Record Mirror* having this to say:

"Lizzy discard their customary power drive for a Status Quo sound-alike song. The sentiments stay the same with twenty-five guys on the East Side and twenty-five guys on the West Side of the city fighting it out for the crown of King hell-raisers. Lynott is fighting hard to stay on side in music but this is dinosaur stuff."

Milton Keynes proved to be the ultimate disaster for all concerned. Lizzy were supported by ex-Mott the Hoople frontman Ian Hunter, Judie Tzuke and Q-Tips. The only act to escape the onslaught from *Record Mirror* journalist Mike Nicholls was Q-tips who he described as, "the pleasant surprise of the day, shrugging off their incompatibility with the open air and loss of a recording contract to offer a set of soaring, spontaneous excellence." The event however was deemed an unmitigated failure by all involved. To make matters worse, the well below capacity crowd of 10,000 was drenched by torrential rain. "There was a lot of pressure on us at that time and of course I arrived early and got drunk and then we were slaughtered by the press," Lynott later revealed.

Next up was Slane Castle, a mere twenty miles from Lynott's hometown of Dublin and crucial in cementing the bands reputation. Following the disappointment of the Milton Keynes fiasco, the band were adamant that the set was tight and the performance consistent. They introduced some of the material that would feature on their forthcoming album, such as "Hollywood". Listening to tapes of the show today suggest that the band were anything but tight – in particular Lynott's bum notes on "Waiting for an Alibi". On the day the band were supported by U2, Hazel O'Connor and Sweet Savage amongst others.

Lizzy wanted to hire a helicopter so they could make a tumultuous entrance, but at first they couldn't find someone willing to hire one at such short notice. U2, being the new boys on the block, had tried the same thing and failed. It was one of many ploys to try and upstage the king of Dublin. In the end, Lizzy managed to acquire a helicopter and flew in during Hazel O'Connor's set to a raptous welcome from the crowd. Swooping so low that Lynott's two-fisted grin was visible, it was all they needed to go crazy and set up a memorable night.

Being the first ever concert at Slane, Thin Lizzy played an integral part in promoting Ireland as a viable venue for a top-level festival. Subsequently, acts like the Rolling Stones, Queen, David Bowie, Bruce Springsteen, Oasis and the Red Hot Chili Peppers have graced the grounds belonging to Henry Mount Charles.

On a downbeat note, August saw Lynott on a drug charge for possessing cocaine and cannabis, and cultivating a cannabis plant. Although the police raid occurred nearly two years previously, it had only just come to court. Under the guise of gas board employees, the police had tricked their way into Lynott's Kew Road residence and searched the house, uncovering a small quantity of drugs. Lynott later tried to rescue the situation in the press.

"Drugs are very dangerous and I would advise anyone following the group not to try to imitate me by taking drugs in any way shape or form. I'm anxious that Thin Lizzy is in no way associated with taking drugs."

By Autumn of 1981, gossip in showbiz circles was rampant that Lynott was to take to lead role in a film about the life and times of his hero Jimi Hendrix. From the onset Phil's cards were held firmly to his chest. As part of publicity for the upcoming release of the new album, Lynott sat down with Liam Mackey of *Hot Press* to discuss recent events.

"I have actually had three US movie offers within the last year. One was like the black guy with the white chick, kind of a *Guess Who's Coming to Dinner*. Then there was the athletic one, something like *Raging Bull*, but nowhere near it in class and of course the most speculated topic of recent months was the Jimi Hendrix biopic. The thing is Geldof's doing enough of that for both of us right now and my time with Lizzy is far more important."[4] According to his management, discussions never went beyond the initial stages.

Despite lingering gossip in the tabloids, Lizzy continued writing and recording the Lizzy album throughout September. The failure of the "Trouble Boys" single was enough to necessitate a re-think on the direction the band was taking. On various occasions throughout the year Lynott took time out to commit ideas to tape for his solo album and "Song For Jimmy", one of the out-takes from these sessions, was issued as a flexi-disc with *Flexipop* magazine. The flexi-disc had originally emerged as a novelty format in the late sixties. Though the recording quality was poor and the shelf-life short it did allow record companies to create demo recordings and make them available as a promotional tool. "Song For Jimmy", despite the misspelling, was in fact a tribute to Jimi Hendrix, and it also re-united Lynott with Eric Bell in a studio for the first time since *Vagabonds Of The Western World*.

With the majority of the material completed, by the end of September it was decided not to include "Trouble Boys" on the new album release. In fact, in an interview Phil revealed it had been the original title of the album.

"The album was actually going to be called 'Trouble Boys', another play on the *Bad Reputation* title a few years earlier but as the single didn't do very well it was decided to abort the idea and think of something else."

In fact, feeling frustrated in the studio Lynott had decided to take a break and walk to a nearby bar where the inspiration for the album title litterally screeched passed him.

"It seemed to go on for ages, nobody could come up with a title for the album," Tsangarides remembers. "By this point, all of the songs hadn't even been mastered never mind worrying about the title. We were in Odyssey studios and Phil had left for a while before all too soon he came running in once more with an idea for the album. He had seen some kid on a bike with a denim jacket bearing the Lizzy logo but also with the word 'Renegade' written down the side of it. That was enough for Phil and consequently he had the title for the album. Also though, he now had the title for the next song he would be working on which would provide him with a stirring track."[5]

Renegade also served to highlight the growing influence of songwriting by the other members of the band. Only two numbers were solely written by Lynott – a regurgitation of the "Lonely Hearts" theme on "No One Told Him" and the vastly out-of-place yet moody "Mexican Blood".

The album opens with eerie keyboard sounds and a trembling bass line over which Lynott sings about the prophecies of Nostradamus. "Angel Of Death" was written by Lynott and Wharton and it proved to be one of the few highlights on the album. It was clear that Lynott had carefully researched the subject matter, as instanced by the following lines: "I was hanging out in Berlin/ In the year one thousand nine hundred and thirty nine/ I've seen Hitler's stormtroopers march right across the Maginot Line/ I've seen two world wars I've seen men send rockets out into space/ I foresee a holocaust/ An angel of death descending to destroy the human race/ Down, down deep underground, a great disaster." Whilst promoting the *Renegade* album Lynott went into a little more detail about the origin of the song.

"Basically I'd just finished reading the *Prophesies Of Nostradamus* and I thought it would be a great idea to write about that. So, I picked two great disasters that he prophesised and I gave the spoken piece where I ask people if they believe it. Then I talk about a personal tragedy – a person watching his father die – a personal disaster and the 'Angel Of Death' coming down to destroy the world or to take you to hell. It isn't full of humour and life is it?"

Scott Gorham on the other hand is scathing about the opening number:

"I hated that song, 'Angel Of Death', even the title. C'mon are we getting corny again? Fucking hell."[6]

"Renegade" once again threw up one of the glorious themes that Lynott had made his own so many times before, a boy from the wrong side of the tracks determined to do it his way, a rebel with a cause. The title track would prove to be one of his finest lyrical achievements of the eighties. Co-written by Lynott and Snowy White the song builds and builds to a climax with one of Lizzy's best guitar solos in years. With White totally revelling in the moody swagger, finally it seems he has found his niche within the Lizzy set-up.

"There's a hard-rocking heavy side to me as well which comes out now and then but I'm more into the mellow direction," recalled White. "The perfect example would be the 'Renegade' track. A lot of that was down to me, the actual mellow side of the guitar and for the group I thought that was a nice change. It still remains my favourite Lizzy piece."[7]

"The Pressure Will Blow" is another standard rocker that is often conveniently forgotten about when discussing *Renegade*. Lynott's rasping vocals hit home in a similar fashion to "Soldier Of Fortune", but its subject matter makes it bland. "Leave This Town" tries to get going, but suffers somewhat from constrained production values.

"Hollywood" would later emerge as a single, and has hit record written all over it. It was a straightforward rocker but still one of their catchiest tunes in years. "No One Told Him" should really have been left off the album.

"Fats" sounds like a band bored by their surroundings, bored by the limitations of rock, and generally willing to try anything to maintain their interest. Though not a bad song by any means, it neither fits the make-up of a Lizzy album nor does it fit the theme of the album. Maybe Lynott's vision had become somewhat blurred by the avalanche of work. "Mexican Blood" also falls well short and further highlighted the tension within the band.

The album exited on another note of soul-searching. Once again co-written by the increasingly confidant Gorham/Lynott partnership, "It's Getting Dangerous" told of the two's private circumstances. Gone was the morbid confessions of "Got To Give It Up" – it was now blatantly clear exactly what the message was really about. Two boys, in way over their heads, finding it difficult to survive in the environment they had created for themselves.

Without a single to promote the new record, the *Renegade* album was to prove a major setback in the Lizzy camp. Going no higher than No 38 in the UK album charts, Lynott and Lizzy were now fighting for their musical lives. In America the album would eventually surface in February 1982 peaking at a lowly No 157 staying on the charts for eleven weeks.

The general concensus among critics was that Lizzy had had their day and that it was now time to step aside and let the young pretenders have a go at the big time. Chris Tsangarides in particular recalls the *Renegade* period:

"Once more the new trends began to take hold in the same way as punk did in the mid seventies. Phil survived that, but he couldn't overcome the

Duran Duran's and all those pretty boy types. Getting back to *Renegade* though, I sincerely thought the material wasn't focused enough. There seemed to be too many styles involved. The focus became diluted when Phil had to commit ideas to tape for his first and second solo albums. Perhaps as well at the time there just wasn't enough input from the other members to counteract this. "It's Getting Dangerous" is one of my favourite tracks to this day."[8]

Another downside was that someone had failed to acknowledge the growing influence of their keyboard player on the cover of the new album. After an interview for RTE an audibly annoyed Wharton stressed his disgust at the situation, though Lynott was keen to play down any fragmenting within the group or the Lizzy organisation.

The album cover would also bring on board some new faces in that for the first time Lizzy employed the services of Graham Hughes. Once more Chris Tsangarides can explain where the ideas for the album sleeve came from.

"The cover concept of *Renegade* came from me, well sort of anyway. At the time I used to smoke Dunhill International cigarettes. I remember Phil pointing to the colour of the box at the console and immediately identifying with a concept in his head. Straight away he was on the phone to the director in the Art Department to get his idea across. So what you see, with the flag on the flip side as well is none other than my ciggie box. I always have a laugh when I think of that."[9]

The year had been somewhat inconsistent as the band's recording schedule had interfered with touring, and they had once again spent a lot of time deliberating about the track listing and final mix of *Renegade*. As an album, it will forever be known as Lizzy's nadir, though this seems harsh considering some of the material is as good as any rock and roll band of the time.

During August and September of '81 Mark Nauseef was recording his own album in Hamburg where he is still resident today. The sessions were held in Tennessee Studios and Nauseef called Lynott to put down lead vocal on a track that he was trying to get together called 'Chemistry'. Nauseef was also having some difficulty coming up with the appropriate lyric, and Lynott came to the rescue.

"A guy called Wolfgang Dreibholz managed to get Phil over. We were working on one of my records, and I had some top heavy guys down there coming up with some great sounds. I knew that the songs we were working on were going to be instrumentals but when a track called 'Chemistry' came together I could hear the vocals. Now I knew that Phil hadn't any idea of odd time signatures, but I did think that he was the guy to do a job on it for me. So Phil arrived in the studio and realised that he had forgotten his notebook, which contained any lyrical ideas he might have. So Phil sent some guy back to London to bring over his notebook, but in the meantime he started playing around with the song and had the rest of the guys in awe of him. There was so much more to him than the public saw, it was quite incredible. He ad-libbed a lot of the vocal and nailed what we wanted down in the second take. Whatever was inside of him came out in the most creative of ways. After the 'Chemistry' session we all headed off for an Italian restaurant and left a note for his assistant about where to find us when he came back with his notebook. Looking back now as a trio we cut a lot of stuff, that is Gary Moore, Phil and me in the Bahamas and at Morgan studios in England. Most of it has never been released, but there are some great jamming sessions there on tape."

The track eventually surfaced on the album 'Personal Note' which contained just six tracks. Though by no means a great song, it nevertheless highlights his willingness to be versatile.

In his personal life, Lynott was intent on creating his version of the perfect family environment. September of 1981 also saw him decide to plunge into a partnership with his mother as they purchased the run down Asgard Hotel in Howth. Philomena remembers it only too well:

"Now that Philip was well ahead in the world making his money and so on and so forth he arrived down to Manchester one day. It was probably in the early part of 1981 and I remember him saying, 'Look at you, smoking and drinking until the wee hours of the morning'. But I had only been doing what all my guests were doing in that that was the kind of hotel that the Clifton Grange was. So then he said, "Go over to Ireland and find yourself a house, I'll buy it for you, go and pick one." So I came over and after looking around I settled on White Horses. After doing all that I said, 'Jesus your putting me out to pasture,' and by then the grandchildren had started to come and I just thought maybe yes this is the time to start settling down. I was fifty at this stage and Philip came over and I was bored, I still thought that I had something to offer. He said look for a hotel and we both bought the Asgard Hotel. Unfortunately after less than a year the hotel burned to the ground. We went through the pros and cons of rebuilding and then all sorts of complications arose so nothing came of it. In the end it proved to be a costly investment for the both of us."[10]

Graham Cohen remembers the running of the hotel out in Howth:

"The Asgard was in an extremely poor condition when it was handed over to us. I had never seen the place and we had to put total reliability on the existing staff and they performed nothing short of a miracle. We built up a great relationship with the staff and the locals, and within the period we had it up until the August weekend we had turned it around from a dump into a thriving place. Whenever Phil had cause to be around, which of course was a little more than usual now with Glen Corr he would always show his face because it gave that little boost to whatever functions were going on at the hotel. Having a rock star as the guest of your wedding tended to bring a lot of positive publicity to the hotel. With Irish music sessions, he was often joining in with them and again this boosted the atmosphere."[11]

Lizzy were back on the road by mid-November supported by Sweet Savage featuring a young Vivian Campbell, later of Def Leppard fame and the treadmill began again.

11

SLIPPING AWAY

As 1982 kicked in, so did the drug problems. Out of the charts, and rather frequently out of their minds on stage, Thin Lizzy was faltering and faltering fast. Husband and father of two, Lynott sat down and tried vainly to rescue what was left of his reputation and that of his position in the world of rock. Re-assessing his marriage would come later, but for now he found himself bereft of inspiration and he turned once more to the splintered cushion of hard drugs. Scott Gorham too had been dabbling with heroin, and both he and Lynott would live out the remainder of their Lizzy lives in a drug-induced rage. Rage at the fact that they could no longer command the large audiences – the fact that the band didn't seem to be getting as big as they foresaw. It was in this frame of mind that Thin Lizzy began 1982, and with another schedule packed with tour dates the performances and sheer power of Thin Lizzy started to fade.

It began badly. The cancellation of several British gigs was officially down to "mishaps on tour". Scott Gorham's initial claims of exhaustion were later discovered to be false. It is now assumed that he was suffering serious withdrawal due to his heroin usage. While the band were in Portugal, a decision was made to return Gorham to London for a recuperation period, and the band marched on as a four-piece for the remaining three gigs.

In Denmark it was the turn of Brian Downey to become victim. Lizzy had by now taken socialising to a new level and Downey became the target of a rampant attack in a local nightclub and was beaten so badly that the Lizzy management insisted on flying him home for treatment. As a result, the band had to call once more upon the services of super-sub Mark Nauseef, who was in a unique position to document the low-key attitude in the band:

"Lizzy had had all the lights and the pyrotechnics in 1978, but things were a little subdued in 1982 when I subbed for Brian. When I originally joined it was Gary and Phil who were going crazy on stage, jumping from my drum riser but by then Gary was gone and Snowy was there. The presentation wasn't all that flash but that's the way they progressed as a band. Snowy for me was a real positive guy, maybe the odd egg in the nest but a lovely guy."[1]

The final two dates of the tour at the Dominion Theatre in London were filmed for a video release but somewhere along the line the plan imploded. The excuse put forward by Lizzy manager Chris Morrison was simply that the shows "were caught on video as opposed to cinematic film." It seems odd that the band put valuable time, energy and work into overdubbing and editing the footage if the material was not up to standard. After viewing the footage it appears that the band seemed to be missing a certain edge. As Phil desperately tried to salvage the performance, Snowy White goes through the motions whilst Gorham wrecklessly shakes a leg here and there to little response from the audience. On the evidence of the Dominion tapes it is clear that everyone's interest, band and audience, seems to be on the wane.

While the group were in Spain touring, the record company finally issued the "Hollywood" single on the 6 March with little result in the charts. It sluggishly made its way to No 53 in the UK charts and disappeared after three weeks – it never surfaced in Ireland. Officially there was no video to accompany the release and maybe this proved to have a dire effect on its progress.

In the age when promotional videos were taking on a new context, and MTV was in its embryonic stages, Lizzy's failure to get commitment from their record company was emerging. Once more the marketing men were at a loss, but how much of the blame can be laid at the feet of the band? Whatever way you look at it, it was promotional suicide to release the debut single from an album that had already been in the public domain for over three months. Lizzy were entering the final stages of self-destruction.

Lynott was however the subject of a TV documentary titled, *Renegade – The Philip Lynott Story*. Produced by RTE, the documentary was one of the most informative accounts of an Irish music phenomenon. It gave previously unseen insights into the workings of the band, their roots and influences, and rather frustratingly remains unavailable to this day as a commercial release. It may well have been out of desperation that Lynott and Lizzy had taken the project on, feeling that the band needed to resussitate their status with the public. It was also one of the last times Snowy White was seen with the band. David Heffernan recalls the process of making a documentary.

"What happened with *Renegade – The Philip Lynott Story* was that I got a call from Philip while I was working at RTE and I was taken aback to be honest. At this point I had never actually spoken to him, but I had seen him when I was quite young playing at the Abbey Theatre in 1971. The gig was great and they really blew everybody away because they were doing something which we thought couldn't be done by an Irish artist, back then you had to be American or English to get away with it.

"So an agreement was reached and we had the usual pre-production period of about six weeks though it would have been staggered. We filmed in England for about four days and back in Ireland for about the same time. So it turned out to be an average ten-day shoot or thereabouts. Post-production then took another five to six weeks. Tony Palmer had done a few touches with Rory Gallagher during the Irish tour of 1974. So we came up with the idea that eventually unfolded into the *Renegade* project or/ *The Philip Lynott Story*. I remember Philip saying, 'Yeah, let's go for it'. At one stage after we had a rough cut prepared and he came in to view it and I remember him being really interested by it. After seeing how engaged he became while watching the rough cut I knew we had touched the subject matter in a way that certainly had a resonance for him."[2]

By the end of the *Renegade* tour Lynott still had to put the finishing touches to his second solo release which was due out that summer. Lizzy were on a hiatus until the Autumn (having committed themselves to a festival in Castlebar) after which they were to prepare material for their next album. The extended break gave Lynott time to compose material as well as prepare for an Irish solo tour. The tour was being promoted by MCD and was going to feature just one Lizzy player, Darren Wharton, who was also musical director. Lynott gave his thoughts on touring solo to Bill Graham.

"It keeps me active. I like to work, I like to play. As for Lizzy, we've just mixed a live video and it sounds really good. I was thinking about playing the 'Renegade' track on this tour plus a synthesised version of 'Whiskey in the Jar' but I'm not sure yet. The majority of the set will be taken from my solo albums. I just hope the people like the other side of me. The musicians are hot, the approach is definitely original and I think there's enough of an audience in

Ireland interested in seeing something different. Obviously if they've come to see Lizzy they're in for a great shock but all I can say is 'tough buns'."[3]

The solo tour also provided time for Lynott to gather his thoughts and reflect on the rut that Lizzy were stuck in. There was less pressure to act like the crazed rock 'n' roll star he was made out to be. He could simply act like Philip – the man who loved to write songs and poems about his daughters or various odes to his wife.

When it came to the bottom line, each Lizzy member had probably had enough. They needed timeout, to re-charge the batteries, rejuvenate the creative juices. Gorham had pulled Lynott aside on numerous occasions throughout the *Renegade* tour threatening to walk away, only for Lynott to convince him all over again that they should complete one more album and one more tour and then they'd bury Lizzy forever – together. Wharton, the relative newcomer had never really added that much needed extra dimension to the band – admittedly in a band like Lizzy it was difficult for him to stamp his mark onstage when he was tucked in away at the back. White simply didn't suit the band, he was the wrong man for the job. Gorham, who was going through a lot of personal problems, had by this point lost interest in projecting onstage. So, much of the responsibility onstage was now bestowed upon Lynott, a mantle he found increasingly difficult as he struggled to control a worsening drug habit.

In recent years it has been the opinion of the Lizzy management that Lynott's descent into chronic drug addiction stemmed from his music business lifestyle. So much of the business is boring, be it the endless travelling or hanging around on the set of promotional videos. The counterbalance is the adrenalin rush for those two hours onstage. In trying to either maintain that rush, or to come down from the natural perfomance high, drugs provide an easy distraction. Whatever the reason, the situation got so out of hand that even the band could do little to deter Lynott. The prospect looked ominous. So, unfortunately, was the outcome.

The Irish solo tour showed the softer side of a hard man. What had started with the tribute to his daughter, "Sarah" taken from the *Black Rose* album, now saw him consolidating his reputation as a man capable of a more tender artistic expression. The solo Lynott gigs were capacious in experimentation – it was an "anything goes" mentality. For the tour, Lynott took with him a selection of some of the finest musicians. Jerome Rimson on bass, Robbie Brennan on drums, Darren Wharton on keyboards, Gus Isadore on lead guitar, Trevor Knight on additional keyboards whilst Lynott alternated between playing six string rhythm and bass.

The Irish tour was a relaxed affair and justly allowed Lynott to off-load a cauldron of ideas he wanted to try live. It also proved to be an effective soundboard for testing out some of the material that was due to feature on his second solo release. Trevor Knight, who was playing keyboards, was actually a member of the Gay Woods led band Auto De Fe, who were supporting the Phil Lynott solo band for the tour. During downtime Lynott would find time to produce Auto De Fe in Dublin. Gay Woods recalls what Lynott was like as a producer:

"I knew Phil since when he was about seventeen or eighteen in Dublin. My ex-husband Terry Woods also worked with himback in the early days, and in the latter days also. I remember working on a song called 'November November' and Phil was going mad trying to get a sound, he was trying everything, a really terrific guy to work with. He wanted to sing on all the tracks we collaborated on and he did a fair few as well. Because I was the lyricist in the band, Phil and I obviously clicked on that level but I was never prepared to relinquish control when it came to my lyrics and he appreciated that."

The gig at the SFX was the final part of the jigsaw for the RTE documentary *Renegade/the Philip Lynott Story*. The cameras descended upon the venue, and the footage stands as one of the only pieces of film showing Lynott performing solo. Though there are glimpses of Lynott in the RTE documentary from the SFX gig, unfortunately all that was filmed was used. The crew only shot roughly twenty minutes footage and made their exit.

The show proved to be an inspired choice for the premiere of his new material. With a rousing version of "Dear Miss Lonely Hearts" the band pummelled the audience into submission, when Philip announced:

"Dear miss lonely hearts, I had to write the letter,
To tell you how I came to Francis Xavier".

The crowd was once again wrapped up in the cosy romance of the rocker, the romeo, the valentino. Whatever your opinion of Lynott, he seldom let an audience away without troubling their heartstrings.

For some reason the band were dubbed the Philip Lynott Soul Band, a name that was somewhat wide of the mark according to Jerome Rimson.

"Well to begin with, my feelings are that most of the solo project, from my take on Lynott, was just filler. It was just something to do. We were never called the Soul Band as so many people have it. Everybody keeps calling it the Soul Band, it was simply the solo band. That kind of offended me, because the only reason they were saying that, was because there was a load of black guys in the group. It was totally wrong. We only went on the tour when Phil said to me, 'I made a lot of money after the *Live And Dangerous* period and I can't stay in this country (England) too long,' hence why he went to record in Ireland. I remember him saying that it was a great tax dodge and also a good way of getting his friends to go on tour."[4]

The solo tour wasn't without the usual hiccups. When the band was in Northern Ireland, they were stopped at the border.

"When the guards came out with the rifles and we were sat there swigging brandy and they scared the shit out of us," Rimson continues. "The Irish tour was actually quite calm, it was quite laid back to the point where we did a lot of drinking and smoked a few joints. At this stage Phil wasn't into the heroin thing to a very obvious extent, to us anyway. The tour of Europe was a different story, well in the sense that heroin was very prevalent."[5]

In July, Lynott released a taster from his forthcoming solo album titled "Together" which failed to chart in the UK but did give him another brief top thirty hit in Ireland reaching No 25. Unfazed by this relative failure, Lynott continued to put an amazing amount of effort into his solo gigs, confirming that the band would reform and play another European tour during the coming winter. Gus Isadore comments on the reaction of fans to Phil's solo material.

"By the time I met Phil in 1982 my good friend Jerome Rimson had already contributed to his solo albums. From then on [Irish tour] I have never looked back. Phil and I hit it off straight away. As far as touring is concerned I served my apprenticeship with Phil, learning the ropes, stage craft etc. The Philip Lynott solo band did cut it with his supporters in my opinion because the band was so dynamic. We were a good bunch of musicians."[6]

On July 18 Lynott joined Rory Gallagher and Paul Brady at the Punchestown festival and all three jammed on a few numbers. Disappointingly the only record of this historic occasion is a photograph, even though RTE cameras were present at the event. Paul Brady:

"We were only onstage for a short time, perhaps fifteen minutes or so. We played one of my own songs called 'Busted Loose' and one by David Lindley called 'Mercury Blues'."

The end of July also brought the news that the hotel that Lynott and his mother owned had burned to the ground. It happened over the course of the bank holiday weekend and proved to be quite a costly loss to all involved as Philomena confirms:

"There was talk of rebuilding and then all sorts of complications arose so nothing came of it which was such a pity because we had turned it around into a thriving business."[7]

Before entering the studio to record the next album, Lynott came up with the idea behind the gem that was "Holy War". It was more or less another run at the Nostradamus theme, though it still needed a lot of work before it could be taken into the studio. Lizzy had agreed to headline a three-day festival in Castlebar on August 1. This would turn out to be the last gig featuring the Gorham/White lead guitar formation. Finally, Snowy had had enough of the whole Lizzy image and Phil's unreliability.

"Phil and I were just on two different wavelengths, putting it bluntly, two completely different personalities. He was the hell-raiser and the hard living guy who just lived solely for his music and the lifestyle it involved. I tended to be a lot quieter which I think everyone noticed. I'd tend to go to bed a lot earlier than the boys."[8]

It was also around this time that longstanding co-manager, Chris O'Donnell decided to call it a day when he announced at a crisis meeting that he no longer felt the band had a direction to take their music. The decision was no doubt prompted by the last two albums. Basically O'Donnell wasn't interested enough to continue working.

With White's departure another nightmare began to unfold as Lizzy were due to commence recording for their next album. This time they decided not to repeat the *Bad Reputation* sessions where Gorham handled the majority of the guitar work, and it was decided that a replacement was needed pronto. During August, Lynott had popped into Lombard Studios in Dublin to visit his producer pal Chris Tsangarides who was working on a session with a young whizz kid guitar player by the name of John Sykes. Sykes was fulfilling his obligations to MCA by recording a single "Please Don't Leave Me" for release the following month. It barely grazed the top 100 despite heavy TV promotion. Chris Tsangarides recalls their introduction.

"It was on my suggestion that Sykes was brought in. I was after sorting out some stuff for Sykes and eventually I secured a deal with MCA to release a song that he had written. We were in Dublin when he asked me if Phil might be interested in recording and contributing to it. So I got in touch and Phil decided he was up for it and we recorded the track with Brian Downey on drums and I think Darren Wharton played keyboards on it."[9]

It was after these sessions that Sykes was officially offered the gig with Lizzy and promptly accepted it. The band was then due to go into the Eel Pie Studios in London later that month to begin recording.

Sykes was born in Reading on July 27, 1959 and when he was fourteen years of age he went to live with an uncle in Ibiza. With the slow pace of life, Sykes took up the guitar and began practising on a daily basis. After less than two years he was back in Blighty without the stability of a job, so he started auditioning for local bands in Blackpool. He eventually joined a band by the name of Streetfighter and apart from the inevitable covers, they recorded a song titled "She's No Angel" which surfaced four years later on a compilation album entitled *New Electric Warrior*.

By 1980 Sykes had been gigging incessantly to little avail, until he answered an advert for a lead guitar position in what turned out to be a gig for the Tygers Of Pan Tang. Sykes recorded two albums with them, the first being *Spellbound* and the second *Crazy Nights*. Though neither were commercial successes, his standing in the music industry was such that Ozzy Osbourne had asked him to audition. Scott Gorham recalls the immediate impact that Sykes had on the band.

"After Snowy left, John came on board for the *Thunder and Lightning* album. To me, John was great because he had a real hard rock edge to him, he had a great attitude and was a very funny guy, though most importantly he was a great player."[10]

Lynott's forthcoming solo album had also gone through significant changes when it was announced that the title was to change from 'Fatalistic Attitudes' to the rather bland 'Philip Lynott Album'. His next solo single, "Old Town" was also being lined up for release and a video already scheduled. The break needed for filming the solo promo cut into the recording time for the new Lizzy album. However, this was eventually remedied by Chris Tsangarides.

"After the *Renegade* session I more or less had my foot in the door, and this led to me getting the production on their next studio album, which turned out to be *Thunder And Lightning*. I remember being in the studio for these sessions and the band hadn't really got anything more than ideas, so I thought, 'Why are we wasting valuable money'. I mean, paying £1,000 a day when all we needed was a rehearsal room to go away and work the songs into shape before going back to the studio to master them. I remember Phil turning around and asking why nobody had ever thought about doing that before."[11]

Bob Collins (producer/director at RTE) devised a slot on the *Anything Goes* Saturday morning show whereby they would air two video promos per month featuring Irish artists. It was an ideal opportunity, especially as Philip had only recently finished writing a song about an individual returning home to Dublin, and of course, this only added poignancy to the promo.

David Heffernan explains how it came about.

"After the *Renegade* project Philip got in touch and he asked me if I could get him on the programme, so I didn't hesitate. So we then spoke about what we would do and put a few questions around various topics and also worked on a few slides together. We struck up a relationship which was mostly professional though I did hang out with him a little bit. I always found out something interesting about him because he was very challenging and a great guy. In a work context, he would have a strong idea of what he wanted to do but he would also listen to how you wanted to treat it.

"After that we did a bit of work together I remember getting a call from him telling me about a song he had which was about this guy coming home. The track was 'Old Town'. So I went over to see him in England when they were recording the *Thunder And Lightning* album at Eel Pie studios. We sat down and went through a storyboard with input from both of us and shot more or less the ideas that came from that session. He had very strong visual ideas about how he wanted to be seen in 'Old Town'. Because this was a solo effort as opposed to a Lizzy track, he saw the male romantic lead role as something that really interested him. I had been doing some work in Dublin with the director Gerry Gregg and we had a decent framework for the song and its presentation.

The shoot for "Old Town" lasted nearly two days, with a very weary Lynott turning up on the morning of the second day very much the worse for wear. "I don't even think he had gone to bed the previous night," recalls Heffernan, "and you can certainly see a tired Lynott sitting at the bar."

"There were a few things that I really wanted to use in the promo for 'Old Town', Heffernon continues, "that for a number of reasons just didn't come off either because of finances or otherwise. For the last shot where he walks down the pier at the end of Ringsend I actually wanted to use a helicopter so that the final shot would be the helicopter rising to see Philo walking towards you and then get a panoramic view of Dublin. I think it was one full day and an early morning because we had to shoot in the the Long Hall bar [the bar/archway still remains, for those who want to catch a glimpse of the Dublin bar] before anybody arrived in to start drinking. When you look at the video you had to know that the song carried a certain romance. It had to be about a town that was synonymous with Philip Lynott. Grafton St looks very different now and the whole sense of Dublin in the eighties is different to the new millenium. I'd like to think that Philip Lynott fronting that period in Dublin is a nice thing to have done and to have it there for people to see. I have always been struck by the resonance it has with people when they see it."

"The girl in the promo is Fiona McKenna, the actress," Heffernan continues. "Frank Murphy, the researcher on *Anything Goes*, suggested Fiona for the shoot. We needed someone who could act as opposed to just model. I am particularly fond of the section where she bursts out laughing at the top of Liberty Hall. We had to put the promo together very quickly and I was happy with the fact that Fiona reacted with Philip's on-camera charisma very well. I remember saying to him that I would really like to see him walking down Grafton Street because I always associate Philip with walking down this street. Whether its part of folklore at this stage I'm not sure but because he was such a standout figure and because he was always at the cutting edge of fashion I thought Grafton Street was the perfect backdrop for this shoot. Philip really wanted to do it as well as did the director. So we got him to walk down the street and what happened was purely spontaneous…

"…We used the Ha' Penny Bridge because we wanted the Dublin landmarks. The trumpet solo in the middle was shot in Herbert Park in Ballsbridge. There was a very old, almost English style bandstand there, which we thought was just right and then there was Gerry's idea to use the ferry that was used to take people from one side of the Liffey to the other. I think this sequence works really well and it is quite funny too, in that I think this Ferry run was on its last day. They withdrew the service after that. We needed an office for Fiona and we needed somewhere that spelt big business, so we used Liberty Hall which would give the view of height and a firm perspective. Every time I see the promo I always wish we could have had that helicopter shot at the end because it really would have helped to enhance the image. 'Old Town' is one of those incredibly identifiable Irish songs. It's always fares well in the polls and I'm quite proud of my contribution to the piece. It has become so synonymous with Philip."[12]

Though the film schedule was tight on occasion it didn't stop Lynott enjoying a selection of double brandies during lunch breaks much to the amazement of the crew.

Philip's second solo release, by this time delayed by nearly three months was ready to be unleashed on the public. However, very few in the record company were reportedly interested in Lynott's new collection of songs.

"One of the last paintings I ever did for Philip," recalls Jim Fitzpatrick, "was the proposed cover for his second solo album, originally titled 'Fatalistic Attitudes'. The album however was not meeting with approval from the record company and they threatened to cancel it altogether. Of course with all this going on, they also refused to pay for the artwork. In my opinion it is probably Philip's finest work, I mean who can argue with a song like 'Old Town'. We were walking along the beach, when for the first time he played the album for me on a walkman with the old-fashioned headphones, and I was simply blown away by what I heard. I couldn't believe the record company didn't like it. At this point I knew Philip was in trouble, he could take neither the rejection of his artistry nor the crap that went with it. We walked on for another couple of hours and I could sense a desperate sadness coming from deep inside him, presumably he was experiencing a great sense of failure. The man I met that day was disillusioned and cynical about his profession, 'running on empty', he called it."[13]

Despite the outstanding video, Lynott's disillusionment was deepened when "Old Town" failed to make any impact on the English or Irish charts, even though it was also backed with the non-album B-side in the shape of

"Beat of The Drum". "Old Town" did however prove to be a big hit single in Holland and throughout Scandinavia.

September also brought the official announcement of the appointment of John Sykes to the Lizzy set-up. The relationship between Sykes and Lynott provided the one remaining constant in the lead vocalist's remaining years up until his premature death.

After taking a break from the recording sessions for the new Lizzy album, Lynott re-grouped the solo band in early October to coincide with the release of his new solo album. The line-up for the gigs saw Nauseef providing rhythm, Wharton and Jimmy Bain on keyboards, Isadore on lead guitar and Rimson on Bass. Lynott's forte was rock 'n' roll on a stadium level and the new solo material wasn't accepted that well by the public.

Like any other tour it wasn't without its hilarious moments. Rimson informed Lynott that he intended asking his girlfriend to marry him when they returned to Dublin, Lynott's roars of 'stag night' were met with much approval. Rimson recalls the events:

"We had been doing a lot of travelling and Gus Curtis was really tired as was Jimmy Bain, so much so that they actually fell asleep in a topless bar while we were out celebrating. Needless to say we and they made up for it during the rest of the tour."

Reports of the European tour are patchy due to the volume of illegal substances that were apparently being used. But Jerome Rimson can recall some of the details.

"Phil decided to do the European tour in two 450 SEL Mercedes limousines and a little estate car. Everybody would be in convoy going down the motorway when all of a sudden you'd see the car with Lynott in it pull over to the side. Of course we would follow suit only to hear this voice, 'Get the fook out' and whoever the hell he'd be throwing out would be relegated to the crappy little estate car. For whatever they would have said or done. People would then be moved up to the car he would be in if he decided he liked them. Everybody at some stage would get kicked out, though some remained in his favour, usually the ones who were most dangerous to have around. On the other hand Isadore was like Phil's protégé, Phil took a real liking to Gus because they both shared the same birth sign so they had something of the same character."[14]

On another occasion Lynott openly abused his celebrity status when it came to dealing with hangers-on and groupies. Once more Rimson takes up the story.

"We were in Copenhagen and Phil pulled this girl who was absolutely stunning. Phil used to play real head games with women. This girl had come to the gig with her father, who was extraordinarily wealthy, and she was totally in love with Phil. He went over to his suite with her and left the door open saying something to her along the lines of, 'I'm going out for a while, don't talk to any of these guys in the band.' Of course we all went to try and sweet talk this woman, and believe me when I say this – this woman would not even say a word to the rest of the band. Phil never even came back; he just left her there. He could be so wicked sometimes.

"He told us what he had got up to the next day when we met up at the airport, but we had missed our flight because Phil had been running late. So Phil hired a private plane and told us he would get a scheduled flight later, because he had some other business to take care of. We had all this baggage and we saw this little plane and there was no way that we could fit everything on. So Gus, being a bit green and naïve, turns to Phil and says, 'What do I do with my luggage?' I can still see the expression on Phil's face as he said, 'Leave it with me.' That was the last Gus ever saw of everything he owned. I'm sure Phil just left it wherever Gus left it."[15]

Lynott's long awaited, and heavily delayed second solo album surfaced during the European tour, and many of the tracks played were taken from the album. Seeing footage of the solo band in action is quite eye catching. It's almost as if Lynott has dispensed with the macho image, especially on the softer material. This was Philip at work, not Philo. These television appearances have yet to find a commercial outlet, which is a tragedy, as he is being backed by an arsenal of sublime musicians playing great live renditions of Philip Lynott songs.

'Growing Up' sounds altogether different when performed live with the solo band. He sings of a father being let go from his job, his child's trouble with school and the struggle to cope with harsh circumstances. On backing vocals is Lynott's cousin Monica, who provides ample support. It is perhaps Lynott's forecast of what was to come in his own life, had he lived long enough to provide direction for his own children and family.

After the success of the re-issued and re-mixed version of 'Yellow Pearl' in the summer of the previous year, Lynott once more chose to include it on the album. It reached No 14 aided by a video directed by co-writer Midge Ure. Featuring a string of Japanese beauties, Lynott opted to continue the theme of Japanese technology taking over. Midge Ure appears in silhouette form in the video and set against a budget of around twenty grand, it served its purpose by putting Lynott back into the British top twenty.

'Together', the first single taken from the album the previous summer has dated badly. The song is known to exist in various formats; one featuring Paul Brady, which never went beyond the demo stage, and another duet featuring Junior, the version on the album has Lynott solely taking the lead vocal. It's just another love scenario being played out, and Midge Ure's heavy influence is apparent, though as Jerome Rimson recalls... 'that was one funky number to play on.'

'Just A Little Water' is a simple, almost angelic twist in Lynott's whirlpool of material. The keyboards are strong, a feature that separates his solo work from that of Lizzy. The song has a catchy little melody, though its repetitive chorus line betrays any real substance. 'Ode To Liberty-Protest Song' is Lynott in fatalistic mood once more. Second only to 'Old Town' on the album, the message appears to be that in order to be heard, you don't have to scream – perhaps this is why Lynott's vocals are somewhat unclear. The mixing of the song is in perfect sync with Lynott's subdued voice, with Mark Knopfler's guitar playing maximising the impact for the listener.

'Gino', a little touch of filler once more, Lynott can't seem to let go of an album without including a track that should have been left on the shelf. Incorporating taped voices from some American religious programmes during the mid-seventies, Lynott just seems to be running out of ideas. Mark Nauseef recalls the time he spent recording Lynott's second solo attempt:

"'Cathleen', 'Growing Up' and 'Gino' were done at Good Earth. I remember Phil was asked, 'How does Mark play?' only to have a reply, 'he walks the tightrope' come flying from his mouth and he was right. If I or we didn't get the take right I just wanted to get right back in there and hammer it out. Most times everybody would head off when it came to Phil doing his vocals, but I used to hang on and watch him until he was satisfied with the outcome. He improvised incessantly in the studio and used an organic way of working. It was amazing to watch."

The final cut on the album was 'Don't Call About Me Baby', and again Lynott was capable of much better than this drivel. Overall the album fails due to lack of organisation. Had Lynott sat down with the various musicians at his disposal and actually planned the album, he probably could have come up with better songs.

With the poor showing of the solo album in the chart, Lynott chose not to gamble on touring it in Britain, possibly for fear that Lizzy would feel the backlash. In any event, Lynott rejoined Lizzy in November to complete the new album.

"When the band had finished up doing their parts," Chris Tsangarides recalls, "be it guitar or drums for the day, Phil would hang around and work up a guide vocal. A lot of his lyrics were made up in the studio but he was always changing them around until he felt he'd done the best he could do with them. All the tracks that appeared on the *Thunder And Lightning* album were recorded at Eel Pie studios while all the overdubs were put down at Power Plant a little while later. I was determined for cohesion.

Because Sykes was a pretty powerhouse player with all the Van Halen aura hanging from him, I thought that this was exactly what Lizzy needed. Now both Snowy and John are great guitarists, but Sykes most certainly fitted the bill in a lot more ways. Snowy had the slower blues style, a great player but lacking identity within the band. A band is all about chemistry, and by late 1982 Lizzy's interest was waning. I suppose they became more despondent as time went on, because once you're used to selling loads of records and the sales start to slip you do begin to wonder. Sykes gave them the kick up the arse that they needed – a renewed sense of interest, of appetite and overall he was a dynamite player." Tsangarides continues.

"In my mind we had to be well rehearsed before we went into the studio. There wasn't going to be any mucking around keeping all the guitar tracks. If it wasn't up to scratch, it was wiped. Phil might say, try overdubbing that bit and then let's hear a playback. I decided that this wasn't going to be the way to do it. We were going to get the parts in check first and then, be it the rhythm guitar, lead guitar, drums or bass and then work from there. The days of keeping loads of shit for little or no reason were gone. If I hadn't chosen to work this way I would have been running from one end of the desk to the other trying to accommodate any overdubs which Phil might want to hear on the playback – that was madness. On the other hand with the vocals, I kept everything. When it came to recording Phil and the band they were always very professional. They were a great band to listen to even at their worst."[16]

With Christmas looming and the general feeling in the camp that the new album was the best they had come up with in years, Lynott once more re-grouped the solo band for a spate of gigs. The line-up included Brian Downey who replaced Mark Nauseef on drums.

12

CAN'T GET AWAY

Just prior to Christmas announcements were made for Thin Lizzy's first, and ultimately only tour with the rookie guitar player John Sykes. Christmas came and went while the band rehearsed their set, and talk in rock circles was that Lizzy were back – though whether they were back to the glory days of previous years remained to be seen.

Behind the scenes, speculation mounted that ticket sales for the new tour were appalling. Due to start at the end of the month, an emergency meeting was arranged by Chris Morrison early in the New Year to discuss the band's future. The tour needed a jolt and the presence of Sykes alone couldn't provide it. Desperate measures led to desperate consequences as one Lizzy backroom employee recalls.

"The tour had indeed been selling really badly and it needed a lot more than sneaky thinking to get the band out of their current rut. So it was decided to make this tour their last, a farewell tour, because in effect, by 1983 Thin Lizzy had had their day."

Embarassingly, newspaper reports suggested that Tony Brainsby, Lizzy's PR agent, had cunningly used below-the-belt tactics to try and sell more tickets by announcing that the band were going to enjoy one last payday from the name Thin Lizzy. Some reports suggested there was as little as £60 worth of ticket sales at some venues, though when the farewell tour was announced the tickets were all snapped up within days. During the course of the European leg of the tour, manager John Salter continued to add shows, it seemed that every town wanted one last lash of Lizzy.

The final blow came on the 18 January when it was announced that Lizzy were to discontinue, both as a touring band and a studio recording entity. Reports suggested that Lynott was sickened by the decision to wind up the Lizzy organisation. He was devastated and hurt as he acknowledged that the group that had for so long been the cornerstone of his existence would be no more. Thin Lizzy was one of Philip Lynott's few emotional moorings, so when it ceased, in many ways so did he. Lynott would have this to say.

"A lot of people of people didn't want Lizzy to break up and I for one, was one of them. The members thought we couldn't move on as we were. I have lived in the safety net of Thin Lizzy for a long time. I would hate Thin Lizzy to live off past glories. Right now I'm looking at going into a bit of production work and I have formulated ideas for a book. With the three books of poetry already done I have completed thirteen short stories regarding the music business and publishers are very interested so we'll have to see how things turn out."[1]

On January 26, 1983 the Thin Lizzy farewell tour commenced at Hitchin, a concert which was broadcast simultaneously on television and radio on the BBC's *Sight and Sound in Concert*. It was the official debut of John Sykes and he graced the boards in true rock 'n' roll fashion in his leathers. His playing was the ingredient that had been missing since the *Black Rose* album and everyone within the organisation knew it.

The band showcased several new songs in the set, demonstrating a strong belief in their latest album. Starting with "Jailbreak", they made their way through "This Is The One", "Holy War", "Baby Please Don't Go" and an eerie "The Sun Goes Down". They then went back to *Live And Dangerous*, and Lynott and Co steamed their way through 'The Boys Are Back In Town' which Lynott rather hilariously announced as a 'medley of our hit' before taking on 'Cuppa Tea' 'Rosalie'. What had changed markedly from the time of their hit live album was Lynott's physical appearance. Dressed in the same outfit as the one that graced the cover of his second solo album, his bloated features came as quite a shock. Also, although the crowd was in high spirits, Lynott's mood was distant, almost resigned. It is fair to say that he wasn't hiding his depression as before, it was obvious that Philip Lynott could hurt, and hurt badly. Smiley Bolger reveals his thoughts during Lizzy's last days:

"The band was shit hot when they broke up. Breaking up Lizzy was a financial decision. Downey used to say that at the height of Lizzy: 'It's like being managing director of a factory employing a hundred and fifty people.' Their driver Gus Curtis thought he'd never be out of a job with Lizzy. I remember him saying it to me. He couldn't believe it. The new punks were coming along and Philip must have felt trapped to a point."[2]

The band continued the tour on the 2 February to coincide with the single "Cold Sweat". It was a Lynott/Sykes collaboration, which was one of the last songs to be included on their new album. Chris Tsangarides recalls the choice of single:

"I was kind of surprised that 'Cold Sweat' was chosen, it was a bit heavy, even for them. By way of promotion they found themselves on *TOTP*, but Phil had a little argument with a stage manager and of course they shafted them off the show. I remember thinking 'God no,' because the consequences for the album would have been positive. They got the album straight in at No 4 and here they are getting kicked off a major TV show at the time, the album ended up doing well, however the singles didn't particularly come off."[3]

Thunder And Lightning, released on March 4, whilst not being one of their best albums, was a step in the right direction. Gorham was extremely pleased with the renewed vigour:

"*Thunder and Lightning* felt pretty good to make, though I wasn't in the best of shape at the time, neither was Phil. It felt like going back to what we wanted to achieve in the first place because things had got a lot softer and easier going at that point. Whether we thought we had a hit or not didn't come into it, because we had returned to hard rock, for which we became known in the first place."[4]

It transpired that newcomer John Sykes handled the majority of the lead solos as John Alcock remembers, "Scott was the quintessential second guitarist. He got off on playing just riffs and power chords with very little lead."[5] Sykes on the other hand was more than happy to be a part of Lizzy and it was unfortunate he didn't have more time to come into his own.

"Yeah, I arrived pretty late in the day for the *Thunder And Lightning* album. The boys had pretty much what they wanted regarding material written and it was literally 'let's get down and record it'. Because I hadn't contributed anything at this stage I just let go with an outline of what was to become 'Cold Sweat', all of that was made up there and then in the studio. Overall the whole experience of doing that album was a real treat for me."[6]

From the ominous introduction, Lynott took Lizzy into their toughest terrain in thirteen years. Although veering toward heavy metal, it still had its catchy moments. The writing credits were shared, as Lynott would solely contribute only two numbers. It was a far cry from the early days. It was the ever-increasing songwriting prowess of Wharton that was coming to the fore.

Though the clichéd nature of the title track's lyric would suggest a re-visit to familiar territory, it still sounds fresh in a new wrapping. The song is laden with imagery that Lynott drew from first-hand experience.

"This Is The One" is by no means a Lizzy classic but nonetheless featured heavily in the set for the farewell tour. Lynott's vocals are somewhat hazy. Though it is a notch above filler, it seems consciously concocted. Lyrically of little substance, Lynott seemed intent on burying his vocals beneath an avalanche of overdubs. Perhaps this is why the song sounds a little misplaced on the album.

"The Sun Goes Down" was a collaboration between Lynott and Wharton, and the helplessness in the song reflected the raw intensity of Lynott's predicament offstage – "Won't someone save this sinner/ I know him too well".

"The Holy War" and "Baby Please Don't Go" were the only numbers solely written by Lynott. "The Holy War" was one of those rare gems that Lynott let rip with on every other album. The song was blanketed with guitar harmonies, with an angry Lynott questioning mortality. It is a powerful song, perhaps the finest musically on the album, but was unfortunately overlooked as a single release. "Baby Please Don't Go", however, was a rather blatant similar offering to the previously released "Please Don't Leave Me". Whereas the Sykes's effort was a cosy tune in the mould of a Lynott solo song, this new track was a Lizzy-ated version. One reporter at the time went so far as to call it, "one of the best ballads Lynott had ever come up with". Perhaps he was a stranger to the Lizzy back catalogue.

"Someday She Is Going To Hit Back" was a Downey/Wharton/Lynott brainwave that had the stench of filler dripping from its opening chord to the climactic cymbal. "Bad Habits" was a Gorham/Lynott collaboration borne out of personal circumstance, though lyrically it isn't as powerful as previous offerings in the same vein such as "Got To Give It Up" and "It's Getting Dangerous". Its accessibility however cannot be denied, and it was another song surprisingly passed over for a single release. It did seem a lot more commercially attractive than the title track, though as Darren Wharton reveals, it didn't quite wash with him.

"'Bad Habits' in my opinion was one of the weaker tracks on the album and even on the re-union tours it hasn't been as frequently asked for as "The Holy War" for example. I never really took to that song to be honest."

The album fades out in a somewhat lacklustre fashion with "Heart Attack" bringing Lizzy's studio life to an anti-climactic end. This was a rare Wharton/Gorham/Lynott collaboration which saw Lynott contribute nothing musically, while lyrically his magic had been on the wane for quite some time.

For the *Thunder And Lightning* album sleeve, Lynott once more tried to enlist the services of his good friend Jim Fitzpatrick. This time however the record company didn't see any need for a heavy investment and deliberately discarded Lynott's idea for a gatefold sleeve.

"The record company didn't have a clue," Jim Fitzpatrick protests. "While they repeatedly wanted Philip to come up with 'The Boys Are Back In Town' part forty, Philip was trying to broaden his horizons. Being an artist myself I knew how impossible it was to compromise or relinquish creative control to become something you're not. I had worked out a few ideas with Philip but in the end they opted for something else, the cheap way."[7]

Early copies of *Thunder And Lightning* came complete with a four-track bonus live E.P. The songs featured were "Emerald", "Killer On The Loose", "The Boys Are Back In Town" and "Hollywood".

It was clear that with *Thunder and Lightning* Lizzy were striving for the sound of the day, but like Lynott's second solo outing, the quality of the material was just not up to scratch. Although the album brought Lizzy back into the top five of the album charts, it did come in for harsh criticism:

"An enormously disagreeable piece of work," said *Melody Maker*, "it isn't so much Lizzy's last stand as their final collapse. Since none of the songs have much to say, Lynott must have been little bothered at not being heard."[8]

It also had as many admirers. "It crackles with the intensity to be expected from one of the most enduring of bands," said a reporter in the *Evening News and Star*.

The *Thunder And Lightning* album still left Lizzy owing their record company one final album. Although the band had enjoyed their most commercially successful period on the Phonogram label, the company could not beat the early success of "Whiskey In The Jar". This proved to be a source of much frustration to Lynott, as Frank Rogers recalls:

"Phil never got over the fact that Phonogram, as big as they were, could never help push a single for Lizzy higher than they achieved with Decca, strange that one."[9]

However, the fact of the matter was that they had signed a six-album deal, which was near conclusion in 1983. After much discussion a proposal was made that as a memento of their last tour, the performances would be recorded and an album featuring the highlights of this final tour presented to the record company as their commitment album. In a way it seemed ideal, as Lizzy's live reputation was what had made them a formidable force in the past. The idea was also mooted that they get back all the previous Lizzy guitar players and have each player guest on the live LP. It was at the

Hammersmith shows in the early part of March that this notion was realised.

Thin Lizzy had recorded thirteen studio albums in as many years. Creatively bankrupt, the final tour was now in full swing. According to Eric Bell, the band's preparations hardly paid off for the Hammersmith reunion gigs, when he admitted the playing was well below par. Brian Robertson recalls similarly.

"After listening to the tapes from Hammersmith, O'Donnell asked me to come to Glasgow to do another recording and I did. They used the version of 'Emerald' from Glasgow on the album. I didn't do many overdubs on that album though."[10]

The Hammersmith gigs did however get Moore and Lynott back on speaking terms as the old hatchet men were brought back together once more. The only Lizzy axe-man who wasn't called to make an appearance at the Hammersmith shows was Snowy White whose wounds were perhaps still weeping from his dalliance with the Lizzy and Lynott machine.

After their Manchester gig at the Apollo on the farewell tour, John Sykes introduced Magnum keyboard player Stanway to Lynott at the Britannia Hotel. The two struck up enough of a relationship for Lynott to offer him the chance to play keyboards on the solo tour through the following July and August.

"After initially meeting Phil in Manchester I later met him at Lizzy's Reading festival appearance," Stanway recalls. "I was playing with Magnum during the first day of the festival but hung around to catch Lizzy's performance. Phil offered me the job of playing keyboards on a Swedish tour and I did not hesitate to accept the offer."[11]

After returning to England to finish off their commitments, the band were once more gearing themselves up to be the subject of yet another RTE documentary, this time an in-depth report on the working of a touring band. The project was aptly titled *The Sun Goes Down,* and it was again presented by David Heffernan who had collaborated with Lynott on the "Old Town" video and the first documentary on the band the previous year. Bob Collins was responsible for capturing Lizzy on film in their hometown for the last two gigs they ever played, at the RDS on 9 and 10 April. Another show in Belfast was also filmed. The first of the RDS shows went well, and Shay Healy recalls the gig with great affection.

"After seeing Lizzy live many times one of the strongest bonds I have ever felt at any concert was at the RDS. Though it was at the end of their career and although I had inkling that all was not well, it was a storming gig with the reaction of the crowd being magnificent. For every twist and turn the crowd were with him every inch of the way. The warmth from the audience rode directly to the stage and he put it back out there through the music."[12]

The second night though proved to be the ultimate burial for Ireland's favourite rock band. Lynott turned up early, got drunk, and continued to drink throughout the set as they tried to remember which song they were due to play next.

"The band's career went into a bit of a tailspin after that," David Heffernan remembers. "I know Philip liked some of what was recorded because he used some of it in the video promo for the 'Thunder and Lightning' single. It was a kind of sad occasion really because it was the last time Lizzy played Dublin. The band were at the height of their powers since the *Live And Dangerous* period and there was certain sense of anticlimax to the whole proceedings."[13]

By the end of April, Lizzy took the farewell tour across Europe. It would be Lizzy's last salute to an array of fans who had pledged their support. During the Scandinavian leg of the tour, there were the obligatory interviews and at one given point Lynott found himself in the company of a youthful interviewer keen on making a positive impression. Magnus Rouden recalls his interview with a highly charged Lynott:

"As a nervous teenager back in 1983 my first job was to interview the front man of Thin Lizzy, Phil Lynott, for the *Rockdepartment*, a music programme. As we made our way through a host of people to get backstage for an interview, we happened upon Robert Hultman, then of Polygram Records but presently at Universal. While guiding us to the dressing room he insisted on telling us how much of a dislike Phil had for reporters.

"The truth was that he was exactly the way I had imagined him to be. Charismatic, with that deep, dark voice, warm, kind and gentle with a sometimes nonchalant look on his face. The hard rock paradox I suppose, soft and hard – tough yet tender. He was an interviewer's dream and gladly provided me with all the relevant material I required for my report. Lynott's consistency as a 'man of the fans' is something that has never been diminished hence the affection that supporters continue to have for him nearly twenty years after his death."[14]

The next Lizzy single to be taken from the new album was the furious title track, which made a brief appearance on the UK charts on the 7 May and then slipped out after two weeks. The single, as was the case with "Cold Sweat", was not promoted with an appropriate video. The marketing wizards at Phonogram once more ignored the best way of promoting a record. The record company spliced together some live performance material from the farewell tour, cutting budget and hindering the impact of the release.

It was reflective of the predicament of a band like Lizzy attempting to survive in the early eighties. After having regular hits for the previous ten years, they weren't afforded the chance of even making a simple and straight-forward performance video to promote their latest single. The footage primarily consisted of the Dublin/Belfast shows the previous month. It also has Phil a good three or four feet away from the mike while at the same time giving a rip roaring vocal.

By mid-May Lizzy had made their way to Japan for their final dates before taking a break to allow Lynott to take his solo band throughout Sweden. John Sykes proved to be a major draw for the Japanese crowd. "We started calling him 'the hunk' after some poll over there voted him as their 'hunk of the month' – he was not amused," Scott Gorham recalls.

The final Japanese dates do not bring back happy memories for those involved. Looking tired and overweight, Lynott repeatedly berated the audience, trying too hard to rally a response. It was rumoured that the upping of indulgence in chemicals was the primary reason for his condition. Their playing was also immensely affected, but numerous mistakes didn't seem to make a difference to the dedicated support of their Japanese audience.

With the possibility of an American tour looming, it seemed the band was plagued by indecision. The sales of *Thunder And Lightning* in the States proved to be less than spectacular. On the 28 May the album stalled at No 159, and promptly tumbled out of the charts after five weeks. The story would be the same in Ireland where the album could do no better than reach No 22, a significant marker confirming that Lizzy were indeed no longer the force that they once were.

Aside of the possibility of the American tour, the band were also rumoured to be considering another visit to Australia. With the lack of success of *Thunder And Lightning* in America, it is easy to see why the band decided not to return there to tour the album. It had been three years since their last visit and each subsequent album release received less and less attention. Australia on the other hand would have been ideal, had it not been for the condition of certain personnel. Though Lynott publicly claimed interest in returning to these territories, it is conceivable that Gorham and Downey saw little point, why bother trailing through these countries once more when the band was going to be wound up anyway? The hassle wouldn't be worth it and considering the return on the investment, wisely Thin Lizzy dropped both the US and Australian legs from their farewell tour.

The disagreements over touring the States really began to grate with Lynott and he later confessed to the press that he really thought the band could make the trip a success.

"I'm hoping that we can get out to the States at some point after Reading. At the moment I've a feeling we could really reef America. To be honest the only thing that America needs is for us to spend a bit of time there. I was of the opinion that we should move away from the European market for a bit and concentrate our efforts on other places but I'm afraid my cries fell on deaf ears. A few of the lads weren't interested so that was it really."

He continued and commented on the media's reaction to the farewell tour announcement in order to sell tickets.

"I wouldn't mind if Lizzy stayed together but they'd all call me a cheeky bastard for wanting all this publicity. Now let's be fair, a lot worse has been said about me so you'll have to believe that I'd lie to keep this band together. For the time being though I'm getting ready to enjoy my holiday in Mozambique with the family so that's the only thing on the agenda for now."

With Gorham and Wharton opting out of the picture, Lynott took off on a solo tour of Sweden with John Sykes on lead guitar, Brian Downey on drums, Mark Stanway on keyboards and Doishe Nagle on rhythm guitar. Known as The Three Musketeers, this would be Lynott's last ever tour in Sweden.

"Scott needed time off and that's where the solo tour in Sweden came into it," recalls John Sykes. "We had got through Europe and it came time to do America but Scott wasn't up for it. By that point it was like he had beaten himself up a bit too much. Phil was no angel, just one of those guys with the constitution of an ox. He'd always be on the case."[15]

While the Musketeers were playing their penultimate show in Sweden on the 6 August, Lizzy issued their last single in Lynott's lifetime – "The Sun Goes Down". Though Phil was quoted as saying, "I think that one is a nice note to go out on. I can see it being played on the radio and fully believe it has great chart potential," it made little impression on the charts, sliding to No 52 during a three-week stay. The sleeve for the single featured a lone Lynott, perhaps a sign of what was to come. There was no official promotional video to accompany the single, as the record company once more reneged on their commitment. The band were left piecing together live footage to accompany the single, but as it languished in the lower reaches of the top sixty, work was abandoned.

On returning to Britain, Lizzy secured the top billing at the upcoming Reading Festival. Due to be the final festival to be held on the traditional site, it would prove to be an inspired choice and an apt swansong for Thin Lizzy's farewell UK performance, where they headlined on Sunday night that also featured the likes of Steve Harley, Little Steven and Twelfth Night. The band put in one of their best performances in years and it was all on tape. The BBC released it some eight years after Lynott's death and it serves to be a worthwhile memento from their farewell tour. Lynott was in great spirits, and it was truly the last time that he was in complete control of Lizzy onstage, and his voice cut through the air. Lynott rallied hard and won the band several encores as they reached the climax of their set.

A couple of days later the band flew to Germany for the *Monsters of Rock* tour and what would turn out to be the final live dates with Philip Lynott at the helm.

The short run of gigs were not without incident as Brian Downey and Scott Gorham got lost on the autobahn right before the second gig in Kaiserslautern. On hand to save the day was Brian Robertson who was also playing the festival with Motorhead. He roped in Motorhead drummer Phil 'the animal' Taylor to cover Downey's position. Lynott then hastily arranged a rehearsal in the dressing room to help Robertson come to terms with the new numbers whilst also trying to convince Taylor how to handle the rhythm section. With Lizzy waiting in the wings to go on, Gorham and Downey finally made their appearance and by the skin of their teeth Lizzy came good on their penultimate live gig with Lynott out front.

The end came in Nuremburg when the band took to the stage one last time leading the crowd through a routine which had begun the previous January. Worn out professionally and personally, the band conceded that they needed time off to recuperate and re-charge their batteries. It was unfortunate for Wharton and Sykes who were entering the prime of their careers just as the band was grinding to a halt.

With the record company accepting the live album as the coda to their contract, Lynott re-entered the studios upon his return from Germany to continue working along with Will Reid Dick on the recordings taken from the farewell tour. It is a pity it wasn't the Reading performance that surfaced because the new live album raised more than a few eyebrows concerning the sound quality. Due to ill health Lynott had been restricted tos co-producer on the album. And for a man who lived, survived and breathed to make Thin Lizzy a success, he was now preparing what was to all intents and purposes his epitaph as much as it was Lizzy's.

Earlier in the summer Lynott admitted that the song selection for a live album was so important that he had to get it right instead of rushing a product out "just because we're in the news right now." The *NME* writer Paolo Hewitt on the other hand had a sweet poke at Lizzy during the summer:

"The only thing worth saying about Thin Lizzy is that a friend of mine had to vacate a studio recently as Lizzy were due in that day to record their forthcoming live LP."

Lynott and Lizzy however stuck with the philosophy that had seen them through so successfully the last time with the *Live and Dangerous* album. As Tony Visconti pointed out that, "The art of making a good live LP was always what you can come up with in the studio."[16]

Live Life was finally released in late October, making the charts in November where it tamely fumbled its way to No 29. Without the back-up of a hit single the album more or less came and went without much applause, despite featuring some great performances from the invigorating John Sykes. He obviously felt he was the man for the job and accordingly afforded some Lizzy standards with some amazing solos. "Are You Ready" and "The Holy War" are the standouts on the album. The band chose to include a lot of material from the *Thunder And Lightning* album highlighting again their belief in the material. Tracks such as "Baby Please Don't Go" and "Cold Sweat" were brisk, but vocally questionable. Brian Downey even admitted that while the recordings were okay, the "mix was so muddy it was awful".

Whilst putting the album together, Lynott and Gorham were in the throes of pain. Years of abusive behaviour towards themselves and those around them put paid to any kind of reasonable future in the industry. By the end of 1983 Lynott's marriage was on the rocks, to such an extent that Caroline had decided to take their children back to Bath in the hope that this would finally shake Lynott out of his consistent abuse of drugs. Facing a fragmented marriage, a defunct band, an debilitating drug habit, Lynott slipped further and further into his addiction. It is fair to say that few people knew the extent of his problem, and accordingly no one took the necessary steps to get Lynott to address the problems he was facing. One source, who wishes to remain anonymous had this to say about Lynott at this point in his life.

"By this stage the drug side of things was in a dangerous area though a lot of people had been kept in the dark about it. What Phil could get away with in London he certainly couldn't get away with in other places, so a man in his predicament would have to have taken chances and take them he did, but all in all it was himself who he was fooling."[17]

The break-up of Thin Lizzy most likely proved to be the final straw for Lynott. However, the band members never really thought that this would be the end of the road. Darren Wharton recalls that the spilt was not meant to be final.

"I never thought for a second that we'd never end up playing together again. The lads who had been there for years needed a break and I recognised that, though I figured maybe in a year or two we'd all be back out on the road. Unfortunately it didn't quite turn out that way. I'll never forget that day at the airport though, we all just filed out one by one and that was it."[18]

Marcus Connaughton on the other hand, remembers bitterly what the establishment did to Lizzy and how it had a crucifying effect in their down-fall:

"When Lizzy finished in 1983 the music industry at the time was in dire straits. Artists with integrity found it difficult to get a commitment from their record company. The sales of singles were way below what they had been just a few years earlier, as were albums. The record companies were looking for a quick kill which they eventually succeeded in doing a few years later and I think Phil Lynott and Thin Lizzy were victims of the policy to come."[19]

Whereas Downey and Gorham welcomed the break, allowing them to sort out their lives and their problems, Lynott rather unwisely decided to keep on working. John Sykes remained in Lynott's company, and encouraged by the positive response to the farewell tour performances, began sussing out the possibility of getting back on the road early in the new year.

As late as October '83, soon after Lizzy's final shows, Lynott was back, producing the Irish outfit 'Auto De Fe'. Earlier in the year he had committed to appearing in a video for another track of theirs he contributed to, 'Man Of Mine'. The set-up for this shoot was under the same proviso that 'Old Town' was made, in that twice a month RTE would finance a promotional video by an Irish artist. Gay Woods, lead vocalist with Auto De Fe recalls:

"It seems so long ago. That video shoot lasted one full day and Phil had a really menacing look about him all the way through, which was of course on purpose. He was really concerned or perhaps confused about which direction his own career should've taken at this point and in a way I suppose he didn't really want to be left behind like so many others had been"[20]

Shay Healy who was also on the set, remembers the day well:

"I remember interviewing him towards the end of his life at Howth Castle where he was shooting a promotional video with 'Auto De Fe'. He started talking about the changes that were happening in his life regarding the children and how he wanted to become a more devoted father. We also spoke at length of his ambitions and it was only much later on that I discovered he was more or less talking to himself. By listening to his own voice and therefore trying to reassure himself that he was still very much in control of his life."[21]

Whether Sykes realised the extent of Lynott's predicament is irrelevant, because others who had known Lynott for considerably longer had tried to broach the subject of his lifestyle. One of these was Jim Fitzpatrick, at the time living a short distance from Lynott's sprawling Glen Corr retreat:

"We usually always took a stroll down around the beachfront and let each other know the latest news, though on this occasion there was something not quite the same. Philip had been having problems with a local musician he had helped out with in the studio and this guy turned on him through a newspaper report. As he explained the situation to me it began to unravel so much to the point that I don't think I had ever heard Philip speak on this level. It was by far the most revealing insight into the man I had ever got and I found it quite disturbing. I thought perhaps that he was suffering the after effects of alcohol or drugs or both but he re-assured this was not the case. He was totally lucid but in the most extreme psychological pain. He had too much pride to let anyone know how he felt inside...

"...After that we sort of fell out for a while and through this I always felt that I became the man who knew too much. When I think about it now it must have been that Philip felt vulnerable when I was around because he knew I was totally disapproving of his use of heroin. On one occasion I had an enormous bust up with him after I found some burned tin foil in the house. Philip enjoyed chasing the dragon but he swore to me that he never injected the stuff and I foolishly believed him. He always used to say, 'Jim, I always have that sussed.' What do you do in a situation like this? Do you disapprove and then risk being cut out of the gang for being a killjoy or do you fake approval in order to remain in favour? I chose the former and duly lived with the consequences. The estrangement in our relationship only lasted for a few months and soon we were the best of buddies again, though it was never quite the same. I cared about him too much to be complacent and as I was vociferous in my opposition to his use of heroin, he slowly but surely distanced himself from me, as he did to all his other close friends. Philip's manipulative qualities were unfortunately sharpened by his addiction to the point of self-destruction, therein lies the tragedy."[22]

Pre-Christmas 1984 Lynott started recruiting for his next musical endeavour. Sykes had agreed to join him on lead guitar and Downey was also up for the new project. Lynott felt it best to go with one lead and one rhythm guitarist, so Doishe Nagle, who had accompanied Lynott on the Swedish tour the previous summer, was brought in on rhythm. Mark Stanway, officially still a member of Magnum, was also asked to join and in due course came on board. By January 1984 this line-up of Grand Slam, as they were called, underwent one of two vitally important metamorphoses.

The first was the exit of John Sykes. Throughout the final section of the Lizzy farewell tour, there were said to be many within the Whitesnake organisation that were highly impressed with Sykes. So much so, that when the band were in Munich in the early 1984 recording their new album *Slide It In*, John Sykes received news of their interest. Sykes recalls his predicament...

"After the [Thin Lizzy] dates in Germany with Whitesnake we pulled the plug and I thought nothing more of it until a few weeks later when Coverdale rang me and invited me to Germany to check the situation out with them. They made me an offer and I turned it down, then they came back with another offer and I turned that down too, when the third slate became clear it was too good to let go so I opted for Whitesnake. In a way I wanted to move on and do something but a lot of my soul was saying, 'Stay with Phil' and keep the Slam thing going. With Scott and Brian opting out the situation was more or less done and I moved on."[23]

Lynott later went on record as saying… "Oh John would have been the Grand Slam lead guitarist but he was ah… paid to join Whitesnake."

Over the following months Lynott, Downey, Stanway and Nagle worked up an amount of material in time for the band's inaugural gig. A short tour of Ireland had been planned to break the band in gently, but not before Lynott had to face the age old battle of finding a suitable lead guitarist. It was Jimmy Bain that presented Lynott with the perfect candidate in ex-Stampede/Wild Horses guitarist Laurence Archer. At a mere twenty-one years of age, Archer had the ability of the likes of Robertson and Sykes. Archer recalls his initial impression of Lynott.

"I first got to know Phil via the Wild Horses angle, previously to that a friend of my dad's called Mick Lawford was road manager for Lizzy. He was an upbeat guy, kind of jolly. At the same time he was a hero of mine. Phil jammed on and off with Wild Horses. After that went to the wall, I was in the frame to join Lizzy around the Snowy White era. We had a chat backstage after a gig, and we did share the same management. I felt that I should stick to what I was doing and turned down the opportunity. At the same time I knew John Sykes quite well and knew he was really up for joining them and he was a good enough player and sure eventually he did get the gig."[24]

Using London as the base for his new band gave Lynott sufficient leeway to get the group into a viable financial proposition for a record company. It was a wise move though one that didn't hold with Brian Downey. The material was unpolished and reminiscent of off-peak Lizzy according to some, and it was another hammering blow to Lynott when Downey decided to call it a day and returned to Ireland just as they were gearing up for the tour. Lynott later went on record to try and play down any ill feeling between Downey and himself.

"Downey left because he didn't want to go on the road again. He'd had so much time off since Lizzy ended he'd got used to being with his family and that. Even though we did make that pact about always working together I guess he made a bigger pact with his wife and kids, you know. I think that one was a little more permanent than the one he made with me. There's no bad blood between us it's just that the time comes when you've had enough."[25]

By April the band had worked up significant new material, though throughout the Irish leg of the tour it was peppered with snatches of Lizzy. It was a decision that didn't wash well with critics, and the set was revised for their showcase gigs at the Marquee the following summer. At the beginning of the year Lynott had written a number of songs that he brought to the band, such as "Nineteen", "Sisters Of Mercy" and "Military Man", and these would undergo several changes by the time of their live performance. Although Lynott was chief-songwriter, this did not stop anyone else within the group from contributing. Archer, Stanway and Nagle would all write material throughout the band's evolution, much of which would never see the light of day.

So, with Downey out of the picture and several English dates pushed back from late May to late June, Lynott recalled an old Irish contact, Robbie Brennan.

"When Brian Downey had enough that was when I got the call to join what was at the time Phil Lynott's new band, they hadn't got a name yet. I was playing with Scullion at the time and I got a call to join the band, and I said I wouldn't mind, but the reaction was that I would have to join in the morning because their first gig was in a few days' time. I had one full rehearsal and the gig went ahead the next day. His supporters just wanted the heavy stuff off him but he was trying to get a few new angles into the equation to make a clean break from Lizzy. At the same time he was very determined to press ahead with it, the only trouble was that he was doing lots of drugs at the time... the basic idea was to get a funky rhythm section though still have it as a guitar-orientated band."[26]

Though Lynott's efforts were admirable, it was always going to be an uphill struggle to bury the past and start afresh.

The majority of the gigs on the Irish tour attracted moderate crowds. As with Lizzy, Lynott cutely used Irish audiences as a soundboard to try and tweak what needed fixing before moving on to the all-important and ever influential British scene. Early in the tour an interesting turn of events occurred when Lynott's new outfit and his old sparring pal Brush Shiels were playing the same town, Lifford, in Co. Donegal.

"I rang him sometime in early 1984 to see if he would tour with my band," Brush remembers. "I'd give him x-amount of money, which was a lot, I may add, because I'd be getting more if he were there. Any money, over and above the usual, I'd give to him. He thought about it for a while and sounded pretty positive but then opted to go with Grand Slam. I wasn't happy about that at all, but then he went on to make a fatal mistake. There's a very strange thing called the showband circuit, which is what Grand Slam toured around Ireland. The way you play it, is by only going in on a certain night. When we met up in Lifford of course he went in on the wrong night. There was more people at my show then there was at Slam's. You don't play the wrong room because the people think that you couldn't possibly be playing there so they don't bother to check it out. I was trying to explain that to him later. To book Phil into such a place was a bad move for the morale of the band. The only useful marker would be to get the band sharp for the bigger gigs, but that may have been his idea all along anyway, so who's to know why he chose going down the route he did."[27]

Lynott and co entered Lombard Sound recording studio right after the short Irish tour. Up until then they had preferred instead to work up as many ideas as possible in Lynott's home studio in Richmond. The band had decided to cancel their UK dates and concentrate on perfecting the material they had written. The demos were then touted to the record companies by Lynott's management, CMO.

Deirdre Costello, one of the directors at Lombard, which is now known as Westland Studios recalls Lynott recording during 1984:

"Grand Slam recorded, to the best of my knowledge, around six or seven demos, during a recording block of about one week. There are no tapes from those sessions in our archives. It was during the autumn of the following year that Westland started up but Philip never recorded at Westland."

It is conceivable that Lynott had worked up a strong arsenal of material since the demise of Lizzy the previous September, but the songwriting credits on the last two Lizzy albums suggest that Lynott was slowing down. Still it does make for some interesting speculation, especially amongst Lynott's collaborators about what happened to some of the material written at this point in his life.

"I heard stories that all the master tapes and anything resembling ideas or demos were thrown into the garbage by Caroline shortly after Phil died," alleges Rimson. "If this is what happened then there is no way we could possibly get the chance to see what direction he was taking with the new material he had written."[28]

Robbie Brennan was a lot closer to the action as he played an integral part in the new Lynott band.

"Because there was a load of new material written by the group, songs that were co-written and so on, these tracks were written and recorded either at Philip's studio in Richmond or elsewhere. It now seems unlikely that they will ever be recovered. God knows who has them or what they did with them. We made a fortune of demos and certainly enough to possibly shape an album live or otherwise. Though some of them did need some work, there is quite a lot of songs that reached what I would feel is their final form."[29]

Towards the latter stages of May, Lynott was promoting the newly christened band on Dave Fanning's *Rock Show* in Dublin, bringing with him the latest Grand Slam recordings. Several names had been thrown around, none however really stuck apart from Slam, a Lynott suggestion. Considering the alternatives, Catastrophe and Reactor Factor, it was a wise choice. Speaking with Fanning proved to be a enlightening session for Lynott, he was enjoying the josh, yet toying with the Fanning line of questioning whilst heartily plugging the new material and band members. Lynott described his new project to the listeners…

"Grand Slam is taking the aggression that Lizzy had and diluting that with the melodic side of my solo material. I mean, when we started the Irish tour we were using 60% of Lizzy's material and 40% Grand Slam. After five gigs we are using 80% Grand Slam and 20% Lizzy… so anybody out there hoping to hear Lizzy better hurry up and come to see us," he added chuckling.[30]

Before long Grand Slam were back in London ahead of their scheduled showcase gigs at the Marquee. There were extensive rehearsals at E'ZEE Studios in London and a few warm up dates to allow the band to find their feet with the new material

Grand Slam had a significant number of original songs, but it still allowed them the luxury of picking a set list sprinkled with a few cover versions. Songs such as Procol Harum's "Whiter Shade Of Pale" and Bob Dylan's "Like A Rolling Stone" had been amalgamated together. These worked so well that existing covers such as "Every Breath You Take" by the Police were discarded as was Robert Palmer's "Some Guys Have All The Luck". They were soon to be replaced by songs like "Crazy", "I Don't Need This" and the mercurial love song "Dedication".

During the course of rehearsals, Lynott gave interviews as the band was a mere two weeks away from making their appearance at the Marquee. He had this to say to a *Kerrang* journalist:

"I'm really fighting for Grand Slam at the moment. I mean, we're here rehearsing 6 days a week, from two in the afternoon until ten at night. I'm really putting a heavy emphasis on my playing and it's standing me in good stead because it has really improved. When it comes down to it though I do feel that the future of the band lies in America. If we head over there and work on it for a time then we can come back here to England and not have to face the usual crap that gets flung in my direction. I'm not fashionable here anymore so once we complete this tour that should be our next move."[31]

Rumours have abounded in the years since Lynott's death suggesting a lack of commitment to Grand Slam. The simple fact is that without Lynott, there wouldn't have been Grand Slam. But stories persisted regarding his unreliability, his refusal to get out of bed for rehearsals, or that rehearsals could be so heart-wrenching and tedious that little headway was being made. Robbie Brennan in particular wanted to set the record straight:

"When we were rehearsing it was from lunchtime through until the late evening with a full PA, full monitor system – it was like playing 3 football matches in one day. The problem of trying to get Phil out of bed has been greatly exaggerated though. The bigger problem was not getting him to do detours on the way to rehearsal. We would be there at the given time with the gear set up and Philip might turn up, but not after getting what he was looking for on that earlier detour. Most of us weren't innocent either, but we would still be on time. Most of us partook in what was on offer but to a much lesser degree than him."[32]

At the E'ZEE Studios in early June Lynott once more crossed paths with his old friends Jerome Rimson and Gus Isadore. At various points throughout 1984 and the following year Lynott would record material with both men, though none of this has yet become available. Isadore and Rimson teamed up to form BlackMail, this was a revision of a concept originally thought up in the mid-seventies. According to Rimson, "The early eighties seemed like an opportune time to re-activate the band." Lynott was so taken with the idea that he nearly passed on continuing with Grand Slam. Rimson in particular recalls the sessions at E'ZEE…

"The Grand Slam thing was a great idea in theory. But you can't leave a band like Thin Lizzy and throw a bunch of guys that are like friends of yours, even if they were decent players, and try to go down the same road that you have explored with another band. Sting did not try to re-produce the Police, he went in another direction. I think that Grand Slam was a big downfall for Phil because nobody really wanted them."

Rimson continued.

"…But at the time that Phil had decided to do Grand Slam, his influence over Gus and me was huge. Gus and myself had it in our heads that BlackMail was going to be an all black Def Leppard type of thing. That's what we were going for, to the point where we had a tentative deal with RCA. We were rehearsing BlackMail in E'ZEE at the same time that Lynott was rehearsing Slam and we were burying them and he knew it. He used to laugh at us when he'd pop out for a bit, so what Isadore and myself were trying to do was convince Phil he should come with us. What we were doing was going to be nowhere near Lizzy and we thought that was how we could snatch him, it wasn't to be though."[33]

Rimson and Isadore remained in close contact with Lynott throughout the Grand Slam period often acting as moral support when things got heavy. Isadore and Rimson were often available to try and rally him and that's where the unreleased track that Isadore and Lynott co-wrote together called "Someone's Outta Get Ya" came from. Rimson takes up the story...

"The track Gus later wrote with Phil, 'Someone Outta Get You' lyrically was all Phil's work, but musically the majority was Isadore. So if he [Lynott] had gone with us I think we could've had something really special. I remember having a conversation with Phil after Lizzy had crashed. As the story goes, told by Sammy Davis Jnr about his pal Frank Sinatra, 'Suddenly my greatest hero was walking around lost'."

Phil Lynott could not get a publishing deal, no record company would touch him. Partially because his writing could've been better, but mostly because everyone knew about his habit. While Phil was trying to get Grand Slam together, the problem was that everybody was indulging in the same thing, so not enough was getting done. Phil was getting depressed, while BlackMail were making major moves with a few companies such as Warners and RCA. Rimson:

"Had Lynott not opted for Grand Slam I still think we could have had a major situation happening. Isadore was writing some quality material and the potential was fantastic. In all honesty though it was a very strange time then with Phil, because he would change his mind about things in a flash."[34]

In the days leading up to their Marquee gigs, Grand Slam knew the predicament they were in. Facing the inevitable comparisons with Lizzy they had an uphill battle, albeit a battle that Lynott thought could be won. There were other concerns, as time was of the essence, considering the amount of money it was taking to keep them together. Another factor was Lynott's reputation in the industry. By the time Lizzy finished, his squabbles with people in the business were enough to freeze any future prospects. So when Chris Morrison began touting Grand Slam, the response was somewhat cool. Whether Lynott had anticipated such a reaction is unknown, but it was still enough to cause concern amongst other band members, such as Laurence Archer.

"We had attracted a good deal of interest from a few record companies such as EMI, but of course somewhere back down the line Phil had stuck out some guy who used to be a journalist and we got shafted. Unlucky for us that he was now head of A&R at EMI, so that was the end of that."[35]

After much discussion it was decided that the band should develop their act into a viable live entity in order to impress prospective executives into taking a gamble. It was with this belief that the band entered their first English showcase gigs at the Marquee.

Lynott's appearance at The Marquee caused concern, his features having undergone a considerable change. Towards the end of Lizzy he had been putting on weight. Though by no means extremely heavy, his bloated appearance was worrying. His facial features had become fuller, his hanging jowls highlighted a marked change. Perhaps he had just let himself go to the point whereby he didn't care anymore.

Grand Slam had showcased seven new songs within a twelve-song set. Though the material was strong, the all-important hit single was nowhere to be found. The band were aware that A&R men would be in attendance at the Marquee, and according to various reports they responded with a tight set of well-rehearsed material. Without leaning too heavily on Lizzy terrain they played two tracks that belonged to Lynott's past. "Cold Sweat" and "Sarah", the latter Thin Lizzy had never played live, though it had featured strongly in the solo tours that Lynott undertook in the early eighties.

"Yellow Pearl" started off the set, harking back to one of Lynott's early solo successes. The emphasis placed on the guitars proved that Lynott was not about to let go of his heavy edge. "Nineteen" followed, sounding a little blunted, as was most of the new material.

"Sisters Of Mercy" slotted in next and although it was one of their stronger tracks, it sounded unfinished. There was far too much instrumental indulgence to hold an audience. At this point, it sounded a little raw lyrically as well as bearing an overwhelming resemblance to the Lizzy classic "Emerald". "Military Man" was an anti-war song that would appear later in a different guise for Gary Moore. The Grand Slam version is certainly noteworthy, though it does seem a little repetitive – it was in all senses of the word a demo.

"Harlem" has a funky feel, and brought a whole new outlook to the band. The song had originated with rhythm guitarist Doishe Nagle, but Lynott put his stamp on it and made it his own. Lyrically he originally had the idea of basing it around his experiences growing up in Crumlin, but sensing that the title "Crumlin" wasn't rock 'n' roll enough he promptly opted for "Harlem".

Lynott then took the audience back a few years and played nostalgic crowd pleasers, even resurrecting his huge hit with Gary Moore, "Parisienne Walkways". They then slowed down the set for a little fun, with a medley featuring "Dear Miss Lonely Hearts", "Some Guys Have All The Luck" and "Every Breath You Take". It was a bold move that seemed to work, and it brought the band back to the stage for the first of two encores, the first of which was their amalgamation of the two sixties classics in the shape of "Whiter Shade Of Pale" and "Like a Rolling Stone" seamlessly stitched together. They then concluded their set with another new track called "I Don't Need This". It was a patchy number and was surprisingly chosen over the bluesy composition "Crime Rate".

"All he had really was the bass riff and a few lyrics," says Archer, "but then the rest of us chipped in and found a way to present the song, a lot of Grand Slam material started out that way."[36]

The band left the Marquee stage to rapturous applause and they were no doubt aware of the importance of earning those encores in front of the all-important press. However, the A&R men were curiously dismissive of Lynott's attempts to update himself within the foundations of a new band.

Whilst the tour continued, it was interspersed with regular bouts in the studio taping the latest songs the band had written. "Dedication" was recorded at EMI's studios in Manchester Square and Laurence Archer in particular remembers the session.

"On various occasions, like when we recorded at the EMI studios, Phil wasn't even there. The first time we put down 'Dedication' he was away, taking care of some other business whilst we were trying to come up with appropriate arrangements for the new songs. We might spend a week in a studio at a time and that's what happened with 'Dedication'. Phil arrived in the middle of the sessions, basically came in and over-dubbed his vocals and that's the version the public got to hear when it was released officially a few years after he died."[37]

July also brought some unexpected good news for Lynott in the form of a publishing deal for thirteen short stories. They were to be based upon first-hand experiences in the music industry, though mostly fictitious in content. For Lynott the notion of recognition as a writer became paramount, though even he admitted, "I'll have to start disciplining myself". However, the publishing deal never came to fruition and the world still waits for what are most likely the unfinished works of Philip Lynott in his capacity as an author. One title that was completed was called "The Roadie".

July was a hectic time for Grand Slam as they were consistently gigging, busy in the studio and making sure that they were filling the columns in the likes of *Sounds, Kerrang* and the *NME*. Their break came in the middle of July when they supported Status Quo on their *End Of The Road* tour at Crystal Palace. It would be Lynott's biggest gig since Lizzy split, with an estimated 40,000 in attendance. Robbie Brennan remembers it well:

"Grand Slam always went down pretty well with the supporters especially at the farewell gig for Quo. We were meant to be third on the bill, but they reckoned Steve Van Zandt's band wouldn't go down as well, so we went on instead and went down a storm. Even after all the positive feedback there wasn't any sign of a deal which I have got to say was pretty disappointing even at that early stage."[38]

Sometime after the Palace gig Lynott hooked up with Quo's Rick Parfitt and demoed some material, though again this has failed to turn up on any official release. The track that they worked on had a working title of "My Father's Son". In one of his last interviews Lynott mentioned that he had written some stuff with Parfit but as to whether it was ever put down on tape and mastered remains a mystery.

More festivals were lined up towards the end of the month, most notably at the Nostell Priory in Wakefield, one of only two shows ever filmed of Grand Slam in live performance. But it wasn't professionally filmed, just an avid supporter in the audience waving a camcorder from a distance. Still it stands as a reminder of what Lynott and the band had to offer.

Fish of Marillion recalls reuniting with Lynott at the festival, the first time the pair had crossed paths since Lizzy's last UK performance at the Reading Festival in August of 1983.

"I remember being backstage and we were just sitting around waiting for the call to go onstage really. We were having a few drinks and because he was the main lyricist in Lizzy, and I being the main lyricist in Marillion, we had familiar ground. He spoke about how nobody really understood his lyrics – well I suppose appreciated them would be the better term. He was slightly hurt over the fact, but not distraught if you know what I mean. At one point he then reached for his bag and gave me a couple of copies of his poetry books, which I still have to this day. The gig itself was pretty good though we had a lot of fun playing on the title of it. Soon Nostell Priory became Nostril Priority. It was one of the last times I ever saw him alive."[39]

Reviews of the Priory gig laid great acclaim at Lynott's feet when a *Kerrang* journalist wrote, "Lynott's charisma and searing talent turned what had been a scene of contrived desperation into one of a spontaneous and unmitigated success."[40] While Archer was described as "a bag full of Blackmores", Nagle was also mentioned for his rhythm prowess.

During September, 'Gay Boys' and a revised 'Can't Get Away' emerged from sessions at Lynott's home studio in Richmond, but he also found time to return to Ireland to provide lead vocals for the traditional group Clann Eadair. Lynott wrote the lyrics and also produced the song called 'Tribute To Sandy Denny'. Only released in Ireland, it remains a poignant reminder of the ex-Fairport Convention vocalist who died of a brain haemorrhage in April 1978, aged just thirty-one.

One of the highlights of October turned out to be the *Kerrang* Weekender in Great Yarmouth. Despite showcasing "Gay Boys" and "Can't Get Away" to an enthusiastic audience, record company reluctance continued as

Chris Morrison poured money into Lynott's latest venture. In the absence of a record deal, he kept the band on the road throughout October and November, still trying to lure interest. Polydor had joined the list of those willing to consider taking a gamble, but wanted to wait to see how the material was taking shape. So far, the band had played up to fifteen original songs but there was a lot more material as Laurence Archer reveals.

"We probably wrote and recorded about 30 songs, to what standard they were recorded I just can't remember. I come across bits and pieces all the time, even now. I remember bringing one song to Phil called 'Is It Any Wonder' and he put down a lead vocal on it but we never got to play that one live. Another one was called 'Hot and Spicy', which was quite heavy, unfinished but there was certainly something there and then of course 'Gay Boys' which we did get to play in the Grand Slam set."[41]

During the course of their early gigs in Britain, Lynott persuaded a fan called Sue Peters to run the Grand Slam Supporters Club and latterly the Philip Lynott Appreciation Society.

"When I started working for him I noticed the change in his attitude towards me, the business side of his character I suppose. He was very demanding and expected everyone to work as hard as he did. He really did push me to the limit and I can't count the amount of times he had me in tears though I did cop onto what he was doing eventually. He was just testing me out, like he did with everyone else, to see if I genuinely cared about the job I was doing and not just hanging around because of who he was. On the whole though he was a hilarious character who enjoyed silly jokes, the company of women and getting up there on stage doing what he did best."[42]

By the time the band went to Scotland for a week-long tour, Lynott was rumoured to have received a solo offer from Polydor. Early in the new-year he did indeed sign a tentative deal with them. Throughout the Scottish leg of the tour the band was plagued with problems. Some of the venues were too small, the physical condition of certain band members was questionable, and equipment failures all helped to bring the band crashing down to earth. One show at The Mayfair was recorded and broadcast to positive reviews, but the last gig of the tour was cancelled under what can only be described as suspicious circumstances according to one onlooker.

"I was at the venue from about lunchtime on and I could hear the owner going frantic as the band was threatening to cancel. A short while later a roadie turned up and took a brief look inside before coming back out and announcing the venue was too small. Arguing that the ceiling was too low and that there was no way the gig could go ahead. He mentioned the trouble at the Glasgow gig and basically didn't want a repeat performance. Later on there were murmurs as to the state of Philip Lynott and that this also played a part in their decision to pull the plug on the gig."[43]

To end the year on a high note, the band intended to release a Christmas single, planned to be the superb Archer song "Can't Get Away". This turned into another empty promise, as the band still struggled for a record deal.

Huey Lewis had been contacted with a view to producing the single, the plan was for him to return in the role of producer for an album to follow. However his existing commitments put paid to that, and the sessions were delayed until January of the following year.

It was decided that if nothing came of the Marquee gigs during December they would have to call it a day. It was proving an expensive endeavour for Morrison, who had heaved upwards of £100,000 of his own money into the outfit, getting nothing in return.

Hoping that the new material featured in the set, such as "Can't Get Away", "Gay Boys" and "Breakdown", would garner favourable reviews somewhat backfired. The press consistently concentrated on Lynott's past instead of the new band. Andy Pell in *Sounds* had this say about Grand Slam in the aftermath of some of their final shows.

"Phil Lynott has lost the need, the hunger which used to make Thin Lizzy so good, and complacency has taken its place, mediocrity was the order of the evening. Whereas the band were tight and competent they were no more than the sort of band who would have been described as second rate against Lizzy at the peak of their career."[44]

It was somewhat unfair to compare Lizzy at the peak of their powers with a band that had only been around nine months and were still finding their feet. Unfortunately the record company executives continued to freeze them out.

On the other hand, *Kerrang* ran with a positive review by Mark Putterford who described the band as "shit hot, with Lynott harnessing their initial explosion of nervous energy whilst settling down with their growing individual rapport. Lapping the band into a controlled and confident outfit". "Gay Boys" being the standout for the band on the night with its playful lyrical content... "I took her to my place/I took her to my bed/ I took off her fine, fine lingerie, revealing...one hairy chest/ I was disgusted/ I was disgusted/ have you sussed it/ I was busted/ I was arrested/ he protested/ Policeman".

Putterford's continued support however was not enough. Too few shared his enthusiasm for the band. Many on the fringes of Lizzy have made their observations as to why Grand Slam never quite cracked it.

"Leading up to the Grand Slam days and then throughout them he was relying more and more on illegal substances," Smily Bolger offers. "People

179

that could have helped him either didn't or weren't allowed to. Television show producers just kept away from him as did other people in the industry. He dug himself a hole and couldn't really get out of it."[45]

Even though the industry was turning its back on Lynott, many supporters continued their allegiance to him. Robbie Brennan remembers:

"He used to say… 'When I'm in England I'm from Ireland, when I'm in Ireland I'm from Dublin, when I'm in Dublin I'm from Crumlin and when I'm in Crumlin – I'm from Leiglin Road and when I'm in Leiglin Road, I'm a Lynott.' He was really proud to be Irish and whenever he was asked where he was from, he sometimes came out with that. Even down to the locality of where he was from he was proud. He was always mobbed wherever he went."[46]

After acknowledging that Grand Slam were doomed, Lynott played down rumours of a solo record deal until after what turned out to be their last ever gig in Walthamstow. In their final throes, Grand Slam had reverted back to using a lot of Lizzy material.

"He was after slipping some of the *Live And Dangerous* material into the set and to be honest it was a bit of a disaster," Lizzy archivist Paul Mauger reveals. "When I was speaking with him he wasn't in the best of moods as I later discovered that his separation from Caroline had finally come through. He did gee up a bit though when he started talking about the option of taking up a deal with Polydor. From the discussion though it seemed that he had to get everything in order pretty speedily regarding who was going to produce it and of course what tracks would be selected for inclusion."[47]

1984 had been a somewhat lacklustre year for Lynott. His drug habit had finally begun to overrun him, his marriage for all intents and purposes was over and due to his hectic lifestyle, access to his two daughters Sarah and Cathleen was limited. Many people within the band and those on the perimeter tried to speak with him, but unfortunately he was simply unable to acknowledge his predicament. Grand Slam had been a failure and many people were only more than willing to remind him of this fact. The ongoing negative press was now at fever pitch. For the moment he could see no way out, the roads he chose to travel were quickly turning into cul-de-sacs. David Heffernan concludes…

"First of all, Philip was an asthmatic, the lifestyle that he led and the way he pushed himself had begun to take its toll. What I did hear of the Grand Slam material was quite laboured. It told me that he should have left the playing field for a while and returned with a fresh angle. So, when things went wrong, for whichever reason, he went down the road that he couldn't get back out of. It was the ultimate tragedy."[48]

Robbie Brennan holds similar views on Lynott's downfall and remembers on more than one occasion trying to dissuade Lynott from compounding his mistakes.

"At the time my one big argument was that he was playing around with other women, but everybody was doing that at the time. He couldn't see why his ex-wife wouldn't allow him too much access to his two daughters without her being there. She never knew what she might find...

"...He actually sacked me out of the band after he said to me, 'Caroline won't let me see the kids,' and I replied with, 'Philip you can't blame her when you don't know what state you're going to be in. You could be in bed, there could be drugs all over the place or women around...' ...So he turned to me and said, 'you're sacked'...

"...The next day he arrived down and apologised. The trouble with Philip is that he surrounded himself with people who wouldn't speak their mind to him and were afraid to broach a subject with an honest opinion. I knew him since he was a teenager and I personally didn't give a shit what I said to him. He had an awful temper and he was liable to fly off the handle but then he'd think about what was going on and apologise the next day. In fact I think I got sacked twice for this kind of thing with him but I was taken back the next day."[49]

13

GOING SOLO

It was never really meant to end like it did, it simply happened. All the possibilities had been exhausted, and without the planned one-off single release during the festive period, Grand Slam folded. All that remained was the official announcement to be made.

Lynott's manager informed him that he would be withdrawing his financial support for the band. This was no doubt an added incentive for Lynott to push forward with a solo career. He decided to use the material he had worked on with Grand Slam throughout the previous year for this new endeavour, which would become the subject of legal issues in later years.

Had Lynott taken his own advice, and ignored his fear of being forgotten, he would have got out for as long as required to recharge his batteries and come back with fresh ideas.

As 1985 blew in, plans were set in place for Lynott's old pal Huey Lewis to produce some material at the Record Plant studios in San Francisco. In mid-January Laurence Archer was to accompany John Salter along with Lynott for what was meant to be a week. In the event Archer spent nearly a month working there, though Lynott would join him later, for other reasons as Archer recalls…

"We headed out to San Francisco where Huey had agreed to produce the sessions. I worked on the backing tracks with his band the News. Phil had lost his passport and used an out-of-date Irish passport to get over to the States. How he did it I'll never know, but we must have been there for a month though it was meant to be only for two weeks. Phil arrived two weeks into the sessions and considering the amount of work we had put in, I felt that Phil hadn't really come up with the goods when I heard the results of the sessions."[1]

As early as January '85 it was rumoured that Phil Lynott had secured a solo deal with Polydor, though it would be time before the terms of the contract could be ironed out. It was based on the recordings Lynott completed with Huey Lewis and his band, the News, along with Grand Slam lead guitarist Laurence Archer. The musicians primarily worked on two songs called, 'I'm Still Alive' and 'Can't Get Away'. The former was a number that Lewis used to sing with Clover, the band he fronted in the seventies, and the latter was the Slam track whose origins began with Archer, though he hadn't quite worked out the lyric.

As Lynott arrived late into the sessions, Lewis and the News set about rearranging the tracks. 'I'm Still Alive' was far more rocked up than its previous incarnation as a country pop song, and the arrangement for 'Can't Get Away' was also improved. When noted producer Robert 'Mutt' Lange arrived and agreed to produce the sessions (even though he was meant to be on holiday at the time) Lewis was left free to help the band rearrange the numbers in time for Lynott to come in and overdub his vocals.

The group are also rumoured to have worked on a few other songs such as 'Bad Is Bad', 'Kill' and 'My Woman's In Love', which have never seen the light of day. However Archer's dismay with the sessions couldn't be hidden, compounding his disappointment at his treatment by Chris Morrison. He also thought the particulars surrounding Lynott's solo deal with Polydor were in need of questioning...

"I went to Chris Morrison as I felt Phil wasn't performing well enough. Huey felt the same and that's where I fell out with Morrison. I told him he couldn't use the track that I had written which was 'Can't Get Away'. I wanted another outlet for my writing because I wasn't convinced by Phil. Now, don't get me wrong, we were friends but he was getting me to write the tracks and he was using them. I wanted to be able to write with other people, but Morrison wanted to pigeonhole me and that's where I decided to jump ship. After America my relationship with Morrison came to an end and Phil and I began to work less and less as a team."[2]

Some close to Lynott felt the solo deal had stipulations within the terms and conditions, as Robbie Brennan recalls.

"Record companies didn't want to go near him after Lizzy broke up until he cleaned up his act. Though he had got a new record deal just before Slam disbanded we had run out of money, so we were only put on hold. The talk at the time was that he was offered money to put a version of Lizzy back together – we never found out. I believe he intended to bring the Slam lads back into the equation because there was a load of new material written by the group, songs that were collaboratively written and so on. And it was on the strength of Grand Slam material that he had got that deal. Tracks like 'No More', 'Can't Get Away' and 'Dedication' were the songs touted around to the record companies. I wasn't a collaborative-writer in the group, but the deal we had, which was never committed to paper, was that if we got an album deal – Philip would own 50% and the rest of the group would share the other 50%. It was a fair deal because he wrote the majority of the material. Nearly all the lyrics came from him along with input on the musical side, and I have to say that I would be very interested in seeing a Grand Slam record released."[3]

Upon his return from the USA, Lynott renewed his friendship with John Sykes who had spent the previous months recording with Whitesnake. They both attended the launch for the new Video Cafe in London arriving at around two in the afternoon. The pair were interviewed later on that evening looking visibly dishevelled, though in very playful form. As the interview came to a close, Lynott rather hilariously pointed out the fact that, "only girls and cold water could separate the two of them."

Lynott had also been approached to star in a new TV advert celebrating the inaugural Stateside flight of Virgin Airlines. The piece was filmed earlier in the year and also featured other stars of the day such as Holly Johnson and Boy George. The *Melody Maker* covered the event and rather appallingly felt the need to tear Lynott off a strip.

"Phil tells us he has flown regularly with Virgin Atlantic since June of the previous year and was more than pleased to promote it. Of course he's about to record a new solo album with various guest musicians, the publicity can do no harm. Right, that's your 15 seconds of fame, Phil, old son, now piss off back to the coffin."[4]

Lynott had in fact worked up a number of songs with a variety of musicians, songs that for numerous reasons have been left in the vault to gather dust. It can be assumed that Lynott had intended on using this material in some context for his proposed third solo album. This however would fail to materialise given his commitments over the coming months. Songs such as "Catholic Charm" (solo), "No More" (w/ Steve Johnson), "Why Don't You Call Me" (w/ John Sykes).

"Why Don't You Call Me?" dated back to the latter part of 1982 when John Sykes first joined Lizzy. It is one of the few rockers that seems right at home in the eighties but somehow transcends all decades, and therein lies its appeal.

With "I Still Think Of You" Lynott seemed to be harping back to the state of his personal life. Perhaps this was his way of dealing with the failure of his marriage.

"Catholic Charm", or "Big Boys Lie" as it is also known, was another song to continue in the same vein as "I Still Think Of You". Its pleasant melody is brought right back down to ground by the lyrical content. Lynott speaks to a girl, a lost unrequited love. He even borrowed a couplet from "With Love" which appeared on the *Black Rose* album.

"Woman you think I don't know what you're up to/ You think I don't know what you're turning on to/ Now you can hate me if you want to but don't forget the things I taught you/ I taught you how to cry and that big boys often lie".

"Samantha" was a track that Lynott and John Sykes had worked up and is without doubt Lynott's last great ballad and was a tribute to Jimmy Bain's daughter. The addictive melody, Lynott's lyrics and tender vocal, Sykes's intricate and supremely delicate playing deserved a wider audience.

"Look In These Eyes" had been hanging around since the *Renegade* sessions, and was a song that Lynott seemed to have a lot of faith in. This was justified when it was re-recorded with Grand Slam, and its merit heightened ever the more when it was re-recorded in the weeks leading up to his death. The song became "No More" and was indicative of Lynott's increasingly commercial awareness by the mid-eighties.

Clearly noticeable from some of the recordings Lynott undertook through the eighties was an obvious defection from Lizzy's rock strategy. He attempted to incorporate funky aspects into Grand Slam, evident on two songs in particular, "Harlem" which later became "If I Had A Wish" and the catchy "Gay Boys".

Also indicative of this new direction was the fact that Junior Giscombe, known as 'Junior', had actually co-written and recorded several songs with Lynott between 1981 and the summer of 1985. Born in London, Junior contributed heavily to the UK R&B/Pop explosion of the '80's with 'Mama Used To Say' which sold over two million copies worldwide.

By the time that Junior starting working with Lynott, Lizzy were on their way down. He recalls the fragmented sessions that disappointingly have yet to see the light of day...

"I recorded with Phil in the early to mid-eighties on a few tracks. We did them at Tony Visconti's place, Good Earth Studios in Soho. We played with Lemmy from Motorhead, John Sykes and Derek Bramble was contributing as well. We tried to get a rock and rhythm and blues fusion going and

I think it worked out pretty well to be honest. We wrote about three songs together, but there was about a half dozen songs floating around at the time. Two of them were mastered, 'Breakdown' and 'The Lady Loves To Dance'. The others were done at Phil's place in Kew, they were demos like 'What's The Matter Baby' and 'Time and Again'."[5]

Lynott had sporadically continued working on the material he and Junior had written in their first encounter around 1980. Though a lot of the songs were very embryonic, there are snatches within several cuts that would suggest that the duo could have fashioned out an album's worth of material if time allowed. Expanding into soul or rhythm and blues could well have proved a lucrative market for Lynott to test out with Junior. Another path forward would have been an album with Gary Moore, considering the success of their efforts of the past. However, one of the tragedies of Lynott's recording career remains that an album with Moore never came to fruition.

For much of their time collaborating together, Lynott was still leading Lizzy, whilst Junior was spending the majority of his time in the USA. So after the Lizzy split and working around Junior's irregular trips to Britain, they set out to try and explore the sound they had experimented with some four years previously. One track, the gentle and sublime 'What's The Matter?' proved to be quite a return to form. Lynott pleads lyrically to his lady whilst Junior provides strong vocal harmonies. Some of Lynott's later songs revert to a commentary on relationships; by the time this track was recorded, during the summer of 1985, his own marriage was to all intents and purposes over. The recording that exists shows Lynott scratching around on his bass over basic drum machine and keyboards. Junior features strongly with backing vocals, singing in falsetto complimenting each other on the chorus.

"What's the matter baby (Lynott),
What's the matter (Junior)"
"What's the matter baby when you're feeling low down,
Nobody loves you when you feel like a clown.
What's the matter baby girl you're still upset,
Get up and dance you know it helps to forget"

The songs that Lynott recorded with Junior demonstrate a far heavier personal emphasis, evident on the demo version of the track 'Time And Again'. Lynott's personal demons were used as inspiration, possibly a forward move on his part, maybe at last he is admitting to being human, and hence suffers for being a mortal. He hurts, he can hurt, but he can also be redeemed, by his own hand or with the help of others if he so chooses. Lynott's bass parts seem as complete as they could possibly be, unlike the guitar parts which have been overdubbed at a later date. Junior and Lynott share the lead vocal on this track.

Lynott seemed to be striving to bring quality to his more heartfelt tracks, 'Time And Again' is an admission that he needs support. With his drug habit ravaging his all-too battered body, Lynott continued to write in code, hiding behind his romanticised image of himself, and it is somewhat sad now to review this material in light of what happened to him a short time after these songs were recorded. This track was most likely demo'd at his home studio in Kew 184, Richmond, London.

Lynott's opening gambit in the "He Fell Like A Soldier" session is: 'this song is for a friend of mine who died'… Listening to the track now, it would seem that Lynott was trying to re-visit the theme of the 'renegade/soldier of fortune'. The lyrics seem a little tacky, eerily putting Lynott in the shoes of the subject, with Junior's almost banshee-like wailing over the chorus lines…

"He fell like a soldier, a victim of circumstance,

He died for his country, didn't have to take a chance,

A man of the people a man of the hour,

Tell my mama it's not too late got to live hour by hour".

Although both parties were happy with the tracks and prepared to lobby for their release, problems arose internally as Junior recalls…

"Phil to me was a very genuine man, a kind guy who very much cared for his friends. My image at the time was of a clean-cut popstar whereas Phil Lynott was hardcore. The image of the hard-man couldn't have been further from the truth – to a degree he was, but there was so much more to him than that and the songs that we wrote and recorded together prove it beyond reasonable doubt. We were both at Phonogram at the time but they didn't take to the idea of our collaboration so they put a block on the material being released. Phil did all he could to try and make them reconsider, he'd lean on his own management to try and convince the executives but it was to no avail."[6]

"The Lady Loves To Dance" is known to have been pressed and delivered to the record company as a 7 and 12 inch but it seems once more that these recordings will never be released.

Junior continues…

"With the music, it was a case of seeing if we could do it and what would it sound like. What we were working on back in the eighties, people wouldn't accept, but now it's the norm. The record company didn't want to see us move in that direction but we thought it could be great for the both of us, also we had Visconti producing it, which we felt gave it credence. All the masters were left at Good Earth but when we went back to it we couldn't access them. Something was wrong, even though we had paid for it, we couldn't use the material. I heard that Phil's management had it, then Phonogram were going to use it but then something else happened and now, God knows who has it. Unfortunately, even I don't have a copy of the material, not even on cassette, though I have requested one. It was hard keeping track of what was going on anyway, because I was in the States a lot, then I might be back for a week and I'd be off again. I would follow them to the studio when I got back and see how the material was progressing."[7]

'The Lady Loves To Dance' is perhaps one of Lynott's last gems – at his most playful and upbeat. The buoyancy in this duet with Junior is the highlight of all their collaborations together. It is also no surprise that this was one of a number of tracks that were submitted for a single release until Lynott's record company put a block on the project. From the opening bass line through until Junior's colourful fade out vocal the pair of them seem to be at their happiest throwing out vocal shapes to each other.

Sadly his work with Junior has never been released, and could highlight the versatility of Lynott, an artist labelled and pigeonholed in heavy rock. Few other artists at the time would, or even could, have attempted such a collaboration.

"Freedom Comes" is another heavy Lynott composition, rough in every sense of the word, and not one of the stronger tracks he came up with during this fruitful period of 1985. It is conceivable that the song might have been included on his third solo album but it certainly needed work.

"Hard Times" is a whole lot better, and this rather politically-orientated number mirrored the turmoil of working class England under Margaret Thatcher in the mid-eighties.

"Hard times… there are people on the breadline…bad days,
There are people that say she is a saint, nobody prays,
Hey mister I have made a mistake, I've taken all the love I can take,
This time is getting rough, it's hard times."

Much of the material was still in demo form but showed possibilities.. Even though his own studio was fitted with a Brennel 1" 8-track machine and an Allen & Heath desk, the songs still needed professional treatment in the comforts of a proper studio.

Lynott knew his attempts at re-establishing his public persona would take time, so he had already agreed to help out his old friend and oft nemesis Gary Moore, who was preparing to release his new single "Out In The Fields". The single hit the charts May 6, crashing in at No 31 before shooting up to No 5, giving Lynott his highest single chart position since the *Black Rose* era, coincidentally when Gary Moore was also playing with Lizzy.

Though Lynott got involved in the song at a late stage, it was his idea about how to market the song into a hit.

The B-side was a Lynott-penned ballad 'Military Man', an old Grand Slam number, revised and re-written with Moore during the recording sessions for "Out In The Fields" at Pete Townsend's Eel Pie Studios. The track had changed from a general anti-war song into delicate human-interest story about Lynott's dedication to his mother and his children. It ached so eerily it was almost like a final cry for help. Moore's guitar playing contributed strongly to the overall theme.

The use of the military uniforms in the video was a wise move suggested by "Military Man". These were interspersed with clips from the studio sessions (it was the only promotional video showing Lynott at work in a recording studio) combined with images of war-torn Belfast proved extremely effective and no doubt contributed to the overall success of the single.

For a while it appeared that Lynott had returned to the shores of creativity, the question remained as to whether he could sustain it as a solo performer. With renewed vigour he threw himself into his promotional commitments for "Out In The Fields". Again he had the corporate muscle behind him and again he delivered the goods. Moore and Lynott appeared on *The Old Grey Whistle Test* on May 6, and ECT on the 10th where a disgusted Moore left directly after the gig when the broadcast faded out at the introduction of the third track they were about to play, an updated version of "Still In Love With You". Television audiences were deprived of hearing Moore playing one of his best solos ever.

This performance was then followed by an appearance on the *Saturday Picture Show* on the 11th before signing off with the *Razzamatazz* show on the 29th. The duo also completed an extensive set of promotional dates throughout Europe where the band would sometimes open the short set with Lynott's "Military Man" for a bit of variety.

It was whilst traipsing across Europe that Lynott once more met up with Fish from Marillion. By the time that Moore and Lynott arrived in Belgium to mime to yet another show he was quite the worse for wear after starting the day with an early drinking session, as Fish recalls:

"It was so boring waiting to go we were going mental. At the studios in the middle of nowhere we decided to try and get a football for a game. Eventually we managed to get this Belgian to make a sacrifice and mainly because there wasn't any chemical friends around we went ahead and had a game. Now we had been a drinking copious quantities of whiskey for a steady duration, so everything on the pitch was a bit wild. Matt Bianco was doing the show as well and of course his band were all in white suits, they of course were destroyed with green stains left right and centre. Phil on the other hand was spotless. All he had to wear were these pointed cowboy boots so of course no one would go near him for fear of being mangled. About twenty minutes into the game Matt Bianco got a call and he went on pissed as a fart in his green stained suit, it was wild."[8]

Summer 1985 also saw another Irishman, in the shape of Bob Geldof, organising the *Live Aid* extravaganza. His idea was to gather the biggest rock 'n' roll acts of the time together for a one-off special concert to raise money for famine-devastated Ethiopia. Many of Lynott's friends were involved in the event, though no-one saw fit to enquire about the possibility of using the ex-Lizzy man's services or even the idea of refuelling Lizzy for a one-off show. The event in itself served a good cause, though some in the star studded line-up played their heart out in a brazen attempt at career resuscitation.

"Geldof approached the *Live Aid* situation purely on the angle of record sales," says David Heffernan. "Had Philip cleaned up a bit after the farewell tour then this could have been the ideal platform to re-activate Lizzy to strut the stuff that they were best at. *Live Aid* at the same time was about something totally different from personal favours or acknowledging people who have helped you along the way of your own career. It was a very focused project with a core objective, which was to make money to relieve the pain and suffering of the people of Ethiopia."[9]

Also during July, Lynott found time to hook up with Moore at his wedding in Lincolnshire, where he got up with Don Airey on keyboards and drummer Gary Ferguson to play a few tunes with the groom.

"Yeah, it was the very last time I saw him and he seemed to be in good spirits," Chris Tsangarides recalls. "Phil Lynott full of energy, he even got up on stage and played for a while, but it was all in good heart. The next time I heard any real news was the following Christmas."[10]

As the Summer reached its peak Lynott begun to surround himself with the old faithful and continued writing at his home studio in Kew, before committing himself to recording for Polydor at their studios. Lynott knew without a definite producer it would be artistic suicide not to record in a big studio. It was interrupted by a brief sojourn to RTE studios in Dublin on July 13 where they auctioned off one of his bass guitars for £900. Jerome Rimson, Gus Isadore, Junior, John Sykes, Brian Robertson, Paul Hardcastle and Steve Johnson would be his main collaborators over the coming months.

Rimson recalls his tenure with Lynott through the summer of 1985 when he could see Lynott slip further and further away.

"Robbo was dropping in a lot because he was only living down the road in Richmond. He was really trying to help Phil get himself back together. At times Phil got really mad and one day I was the victim. He had a go at me when I was moving out of Kew 184. He came in one day from the studio and I just happened to look at him and he turned and said, 'You're like me bleeding conscience.' I just turned back to him and asked, 'What the fuck are you doing? Here you are with enough money in the bank, two or three houses and a great family, why are you doing this at this point in your life?' At this stage I said it to him to take a bit of time out and get himself back on track. But it's my opinion that Johnny The Fox was working at his brain."[11]

The pressure that Lynott was under professionally at this point seemed insurmountable. He had even bigger issues to deal with when his relationship with his ex-wife worsened – estranging him further from his children. Lynott's inability to separate his professional life from his personal one would ultimately be his undoing, and it is sad that neither management nor close personal friends ever managed to get through to him.

In the meantime the Supporters Club were happy to report that, though the members of Slam were no longer together, the individuals were working successfully on other projects. At the fore was the emphasis on Lynott's third solo effort. It seemed clear that Philip was now prepared to include "I'm Still Alive" which he had recorded the previous January, plus material he had worked on with Grand Slam. The report also suggested the album would be ready to come out as early as September of that year. There was also talk of Philip working on a fund-raiser for Ethiopia with Jimmy Bain, though nothing ever came to fruition.

Though there wasn't any pressure on Lynott to have the album out particularly soon, he had committed himself to having two singles ready in double quick time. He had regularly been meeting with Robbie Dennis, who was product manager at Polydor from 1980 through to the acrimonious take-over by Universal in 1998.

"At the time when Phil Lynott came in there was maybe three or four of us in that position," says Dennis. "Though I had enjoyed his music with Lizzy it was certainly from a distance, I mean I wouldn't have been running to the venue he was playing at in town, but there was definitely an appeal in there for me. So when his name came up at the office I put up my hand and it was as simple as that – Phil Lynott was my project. From the way he was speaking at a meeting with the promotional man and press man it was easily noticeable he wouldn't suffer fools. Any meeting that we did have would have been attended by the head of A&R, Alan Sizer and my recollections of those times were that they were extremely constructive affairs."[12]

Lynott's much-hyped third solo album was still nowhere near completion when he decided to holiday in Marbella during August, though he had invited Gus Isadore to record at his home studio upon his return and polish off the anthem they had worked up called "Someone Out To Get Ya". Philomena Lynott remembers this holiday, though for all the wrong reasons…

"As the summer was moving on Philip had asked me to go on holidays with him to Greece with the children. He wanted to take it easy so he went ahead to try and book a couple of weeks on the Greek island of Kos. He had had enough of the party scene and just wanted to spend some quality time with his family. I thought it would be better to go to a lively place and convinced him to book for Marbella instead. Of course I didn't know at the time why he really wanted to go to Kos, he wanted to get away from the drug scene. When we headed for Marbella it was straight back into the area where he wanted to avoid, but I simply didn't know this at the time. But even though he was on holidays he still played a gig out there. He never really gave himself a break and even flew some of the Grand Slam boys out there for that gig."[13]

The gig in Marbella was a favour to Maurice Boland, an old friend who was running a club out there at the time. As Philip needed a band he called on the services of two ex-Grand Slam members, Doishe Nagle and Robbie Brennan. Brennan flew out on August 3 while Nagle was temporarily stranded for a couple of days with passport problems. With one day of rehearsals the band went ahead and played the gig on August 6. Lizzy supporter, Paul Jenkins witnessed the unfortunate event.

"I was in Spain with my wife at the time when I came across a poster about a Phil Lynott solo gig at a club in Marbella. It was quite a distance to the club though and we didn't arrive until about seven in the evening. Luckily after finding a poster on the bus we soon found the club and after getting in whom should be sitting up at the bar but old Philo himself. We made our introduction and I was delighted to meet the man though less than happy when he informed us that the band weren't due to go on until midnight. Because we had travelled so far I thought, 'Why not, we've come this far.' This would soon change. The band took to the stage at 4 in the morning and opened with a shambolic version of 'The Boys Are Back In Town'. The band stopped playing when they realised how bad they were except for Robbie Brennan who continued on playing. They tried to start again but failed miserably and then left the stage to return to the dressing room. At this point I had had enough and left and that unfortunately is my last memory of seeing Phil Lynott on stage."[14]

Robbie Brennan recalls the same events.

"Was I willing to play a gig in Marbella, what a silly question that was. I got a phone call from Philip, as did Doishe asking if we wanted to go out there. He wanted to do one gig out there and he found some guitar player who was playing with Julian Lennon at the time as well. That was his holiday, yet he still rehearsed and did a gig out there. We went out for a free holiday, got paid for it – picked up at the airport – got put up in a hotel and we were back after about a week, it was great. The gig on the other hand was not. We just had too much drinking time before we went on and the end result was atrocious."[15]

By this stage in the press Philip's name was synonymous with drugs. So many friends tried and failed to get him to kick the habits that were beginning to destroy him. It was brought up in one of many conversations Philip and Smiley Bolger had when he returned home to escape the pressures of London.

"Philip had an addictive personality and you couldn't really tell him what to do," Bolger reveals. "I had one very serious conversation with him one day at his home in Glen Corr and he literally kicked my ass out the front door. I wasn't in any fit shape at the time and after walking half way across Dublin with sporadic vomiting along the way. I finally stuck out my thumb, hitched a lift and got home. The next morning the phone is ringing and it's Philip on the line apologising for his behaviour the previous day.

"…With drugs, Philip had more or less tried them all and maybe believed he could handle them, he never for a second thought that they may be stronger. His wife Caroline stopped, he didn't. They both went to Drugs Anonymous at one stage. The result being she quit, he didn't. Through this and other factors his marriage broke down. It would be my feeling as well as many others that the loss of his marriage/kids/band all but destroyed him. His habits isolated him though at the time he thought he was being left out in the cold. He was pushing himself and I don't know if he ever saw that before he died."[16]

Upon their return to England, Nagle and Brennan retreated to Ireland while Philip remained in London to continue work on his solo album. Another single had been planned for September as delays meant the album would not surface until the New Year. The unavailability of certain producers was one of a number of reasons being thrown around by Philip at this time. He had more or less two year's worth of material down on tape and therefore felt it was worth waiting a few more months to get the right people.

"He brought in about nine or ten demos to me," Robbie Dennis recalls. "And instantly we thought there was at least three great songs among them, good enough to possibly feature on a single issue. Tracks like "Military Man", "Sisters Of Mercy" and "Breakdown" were the standouts and I'd have to say we were really excited about the prospects of this relationship."[17]

By September, Lynott was back in the studio, this time working on another old Grand Slam number. "Nineteen", just like "Military Man", underwent a metamorphosis both musically and lyrically – and not for the better by any stretch of the imagination. Originally Lynott had wanted John Sykes to play guitar on the track but he was busy recording in Canada with Whitesnake. One or two other names were touted but Lynott eventually settled on Robin George whose album Lynott had guested on a year earlier.

"At the DJM studios Phil contributed some spliff as well as bass," George recalls. "My first impressions from those sessions was what a nice guy and a hell of a musician, at the time I was more so overawed at the fact that he wanted to play on my track. It was a great thrill for me that someone who was a star could rate an up-and-coming performer like me. It in a way gave me hope that my music could make a difference or even matter in some way to someone.

"For the 'Nineteen' sessions we headed to the Roundhouse studios. The sessions were relaxed, though always with a professional edge. For the entire duration of our stay the 'Nineteen' track was our sole focus, there weren't any other tracks worked on at all."[17]

Lynott roped in Paul Hardcastle as producer who had recently had a huge No 1 hit with a song also named "19". The unlikely union is explained by the fact that Chris Morrison (Lynott's manager, who later hit the big time with Damon Albarn's Blur) and Simon Fuller (then of Chrysalis) co-managed Hardcastle. In any case it proved to be a big thrill for Hardcastle to work with someone like Lynott.

"It was actually at the CMO offices where I first met Phil and before long we were at the Roundhouse Studios at Chalk Farm recording. On the recording itself we got in Robin George on lead guitar who Phil knew and then used a drum machine for rhythm. I handled all the keyboards. The song did suggest teen angst and Phil related to that sensation. It was while we were in the studio that the notion of trying to get a motorbike sound on the track came about. We soon walked out of the studio and down the street to the nearest bike shop. Phil casually walked up to the assistant and inquired about borrowing a bike for an hour. The assistant never recognized him at first but when Phil explained the situation to him the poor guy behind the counter shriveled up. Though Phil laughed at the whole episode, I have seen other stars in that position get really sticky about that, Phil would literally refuse to take offense to that sort of thing. So we got the bike into the studio and set everything up. The engineers didn't know what to think but Phil was having a laugh. All I expected was a minute or two of revving it up but Phil just sat on the bike for about ten minutes revving her like crazy. By this point the studio was filling up and the place was in chaos, everyone had to clear out, but Phil just sat back looking on hilariously at the disorder he had caused, whilst everyone was suffocating in carbon monoxide."[18]

"I told Paul I wanted to experiment with putting a dance production to a rock song. ZZ TOP has done that successfully. Eddie Van Halen worked well with Michael Jackson."

He continued... "I had this idea of trying a scratch mix with a heavy song and I already had 'Nineteen' written from last year. But it also appealed to Paul 'cos he wanted to show that he's up to doing more than disco mixes, so we just decided to go into the studio. I've landed on my feet after all the troubles of the past two years and I'm still hard and heavy."

The recording of the sessions also demonstrated that, contrary to the belief that he was losing interest in his music, Lynott was still prepared to push hard for the performance he wanted from a musician.

"Phil was happy with Robin tackling the lead guitar part but he wanted him to play the solo at 5000 mph," Hardcastle remembers... "Now Robin was doing everything right, the playing was good the sound was fine but Phil was still giving him a really hard time. Because I suppose he had already worked with some of the best guitarists in the world and maybe that was his way of egging on Robin and trying to show him that he can still improve as a player. During another episode in the studio Phil was formulating bass parts and having trouble with it. So he put the bass down to take a break and headed out back for a while. Now I just started thinking I've got one of my heroes by my side in the recording environment and his bass guitar is lying helplessly on the ground. I wasn't a bass player by any stretch of the imagination but I picked it up and started throwing out these funky rhythms. I recorded it and mixed it in and played it for Phil later, he loved it and decided that it should be left in the finished mix. Now some people are touchy about their instruments being used but I never got that feeling from him, he was or seemed to be impressed by my contributions to the record."[18]

Lynott, Hardcastle and George spent about two weeks re-recording "Nineteen" and all were reasonably pleased with the outcome as September was drawing to a close. For the next few weeks Lynott and Hardcastle met for some photo shoots at Kew.

"The first thing I saw when I walked in was one of those old jukeboxes," Hardcastle recalls of Lynott's Richmond home. "I was well impressed with it and Phil realized this. A few days later coming up to my door at home are two huge bouncers bearing a gift from Phil, it was the jukebox – what a gesture. I had also recently got married and as an apology for keeping me away from my new bride Phil sent flowers to 'Mrs. Hardcastle – sorry for keeping Paul out so late', there isn't many guys like that around if you know what I mean."[19]

In late October, Lynott flew to San Francisco with his management to film the promotional video for "Nineteen", thereby forgoing a possible reunion with Gary Moore, who was undertaking some Scandinavian gigs as part of his European tour.

The promotional video features Lynott befriending a group of bikers in the desert and then being rescued by them in the city. Lynott looks disinterested and tired, almost hunched at times. For some reason he never quite maintains his eye contact with the camera, nor can he summon up the old vigour to entice us into the world of the 'Nineteenth Chapter'. In the end, Robin George is all but cut out of the promo.

"For the video I only appear in snatches while Phil is obviously the primary focus of the shoot. Phil later told me that my main part was edited out because I made him look too rough. He was very apologetic about it but that's just the way it went."[20]

"Nineteen" was released on 8 November and though it made an impression on the heavy metal charts it hardly broke a sweat in the more important mainstream top forty. The song grazed the top 100, peaking at No 76 before disappearing without a trace. The rejection of the single was a further blow to Lynott, but reflected public opinion. Once again, only Mark Putterford welcomed its release with the parting line, "rush out and grab yourself a taste of the new Lynott seven incher."[21]

Sounds and *NME* on the other hand had had quite enough of the Lynott legend.

"Far too many clichéd riffs," was the conclusion in *Sounds*, while the *NME* said, "…Lynott is well beyond teenagedom and the only battles he has to fight are fruitless struggles to put rubbish like this into the chart."

"Nineteen" was a simple song with a simple message and banal lyric that was well below Lynott's capability as an artist. Whereas previously his songs suggested rather than stated, his inability to do either at this point proved to be a major set back in his attempts to re-launch his career.

Paul Hardcastle has his opinion as to why the single never took off.

"In my opinion the failure of the "Nineteen" single lay at Polydor's feet. The sleeves got mixed up, the A-side and the B-side got mixed up and people weren't listening to the song that we intended them to hear as a single. The single did get limited air-play though, Gary Davies for one, gave it a lot of time on Radio 1, primarily I think through his interest in the rather odd combination of me and Phil."[22]

Robbie Dennis refutes Hardcastle's version and suggests that Lynott was a hard man to sell to the radio in light of his reputation with Lizzy. He tells his side of the story...

"The 'Nineteen' track when it was released it didn't fare out too well on the charts, but there could have been a variety of reasons for this. One that doesn't hold, is the notion that the printing of the single was botched up as was reported in the music press. The reason it didn't chart well though, was primarily that we just couldn't get it on the radio play lists. They have a play-list committee that chooses what song gets on air and what doesn't. At the time the anti-drugs issue was rampant and they probably had an inkling to how the public might react if they started playing Phil Lynott's records again in light of his bad reputation with Lizzy."[23]

The failure of "Nineteen" heightened Lynott's alienation from the music world and the pressure was so severe that he never recovered. He continued working up until a few days before Christmas and had numerous promotional trips that took him through to filming on 17 December in Newcastle. Before that however he made an appearance on the Norwegian TV show, *Kanal* whereupon he was forced to mime including the feigning of a lead solo. His performance was reminiscent of Elvis with all his moody posturing while decked out in black leather. However, his energetic display and appearance belied his physical condition.

It was also around this time that his Aunt Marian recalls seeing him for the last time.

"The newspapers for some reason were always giving him a hard time and especially so around this point," she explains. "It was around November when I last met up with him. The thing about Philip is that every time I saw him he had a smile on his face and wanted to know all the latest news whether it was about my family or telling me about his. He was trying hard at this point in his career and I admired him for doing that."[24]

For the first couple of weeks of December, Lynott had been toying around in his home studio with guitarist Steve Johnson. Johnson had been keen to work with Lynott for some time.

"It was sometime after Lizzy broke up that I first met Scott Gorham," Johnson recalls. "There was an ad in some magazine and basically he was auditioning players for a new band. After we had finished playing I asked for Phil's number because I had always been a huge fan of Lizzy and Phil in particular, so to play with him would be a dream. But I think Scott got annoyed at that, so I got in touch with John Salter. So quite regularly I would ring Salter's office explaining my case all the time trying to get a break with Phil. I passed on a tape to Salter, which I made in my garage on an old eight-track machine, Salter eventually passed it to Phil and he liked it. But at this stage Phil was already working on the '19' record so I missed out, but I did travel with him quite frequently whilst he was promoting the record."[25]

Working with Lynott wasn't without its funny side:

"When I started hanging out with him I was quite young, says Johnson. "I mean there were some unusual atmospheres at the house on occasion, but like I said I was quite young. I would get up every morning at seven and be frantically raging up and down the fret board. But he would disappear for hours on end to his room and sometimes mightn't arrive to the studio at the end of his garden until twelve at night by which time I was in bed. He'd drag me out of bed wanting to play through the night. At the time I remember that Polydor had a deal with him for a solo album but they weren't happy with the tracks that he had come up with, so we then set about writing 'Revolution', which was the best of a fair few tracks in the can."[26]

Johnson and Lynott initially began work on just two tracks, one of which dated back a few years but had yet to surface on any album. In its original incarnation it was called 'Look In These Eyes' but had undergone both lyrical and musical changes. Renamed 'No More', it became a prominent feature in the 'Three Musketeers' set during the summer tour of Sweden back in 1983. It then went through Grand Slam, who were never really sold on it and finally Lynott decided to resurrect it for his new solo album.

The last track that Philip Lynott ever worked on was a song called 'Revolution', though it has also become known as 'People Get Ready', after the opening line of the chorus. Lynott had worked on an early version of the track with Robin George, the guitarist on the 'Nineteen' single, but eventually Steve Johnson helped to bring it to a conclusion. 'Revolution' was one of the strongest songs Lynott had written since the demise of Lizzy, and in a way it is very Lizzy-esque. Though he hadn't quite worked out the verses, the chorus is strong and Lynott sings out almost in defiance.

Lynott's recording contract with Polydor stipulated that he had to have two singles ready for release in a short space of time, one which would be issued before Christmas and another due to be issued in the early part of February '86. Some claim the revised 'Harlem' in the form of 'If I Had A Wish' would have been the first single, others maintain it was going to be the track he recorded with Huey Lewis, 'I'm Still Alive'. It is also conceivable that Lynott was going to use 'No More' as the B-side. However, as Johnson was due to join Lynott again in his home studio during the first week of January before settling into a professional studio in mid January to record the album, 'Revolution' most probably would have been the next single issue. 'Revolution' is a stronger track than the other two songs, has more commercial appeal and screams chart potential.

"They hung him, hung him out to die, standing in the line,
Tell me what's going on,
Freedom standing in the rain, don't you feel the pain,
Don't you feel the pain…
…People get ready for the revolution,
People get ready for the overthrow,
Now the time has come to use our guns,
Now is the time to let it all go".

These lyrics were the last ever written by Philip Lynott.

During one of Lynott's last interviews with *Hot Press* magazine he expressed many desires for his future. Talk soon swung to a previously unexplored territory, a film soundtrack. Lynott's name had been linked with a big budget epic titled *Soldiers Of Destiny*, which was due to be shot in Ireland later in 1986. The plot supposedly revolved around the activities of the notorious 'Black And Tans' during the struggle for independence. Though nothing concrete had been settled between Lynott and the film company, this may have been an interesting diversion for Lynott to follow in his attempts to resuscitate his flagging career.

However, everything came to a head one evening, when unbeknownst to Lynott, a Polydor representative arrived at Kew inquiring into the progress of the material, as Johnson remembers.

"He was struggling with writing the album and then this guy from Polydor arrived to check on his progress. Of course Phil wasn't prepared and tried to fob him off with the revised version of 'Harlem', it didn't work and so an even heavier depression settled upon him. A lot of the Slam material was cropping up in the recording for the solo album and he wanted to develop this with me because a lot of it was just thrown together. I in turn couldn't wait because I wanted to put my mark on it. For the track 'No More' he asked me to sing harmonies and I was up for it and he seemed to be very pleased with the result."[27]

With the "Nineteen" single on the fringes of the charts, Lynott ploughed on mercilessly with promotion, appearing on the special Christmas *Razzamatazz* show which was being hosted by his old friend David 'Kid' Jensen. It aired on 23 December with Brian Downey back with Phil after two years. Lynott kicked off the show with "Nineteen" but his physical demeanour revealed an ashen face and glazed eyes. Brian Downey recalls the brief re-establishment of his relationship with Lynott.

"I went over to play on TV with him just before Christmas. He was talking at that time of getting Thin Lizzy together again the following year. After the session we went out celebrating but nothing over the top. However,

199

I suppose he shouldn't have done that in retrospect. He was under doctor's advice then to lay off, but that was Phil for you. He'd always been a bit of a maverick. It was like that with Lizzy: the management was never really in it. It was Phil who really directed what we were doing."

Lynott had invited Downey to stay at Kew but upon their return to the house he decided to decline the offer of a conversation about a Lizzy-reformation and made his way back to the hotel in Hammersmith. He persuaded Lynott to leave the chat until after Christmas. Downey boarded a flight for Dublin the next morning and never did get to finish the conversation.

There were many visits by old friends during December with ex Lizzy axe-man Scott Gorham turning up to check out the latest news with his old friend. Gorham had purposely got away from the music scene in his attempts to purge himself of the lifestyle, a move Lynott had rejected.

"I knew when he answered the door that he was still in a bad way," Gorham recalls of his visit. "He had put on weight, his breathing was heavy and though he spoke positively about the future I just thought it would take a little time before he got back on form again. So we kicked around a few ideas, had a chat basically and wished each other a good Christmas and said that we'd meet up soon."[28]

Though Lynott had not yet recorded at the Polydor studios, preferring instead to work up ideas at his home studio in Richmond, he had booked time to record his third solo effort from 16 January. He resolved to avoid the mistakes he had made with his previous solo efforts, when time was so tight that he fitted recordings in between bouts with Lizzy.

In the meantime, however, with the holidays beckoning, Lynott decided to spend Christmas at Kew before returning to Ireland for the new-year celebrations. He had been to a staff night out leading up to Christmas day and it seems in the aftermath of this party he began to feel gravely ill, but as Philomena reveals his demeanour at this stage didn't give cause for concern.

"His lifestyle was such that a lot of his work was done at night, at gigs or in the studio and consequently we lived in two different worlds. Showbiz people are generally night people and that was how I rationalised the situation when it occurred. He didn't look well but at the same time insisted that all was okay, who does look okay with a hangover?"[29]

The reality of the situation was that over the recent twelve months, his physical appearance had changed dramatically as had his personality. He had spent a great deal of time in England worrying about the state of his career, his marriage and his relationship with his children. It is the opinion of many that he concealed his involvement with drugs, primarily heroin, from those people who may well have been able to help him. Philip Chevron of the Pogues tries to explain the unfortunate downturn in events.

"When I spoke to Phil he spoke lovingly about himself as a family man, but in truth he was just constructing another mythology which he thought would help him to live his increasingly difficult life. Philip was his own worst enemy. He never let people love him enough to be able to tell him how things really were. When he really needed help, he didn't know whom to ask. And, in truth, I think he had us all believing in the myth too."[30]

Philomena herself arrived at Kew 184 just a few days after Lynott's last TV appearance on the *Razzamatazz Christmas Special* looking forward immensely to spending the holidays with her son. Though relations were very much strained between the Crowthers and Lynotts, both Philip and Caroline had initially agreed to spend the holiday period together, most especially for the children Sarah and Cathleen. This arrangement was changed when Philomena received a phone call from Caroline informing her that she would be unable to join them. Caroline had in fact apparently asked Philomena to try and convince Philip to spend Christmas in Dublin, and though Philomena tried to bring him round, it had been settled that he would only be returning home for the new-year celebrations.

During the following days Lynott rarely ventured from his house. Philomena picked up Sarah and Cathleen in Bath, thereby easing the possible tension between the two families had Phil turned up to collect the children himself.

After arriving back in Richmond with the children the next day, Philomena decided to go shopping in the nearby town and pick out a present for Philip. Previously when asked what he wanted for Christmas, Lynott informed his mother that a beautifully crafted lamp he had spotted in town would be perfect for the living room. When he mentioned the sum of £330, Philomena quickly dispelled any possibility of paying that kind of price and the two of them joked about it.

On Christmas Eve morning, Lynott again successfully hid his urgent need for medical attention. His failure to even dress himself, preferring to lounge around in house clothes, gave rise to considerable suspicion on Philomena's behalf. Once more several visitors arrived, 'Big' Charlie McClennan, Brian Robertson and Jimmy Bain would all stay for short periods of time. Bain, who had previously irritated Philomena with his foul and abusive language, endeared himself even further by using Lynott's own Christmas wrapping paper to wrap his own presents. Though appalled by his behaviour, she refused to let this upset the festive spirit in the house, especially with Sarah and Cathleen in their father's abode.

It was later that night that Lynott became increasingly ill and a doctor was called. Thinking her son may be suffering from the usual Christmas excesses, the doctor simply prescribed medication for flu. The negative effect this had upon Lynott's ever decreasing immune system began to frighten Philomena and she in turn would call Dublin to try and find a solution.

It was agreed that family friend and confidant, Graham Cohen, fly over from Dublin as soon as possible to try and help ease the strain on Philomena and hopefully provide a solution for the fragile state of Lynott's health. His condition was to remain stable until the morning whereupon Brian Robertson dropped by to wish everyone a happy Christmas only to discover that his good pal Philip Lynott was in a very bad way indeed. After trying to calm Philomena and sitting her down in the kitchen, Robertson informed her that her son had been using heavy drugs since the mid-1970s. An astounded Philomena was also informed by 'Big' Charlie, who arrived later that afternoon that Philip had a serious heroin habit.

On Christmas night they arranged for Philip Lynott to be booked into a clinic known as Clouds near Salisbury in Wiltshire. Less than an hour after his arrival Lynott was then transferred to Salisbury General Infirmary after failing to respond to treatment.

For the duration of his stay he was kept company and nursed by family and friends. On a couple of occasions Caroline visited the hospital, one time with the children who she had taken back to her home in Bath for their own protection. The media, who had by now heard reports that the former Lizzy frontman was very ill, started gathering, only to hear confirmation that Lynott was indeed fighting for his life. Whilst in hospital Lynott drifted in and out of consciousness, tenderly cared for by his ever-adoring mother. Philomena then brought it to the attention of the medics at the hospital that Lynott had not urinated since his arrival, which suggested that his kidneys had started to fail. Quickly being placed on a dialysis machine helped to restore their function, but Philip Lynott's body was approaching the shutdown stage. The many years of heavy partying had simply taken their toll. After developing pneumonia early in the new-year, he began to slip away and finally on the evening of 4 January, Philip Lynott died of total system failure.

Before the news had filtered through to Caroline and her dad about how gravely ill Lynott was, he was gone. A press release was prepared. Rumours about the way in which the statement was made have varied through the years but one onlooker who wishes to remain anonymous remembers.

"I can recall being outside when the statement was read out that Philo had passed away, autographs were being signed by certain individuals, I thought how can they at a time like this, it was horrendous."[31]

Though many people considered his death to be inevitable, nobody for sure thought he wouldn't pull through. Graham Cohen recalls the effect Lynott's death had on the staff during that difficult time.

"The staff at the hospital wouldn't believe for a second he was going to die and they were really brilliant to him. They were genuinely aggrieved and really did feel the impact of his loss."[32]

Philip Chevron, having supported Lizzy in the mid-seventies with The Radiators From Space says, "the reason his death came as such a shock to people was that everyone had him marked as bullet-proof."[33]

Though Philomena was not at the hospital when Philip died, having being taken back to Kew after the strain of the previous week, she was briskly collected and taken back to the hospital. In her despair she was unable to identify Philip's body and the task was bravely undertaken by Philip's ex-wife Caroline and Graham Cohen. A couple of days later a post-mortem was conducted and the findings by chief pathologist Dr. Angela Scott reported that Lynott had developed 'multiple internal abscesses and staphylocccal and streptococcal septicaemia', which led to total body failure. Philip Lynott had simply died of neglect, by his own hand and his refusal to seek help and by the refusal of all else to see that he was as mortal as the next man.

The manner in which he died meant that the media started to circle like vultures and paid little heed for requests for the family to face their harrowing ordeal in private.

With the funeral arrangements finalised, Lynott's body was taken to St. Elizabeth's Church in Richmond, where just shy of six years earlier he had married in a blaze of publicity. The funeral was attended by a wide array of industry people, family, friends and everyone who was even remotely connected with the Lizzy organisation. A final farewell to Ireland's black rose took place at the Richmond Hill Hotel where everyone re-told their adventures with Philo.

Lynott though, was to be buried in his beloved homeland of Ireland and on 10 January he made his last journey home. It was the following day, a Saturday, when a second service was held for Philip Lynott at the Howth Parish Church, attended by a similar crowd that had turned up to pay their final respects in London. The ex-Lizzies were there, members of U2, the Irish Premier Charles Haughey, several members of the Pogues, Bob Geldof and Paula Yates, David Heffernan and his wife Tina plus intimate members of the Lynott inner circle. Lynott's coffin was removed from the hearse at the entrance to the church and passed over the vast array of men in the village, right to the church door.

After the mass, Lynott was taken to St. Fintan's Cemetery and buried in the St. Polan's section in plot number thirteen. Philomena being so distraught was escorted from the cemetery in tears and brought back to Glen Corr whilst the service continued. Lynott's two daughters, Sarah and Cathleen each placed a red rose on his casket in loving memory of their father, repeating their act of the London service. Many attended both services and the sorrowful sight got wide coverage on national television.

For Philomena however the event proved to be traumatic. Having not seen his body she refused to believe he was dead, merely trying to fool herself that he was away touring. It was a belief that she would contend with for some time after his death. Philip Lynott had left behind two daughters aged seven and five, and an estranged wife. On a professional level he left an unfulfilled contractual obligation which has yet to reach a satisfactory conclusion.

For a time, Lynott's grave was marked by a simple white cross, a reminiscent feature of the cowboy tradition. In time this was ultimately replaced with a flat stone, so as not to disrupt cemetery regulations. Lynott's old friend, Jim Fitzpatrick designed the inscription in Irish, which translates to "Sleep In Peace, Our Black Rose".

For many the first weeks of January remained blurred by painful recollections and time has done little to dim the pain of a lost loved one. Philip Chevron recalls this time...

"On 4 January, 1986, myself and Terry Woods spent the whole day crying on each other's shoulders. We just wept and wept. I wept again at his funeral. I really don't know why exactly. I didn't much like him and he didn't much like me. But I think I loved him all the same. I loved him for the man he was, before his drug abuse began to distort his life. And maybe we also knew then that Ireland could ill-afford to lose a man of such enormous character, talent and personality. In the end Philip Lynott was an enormously complex man and unknowable sort of man and, oddly enough, he didn't leave that many clues behind about himself."[34]

Many within the business knew of his self-destructive nature, but he never let people near enough for them to recognise just what a perilous road he was on. The effect of Lynott's death reverberated through the industry, and almost immediately a concert was organised to bring a wider awareness of the scourge of heroin. Nik Kershaw booked the Hammersmith Odeon during May of 1986 and acquired the services of many well-established chart artists prepared to put their muscle behind such a cause.

Then there remains the issue of Lynott's last known recordings. The decision to leave these unreleased is all the more hard to accept on hearing friends and work colleagues describing with great interest what direction Lynott was taking musically before his premature demise. Shay Healy, director of *The Rocker* documentary on Lynott had this to say about Lynott's final career moves.

"There have been many stories relating to the movie on his life but for me one of the more intriguing topics would be the work he put into his final solo album, which has yet to find its way into the public domain. Previously his solo work had been fascinating musically though not particularly commercially successful. He seemed to be developing all the time as a songwriter, which had to have been further enhanced by the different types of music he listened to. His craft is something that he was trying to perfect every time. As a fitting tribute to an extraordinary talent the release of this material would be the feather in the cap as it were. To let people know exactly what direction he was taking with his songwriting and show what point he had reached before his death."[35]

1986 had begun with a sense of loss for all within the Lynott inner circle, but few suffered as furiously as Lynott's mother, Philomena. Her rapid decline became glaringly obvious to all her close friends, as she would rarely venture out, preferring for nearly two years to just lay on the settee in Glen Corr.

"I died really…," Philomena recalls. "It took me a long time before I got the click to come back to life. I was just like a zombie, completely and utterly gone. On one occasion I was out walking the dogs, and I used to hear people saying once I had passed them, 'God look at her, she's after losing it, she's gone'. I knew what they meant and I was very aware that people were looking at me and thinking that I had gone mad. In a way I suppose I had gone to the edge of the cliff but I didn't fall over. There were a few things that brought me back to my sanity. I remember being at the graveyard visiting Philip when I was mourning the loss of one child and I discovered another woman grieving over the loss of three of her children.

"There were other things as well. I was lying down on the settee one day in the front room and I couldn't stop crying, I couldn't eat, I was losing weight. I cried rivers for Philip and he was worth every single tear. I can recall watching TV one day when it transpired that a youth had been murdered. The body had been sexually assaulted and I just thought, 'Imagine that policeman having to tell the parents of that child'. That situation jolted me out of myself and I lay in bed crying for that woman. Knowing that other mothers were out there suffering and here I was crying my eyes out day and night for Philip. But as I said he was still worth the tears, but I came back, I'm back…I'm okay now. I still cry over him, Jesus I even have a rant at him now whenever I go round to see his resting place."[36]

This feeling was mirrored throughout the rest of the people who had the privilege of meeting Lynott – those who had either shared his generosity, flew with him on his musical adventures, or had any remote contact with the man. Whether he was licking his wounds or smiling in his triumphs, Philip Lynott made an impression.

"I remember him with real affection," David Heffernan recalls. "He was one of those people that you come across that you're really glad that you've worked with and one of those whose company you were glad to have kept no matter for how long or short a time. I think he was a really generous guy. When things went wrong for whichever reason he went down the road that he couldn't get back out of. It was the ultimate cul de sac. I think you can shed a tear about Philip every now and again. He was a very complex human being but I remember Brian Robertson on Shay Healy's documentary *The Rocker* saying that he still dreams about Philip and I can understand that. There are times when Philip will come into your consciousness or your dreams for no apparent reason and in some respects it sums him up because that's what he wanted to achieve, to make an impression. He wanted to be part of people's lives and to prove that where he came from, you could achieve something. Essentially he did all those things but I can't help but feel when I do think about him an overwhelming sense of remorse and loss."[37]

Renowned video director, David Mallet is another who holds nothing but good memories of Lynott.

"Philip was a poet and that was always the one thing that struck me about him. His lyrics were his strong point alongside his prowess to conjure up a melody, and these ingredients combined made up his fascinating character. My overall impression of him is that he was so clever with the way he went about his music. There were only a few people back then who used certain methods for success and he had mastered them by the time I came to work with him. On the occasions I worked with him, he was a very exciting person to be around at that time in his career."[38]

Marcus Connaughton is another who still tries to come to terms with the fact that Philip Lynott is no longer with us.

"Even so long after his death I don't think Philip Lynott has yet been given the recognition that his work within Lizzy and outside of it deserves, but I do believe his time will come. When he did pass on I was extremely upset because I felt he was robbed and he was taken from us. To me he was somebody special. The way I remember Philip is probably the way a lot of the people who were closer to him than I was remember and that was as a generous spirit, a gentle guy and a sweet man."[39]

One of the last musicians to have worked with Lynott, Paul Hardcastle describes the time he heard of Lynott's demise...

"When we were in the studio together I didn't realise that his health was as bad as it later turned out to be. We were working together even about six weeks before he died so that's why I couldn't believe it when I heard the news of his death. I was at home when I heard. The only thing that seemed a little off with him was his rasping cough."

Steve Johnson also has vivid recollections of the time.

"It was actually Don Airey who rang me to tell me Phil had died. Phil was a broken man, between his marriage, his drug problem and the Lizzy break-up. He was struggling and the last thing he probably needed was a young Yorkshire lad who would pretty much tire him out with enthusiasm. Of course Phil had the hangers-on and what was easily apparent was a lack of real friends, he was such a lovely guy and if he had had steadier people around perhaps things might not have taken the turn they had."[40]

Frank Rogers, who nurtured the young Lynott during the Decca years, found it all so sad…

"I was so fond of him, I can't put it into words. I knew he was ill but when I opened the Sunday papers and saw the announcement it really nailed me. There was so much more left for him to do."

The media too did little to deflect attention from Lynott's anti-social habits, hissing mercilessly and scavenging for the last gory detail, and all this mere weeks after Lynott's death. What hurt most was the sordid recount of gossip columnist Heather Mitson, at the time known as Heavy Metal Heather who dished the dirt, baseless scandal on her wild times with the one-time Lizzy frontman.

"All in all it was a bad time to die of drug problems," recalls Smily Bolger. "When Brian Jones, Hendrix, Joplin and Morrison of the Doors died it was not so much so cool, just more so widely accepted that this is the way that some musicians go. When Philip died, out came the knives disguised as pens and so began the annihilation. The English press crucified him over his bad habits. But before Slam started he was on a slippery slope. Little by little the art of disassociation became very, very obvious."[41]

During the early part of February, Huey Lewis and the News were back in Britain having been nominated in the category of Best International Act at the BPI Awards. Bob Geldof and Midge Ure were there to collect awards for their efforts with the *Live Aid* extravaganza, yet neither made any reference to the recent passing of a man who had encouraged them immensely when they were starting their careers. Huey Lewis made amends and when he won the award for Best International Act he immediately pledged the award in honour of his pal, Philip Lynott.

Over the course of the previous two years it was noticeable that Lynott had been given the cold shoulder by many within the industry. Few others were brave enough to mention Lynott's name and this explains why Huey Lewis remains a favourite amongst Lizzy supporters worldwide.

Over the coming months plans had been set for one of the biggest events in Irish history, *Self Aid,* a spin-off of the previous year's success in England, once more organised by Geldof. The event took place on 17 May at the RDS with a variety of musicians playing. Paul Brady was there, Rory Gallagher, U2 and as extra special guests to cap off the finale, a reformed version of Lizzy took to the stage. Gary Moore handled the lead vocal on "Don't Believe A Word" whilst Geldof threw out "The Cowboy Song" and the whole pack fought on for "Whiskey in the Jar". Downey, Gorham and Wharton were also there with Gary Moore's bass player, Bob Daisley. The performance itself was a mess due to insufficient rehearsal time, and the overwhelming emotional low of not having Lynott to lead them through their most famous numbers hit them hard. Indeed the emerald cowboy was sorely missed. As Brian Downey later commented, "What in the name of God did *Self Aid* mean anyway?"[42]

The remainder of 1986 faded without much news of any Lizzy-related release. It seemed the public would have to wait that little bit longer for any fresh material. Matters were complicated however when it was discovered that Lynott had died in testate.

14

LIFE AFTER LYNOTT

In January 1987 plans were set in place to release a compilation album to coincide with the first anniversary of Lynott's death. Released on Telstar, it was entitled *Soldier Of Fortune* which combined the best of Lizzy with a sprinkling of Lynott's solo work. All material was previously available and it limped its way to No 56 in the charts and disappeared a short three weeks later. It was clearly a reminder for how far Lynott and Lizzy had fallen in the public eye.

Newspaper reports at the time of Lynott's death suggested a dwindling fortune with his net assets reported at around £200,000 sterling. There was still the question as to whether the properties Lynott owned in London would be retained or sold. Glen Corr in Dublin was presently occupied by Philomena, her partner Denis Keely, and Graham Cohen. In her attempts to recover from Philip's death, she remained in the home he had intended to grow old in. For the meantime, White Horses, which Lynott had presented to his mother as a fiftieth birthday gift and from which she was drawing her only income, proved to be a necessary distraction from her grief. By attempting to get back into the day-to-day running of a household, Philomena was fighting her way back.

Relations between Caroline and Philomena continued to deteriorate and

Philomena only had limited access to her grandchildren. This continued over the coming years to the point where they would eventually have their differences settled in the Irish High Courts. The Court issue also involved property, Glen Corr to be precise – Caroline had already decided to sell Lynott's Richmond residence at Kew 184.

Before its sale, Lynott's studio had lain dormant at the end of the garden with tapes littered throughout the garage. The Kew residence was also peppered with Lynott's personal belongings, clothes and the demo tapes he had been working on prior to his death. With Kew put on the market during the latter part of 1987, interest in the property was said to be good, but it wouldn't be until the following year that the deal finally went through.

The scene within Kew proved to be quite shocking however, all Lynott's personal effects were just lying around. There had been no attempt by anyone to do anything with it. Philomena and Graham Cohen along with a few friends were encouraged to take what they wanted from the house after Caroline had taken what she needed. So the Lynott clan retained Philip's belongings, packing as much material as they possibly could. One close family friend was upset at the scene…

"Anybody who was moving in would have just binned this stuff that was lying around. Little attempt had been made to respect his memory, so all in all it was pretty disgusting."[1]

Lynott was known to be precious about his newly recorded material and it has been revealed in recent years that he hid much of it in a secret compartment built into the wall in his bedroom. It was from here that the material was supposedly removed and has since fallen into the wrong hands. Although this is supposition, Philomena Lynott herself maintains that certain objects have been stolen over the years from her possession. Whatever happened to these demo tapes is enveloped in mystery – one that seems destined to continue for the foreseeable future.

One commendable venture was the effort of Lynott flame-bearer Smiley Bolger in holding the first 'Vibe For Philo' in London on the anniversary of Lynott's death. Every year thereafter he has put together an event that has subsequently been held in Dublin with the most memorable being held at The Point in January 1996 to commemorate the tenth anniversary of Lynott's passing. In the interim Bolger also put together a collection of tribute albums in celebration of Lynott's work roping in many Irish artists who knew Lynott. Phil Chevron is one man who contributed.

"*The Ode To A Black Man* project was such a labour of love for Smiley. It seemed to be around for years but at some point the CD version finally arrived. I made my contribution at quite an early stage. I can recall standing in front of a microphone and reciting some of Philip's lyrics, some from

'Still In Love With You'. In truth, I got involved in this more out of fondness for Smiley than in memory of Philip. Smiley was clearly heartbroken by Philip's death. And if this project helped him in some way to cope with the shock, taking part was a small thing to do."[2]

Lizzy news was thin on the ground as the decade drew to a close, with a variety of projects going on for ex-Lizzy members. Brian Downey had started up a drum clinic in Cork, Ireland, whilst still maintaining his links with the local blues circuit in Dublin. John Sykes continued to work with David Coverdale's Whitesnake throughout 1986 playing on their American breakthrough album *Whitesnake 1987*. Though hardly reminicent of the Moody/Marsden days, Sykes had contributed enormously to the writing of the album, but when it came time to tour he had fallen out of favour with Coverdale.

Darren Wharton had also been making significant strides with his new band Dare. After Lynott's death, Wharton had been doing sporadic session work whilst working on a tentative deal for a solo release. In the end, he scrapped all the material he had written and concentrated his energies towards Dare. The first fruits of this new endeavour was *Out Of The Silence* released in 1989 on the A&M label. Their initial success came via European markets where they supported a variety of people such as Gary Moore. They would also find some success in markets as far flung as Japan and Australia. After a follow up in 1991 titled *Blood From Stone*, their next album *Calm Before the Storm* was five years in the making and again met with moderate success.

Scott Gorham had by this time put together 21 Guns. The aim of the band was to produce an accessible rock and roll melodic quartet, judging by their debut album *Salute*, released on the RCA label. But as grunge became the new rock 'n' roll, 21 Guns were dated before they had even begun. Though *Salute* met with positive reviews, it suffered commercially and the band never got out of the starting blocks. A second album followed some six years later, titled *Nothing's Real* which suffered the same fate as their debut and sunk without a trace. Gorham's next move would be the re-activation of Lizzy.

Snowy White had re-started his career in a somewhat mercurial manner since his departure from Lizzy. He got together with bassist Kuma Harada, drummer Richard Bailey and keyboardist Godfrey Wang to produce his first solo album *White Flames*. It included a re-recorded version of a track he had demo'd whilst still in Lizzy called "Bird Of Paradise". After re-working the arrangement and vocals, it was later decided to issue the track as a single and it rose to No 6 on the UK chart.

"I was starting to be thought of as a ballad singer who happens to play a bit of guitar," White recalls. "There was a lot of pressure on me to come up with another hit, but the reality was that I wasn't really a singles' artist."[3]

White's follow-up album simply titled *Snowy White* failed to repeat the previous acclaim and the single taken from the album, "Peace On Earth, Land Of Freedom and Fortune" failed to sell. After releasing another album *That Certain Thing*, White eventually parted company with his record label and by 1988 had set up the Blues Agency who toured throughout Europe and released two albums titled *Change My Life* and *Blues On Me*. Another solo LP followed in 1993 titled *Highway To The Sun* with special guests including Dave Gilmour, Chris Rea, Paul Carrack and Gary Moore.

By 1990 rumours abounded that there would be something special concerning a Lizzy release. It soon became clear that talks had being taking place with a view to re-recording some of the old Grand Slam numbers. "Military Man" had already featured on the "Out In The Fields" collaboration with Gary Moore so that was ruled out. Chris Morrison, who was still handling the Lizzy managerial affairs was adamant that a song was put out for the fifth anniversary of Lynott's death. The idea was to promote a compilation package already in the works, designed to appeal to the mass market.

Initially both Scott Gorham and Brian Downey were sceptical. The Grand Slam song "Dedication" was chosen, originally written by the Slam lead guitarist Laurence Archer. According to Archer the song wasn't in any state to be released without sufficient re-working, so Morrison put out feelers to ex-Lizzy members about contributing to a re-recording of the song. Gary Moore was approached and agreed, though Gorham and Downey were still refusing. In the end, as the track was to be released anyway, they were forced into submission and agreed to supply overdubs.

By late October, Gorham and Downey along with Lief Johansen, the keyboard player with 21 Guns, started work on the track. After listening to the original demo it seemed that the old Lynott magic was still hanging in there. Lynott was in fierce voice and with the benefits of modern technology they prepared the song for release. It left one problem though, the sleeve for the single suggested that it was a Lynott-penned song.

"I never knew the song was going to be on an album of Lizzy's greatest hits," Laurence Archer explains. "A friend called me to tell me my song was on the radio, though it had been released as a Lizzy single. Morrison however didn't have a leg to stand on as I had registered the song before I ever hooked up with Phil. In the end I ended up signing away the rights to another selection of songs, like "Sisters Of Mercy" and "Military Man". A lot of political shit went on and if I knew then what I know now, there wouldn't have been any way any of it would've happened."[4]

The "Dedication" single was due to be released on 4 January but a delay was caused by the apparent lack of visual footage to accompany the single. It was decided to use footage of the classic *Live And Dangerous* line-up of the era, but there are also snippets with Eric Bell. The lip-sync was well off, but it was necessary to use footage showing the man at the peak of his game. It was eventually released a week late on 11 January and though the video featured Brian Robertson, at no stage was he approached to contribute to the revised version of the song.

"I wasn't annoyed about not been asked to do the single at all," Robertson says, "I mean Laurence Archer wrote the song for Christ's sake, a non-Lizzy member, so it all seemed to be quite a strange time when that came out under the Lizzy banner."[5]

"Dedication" reached No 35 on the UK charts. Excepting "Cold Sweat" back in 1983, it fared better than any Lizzy related release since 1981. But in a typical piece of bad luck, when "Dedication" was due to be screened on *Top Of The Pops,* an extended news bulletin regarding the Gulf War meant it was swept to the side. On the Irish charts it zoomed to No 1, reinforcing the strength of Lynott's home following.

In February the compilation album followed. Titled *Dedication – The Very Best Of Thin Lizzy,* it made it to No 8 on the UK charts proving that the band was still popular. However, in March a second single, a reissued and remixed version of "The Boys Are Back In Town" died a death with few people interested in going back out to buy the single for the umpteenth time. A wiser move might have been to go back and review other post-Lizzy material, perhaps one taken from the Huey Lewis sessions and re-record it, as the Lizzy management had done with "Dedication".

Although the year began positively with the release of the greatest hits, all was not well behind the scenes. The early nineties proved to be a painful period for those concerned with Philip Lynott's estate. It was some six years after his death when the wheels of justice were called into play. Caroline remarried in 1989 and challenged Philomena for the rightful ownership of Glen Corr. The disputes eventually led to a High Court battle. The fact was that, when the children came of age, the house would revert to them anyway. In the end the law had to be implemented and Philomena was ordered to leave Glen Corr. The property was sold and she retired to her own home White Horses, where she still lives today.

For a number of years the idea of setting up a trust in Lynott's name had been toyed with by family and friends. On 4 January, 1994 this vision became a reality. It coincided with an anniversary gig set up by Smily Bolger at Fibber Magee's on Parnell Street. The 'Roisin Dubh Trust' was in essence set up to commemorate the artistic life of Philip Parris Lynott and to co-ordinate commemorative activities undertaken in his name.

In the summer of 1994 there was the surprise announcement that a Lizzy revival was on the cards. In November a reformed Thin Lizzy were pencilled in for a short tour of Japan with John Sykes, the last guitarist to join Lizzy with Lynott still at the helm, taking over the vocal chores. Gorham was back, Wharton on keyboards, Brian Downey was back in the drum stool and Marco Mendoza played bass.

Mendoza had pretty big boots to fill:

"What really impressed me," he says, "was how he used to play with the melody, because he was much more so a songwriter than anything and that reflected in his bass playing as well. He really wouldn't stretch that much on the bass primarily because his main thing was to sing and get the vocal out there, which is a real skill in itself to be honest. Getting to play with Brian Downey was cool and he was another who had developed his own style and I could see how he and Phil worked so well together."[6]

In some quarters, the objections to Lizzy reforming veered towards the venomous. To continue with the name without Lynott seemed like the ultimate betrayal for a substantial number of supporters. Several alternative names had been suggested, but at the end of the day the band was playing tracks solely from their heyday. It was advertised as a tribute to the man and essentially that is all it was, and doesn't stretch beyond those boundaries. It would be an entirely different matter if they were recording fresh material under the Thin Lizzy banner. "There is talk about the current line-up sitting down and recording some new material, but we all have to decide if this is something that we want to jump into,"[7] says Marco Mendoza.

Around the same time as the Japanese tour, Philomena was undertaking a rather important project of her own. In the aftermath of the trial regarding Glen Corr, she was approached about publishing her memoirs. So she began the painful process of having to delve into the depths of her previous despair to uncover the lasting meaning of her relationship with her son. It was a process that highlighted a lot of aspects of her bond with Philip that she had previously not recognised or overlooked. The book was to be a collaborative effort with *Hot Press* general manager Jackie Hayden. It was Hayden who interviewed Philomena for hours upon end trying to unravel the hardship she endured as a single mother in the 1950s. The book turned out to be a very candid read and stands alone as an ultimate declaration of love between mother and son. *My Boy* shot straight to the top of Irish bestsellers list and was later released in England by Virgin Books. Mark Putterford's biography *The Rocker* was published in March 1994. Putterford, who had not been well whilst writing the project, died in November of 1994. He was one of the few journalists who championed Lynott's post-Lizzy efforts.

On January 4, 1996 the Point Theatre in Dublin hosted a tribute to

Philip Lynott titled King's Call. Gorham, who had previously refused to become involved in any tribute event unless it was run in what he deemed a professional manner, agreed this time around. Bolger, the tribute mainstay, had to a degree been pushed aside as the big boys such as Denis Desmond took hold of the night. Sykes also came on board especially after the successful Japanese encounter. The wise inclusion of Irish acts proved just how influential Lynott had been.

Another biography appeared in 1996 in the form of *Ballad of a Thin Man* by Stuart Baillie. To coincide with the passing of a further anniversary of Lynott's death, yet another compilation album was released titled *Wild One*, though a curious title as it omitted the track itself.

The onset of the Internet brought various Lizzy websites, including official sites and some not so official. Announcements came and went suggesting Lizzy related releases, few of which ever came to pass. All of this coincided with the Universal Records takeover, which, once more delayed any more Lizzy-related product. As a result, the only new material were the numerous tribute albums, the best of which was the Record Heaven release *Spirit Of The Black Rose* which featured such luminaries as Robin George, Primal Scream and Randy Bachman.

Finally, towards the latter months of 2001, it was announced that a Thin Lizzy box-set called *Vagabonds, Kings, Warriors, Angels* was to be released. However, it featured little that was of any value to the hardcore collector. At least it did acknowledge Lynott's post-Lizzy shelf life by including "Sisters Of Mercy".

2002 brought the limited edition release on ZoomClub Records of the long-awaited post Lizzy recordings made by Grand Slam. This was actually preceded by a special edition Three Musketeers release, recorded during the break in the farewell Lizzy tour in the summer of 1983. Both albums were compiled from the private archives of Mark Stanway, keyboard player with Grand Slam. The fact that the recordings were not released officially on the Universal Label, harks back to the fact that Grand Slam never obtained a record deal.

"The reasons I had not released this material are very personal," says Stanway. "Needless to say Phil's death was very saddening and a major loss to rock music, and at the time people were blatantly cashing in on his death."[8]

To date, there still remains a lot of material, albeit some in demo form from the 1980s that remains unreleased. The reason for these recordings being withheld are uncertain, especially as some of it is strong material. Perhaps the lobbying that has gone on has been aimed in the wrong direction.

Aside from the material that Lynott recorded in the final three years of his life, there are also those who claim that Lizzy might have a cache of material left over from their studio days with Phonogram, although it would be almost impossible to guess how much would be worth working on.

Brian Robertson claimed that there were as many tracks left over from the John Alcock sessions as there was on the albums, *Jailbreak* and *Johnny The Fox*. Robertson remembers one of these tracks in particular:

"Scott and me had this riff of a track called 'Dealer' for years, but we couldn't get it together for ages, sometime around the first *Wild Horses* album I think."[9]

'Crawling' is another track written by Gary Moore and played live by Lizzy in the early days. A tape is thought to exist with a Lynott vocal recorded before the *Fighting* album sessions commenced. The studio version of 'Are You Ready' also awaits a compatible home as does 'Leaving Town', a song which contained a couplet later resurrected for the *Jailbreak* album track 'Running Back'.

There's also the early track 'Blue Shadows' along with the rejects from Lynott's solo endeavours 'Somebody Else's Dream' and 'Hate'. There are many versions of 'Hate' in existence, some featuring guitar and others featuring a heavily synthesised sound, although none has yet appeared in any official capacity.

Frank Rogers who worked with Decca Records up until 1990 can recall a quantity of material in their archives:

"They had a great archive, which was under some railway station, could've been Victoria Station. I would say most likely that there is some material there that has never seen the light of day, along with early versions of songs that for whatever reason were never utilised."[10]

In the summer of 2003 an announcement came via Radio Clyde in Scotland claiming that rare recordings featuring Thin Lizzy and a host of other top artists will be officially released through the Universal Records label. Considering that so many people were under the influence of so many different things, what studio recordings may exist could well exceed all expectations. Phil Chevron, who interviewed Lynott during the recording of the *Renegade* project, recalls Kit Woolven showing him the band's tape store:

"There were literally dozens and dozens of half-baked and half-forgotten ideas on tape. Philip had by then taken to singing his vocals not even line by line (which is not uncommon) but word by word. His sinuses were completely fucked."[11]

There are also the recordings that Lynott made with Terry Woods during the early eighties. 'Tennessee Stud' for example exists as a duet along with numerous other tracks the duo ended up jamming on whilst recording the standard. Woods had in fact been a roaming member of Lynott's pre-Lizzy outfit Orphanage so the ties went back a great distance.

The issue of credits, as with most bands, continues to be a source of unrest. Even throughout the Grand Slam period other members had brought ideas to the group, though in the end got little credit for it, if any at all. It can be easily explained. Laurence Archer, Slam's lead guitarist brought songs like 'Dedication' and 'Can't Get Away' to the band, but they were not fully-fledged tracks. The early demos of both songs have completely differently lyrics. Lynott's lyrical contributions have caused consternation over the years as to who owns what song.

The 'Dedication' demo is musically more or less all in place, but Lynott rewrote the lyric. On the other hand 'Can't Get Away' seems musically and lyrically unfinished, which perhaps tarnishes Archer's claim that the tracks should solely be credited to him. The various demo's show the development of the track, and in some ways the sorrow of the demo is lost in the eventual mastering that Archer and Lynott made with Huey Lewis.

Aside of the unreleased material already mentioned, there is also the Lynott/Wharton composition 'For Always' as Wharton recalls:

"It written and recorded sometime before the *Thunder and Lightning* sessions. It was a melancholy number but Phil really liked it. It's a pity it never found a home on any album, but it's still hanging around somewhere."

"Don't Let Him Slip Away' is another track that Lizzy worked on during the late '82 period. Although many versions exist, it never made the final cut of any album. 'Blue Parris' has its origins around the time Lynott was producing his second solo effort. Though rumoured to be a follow up to 'Parisienne Walkways' the downbeat nature of the song rendered it to the cutting room floor.

So is there enough Thin Lizzy or Philip Lynott material in the vault to fashion an album? Mostly likely there is, but is the market still there? This was tested back in the early months of 1991 when 'Dedication' was issued under the Thin Lizzy name. It charted, and it's possible that there is more Thin Lizzy, Philip Lynott and Grand Slam material which deserves release.

Perhaps the last word should be left to the woman who was never that far from his thoughts… Philomena Lynott.

"I want him to be remembered for his music, his poetry, his sense of humour. At the end of the day he'll always be remembered for his stupidity in getting involved in drugs which are a killer, but lets be terribly fair drugs are still out there, they are a temptation, he got tempted and sadly I lost him on account of it. Also let's not forget that he was on this planet and he left us some great memories, his music and his lyrics."

15

FINAL WORD

It is always difficult to summarise the achievements of someone who was part of a different generation to one's own. Philip Lynott's authority has never been in doubt, nor has his influence on the vast array of musicians who parade modern rock 'n' roll to an ever-hungry public. What is in doubt is the manner in which he went about it. Had he survived, one can only wonder as to what he might have been producing musically.

As Brian Robertson said towards the climax of our interview in Dublin in January of 2001, on being asked about whether Philip Lynott would have dared to tackle dance music, "I'm sure he would have had a hell of a go at it."

Nobody would doubt that, except maybe Philip Lynott himself. It was perhaps these seeds of doubt that ultimately robbed the world of an extremely talented human being.

His partners in crime, the Lizzy's, have trodden the lonesome road since his departure and continue to think of what might have been. Philip Lynott has certainly left behind a legacy. Philip Lynott achieved more than most. In his lifetime he strived for a perfection that was as elusive as that 'last honey by the water'.

As the years pass, few will ever scale the heights of the boy who stormed

Dublin, and then took on the rest of the world. Armed with his trusty bass and an avalanche of lyrical genius he stands as one of the most influential Irish recording artists. And despite that, so long after his death, there aren't any landmarks in his hometown of Dublin acknowledging his status, though this is sure to be rectified in the near future.

Lynott's ability to communicate through the power of verse stands unchallenged. He remains a significant influence on the history of rock 'n' roll – a renegade, a warrior and ultimately a soldier of fortune.

Behind the façade Philip Lynott constructed for himself, there was an extraordinarily gentle and fragile soul who never quite figured out how to keep from getting hurt.

NOTES AND SOURCES

CHAPTER 1

1 Interview with Alan Byrne Summer 2000
2 Interview with Alan Byrne Summer 2000
3 Interview with Alan Byrne Summer 2000
4 Interview with Alan Byrne Summer 2000
5 Interview with Alan Byrne Spring 2000
6 Friday Night BBC One Broadcast, Tommy Vance, 8th jan 1986
7 Interview with Alan Byrne Winter 2000
8 Interview with Alan Byrne Summer 2000
9 *The Rocker*, by Mark Putterford
10 Interview with Alan Byrne Summer 2000
11 Interview with Alan Byrne Summer 2000
12 Interview with Alan Byrne Spring 2000
13 Interview with Alan Byrne Autumn 2000
14 Interview with Alan Byrne Autumn 2000
15 Interview with Alan Byrne Winter 2000
16 Interview with Alan Byrne 2000
17 Interview with Alan Byrne ,
18 *Hot Press* Sept 2nd 1977
19 Interview with Alan Byrne
20 Interview with Alan Byrne
21 Interview with Alan Byrne
22 *The Rocker*, by Mark Putterford
23 Roddy Cleere Interview Summer 2000
24 Interview with Alan Byrne
25 Interview with Alan Byrne
26 *Hot Press,* Sept 2nd 1977 .
27 Interview with Alan Byrne
28 Interview with Alan Byrne
29 Interview with Alan Byrne
30 Interview with Alan Byrne

CHAPTER 2

1 Interview with Alan Byrne
2 *Hot Press* Dec 10th 1978
3 Friday 8th January 1986 BBC One Radio broadcast, Tommy Vance
4 Jim Fitzpatrick Website
5 Interview with Alan Byrne
6 Interview with Alan Byrne
7 Oct 1988 BBC 1 Radio broadcast, Shamrock 'n' roll
8 Interview with Alan Byrne
9 Interview with Alan Byrne
10 Interview with Alan Byrne
11 Interview with Alan Byrne
12 Interview with Alan Byrne
13 Interview with Alan Byrne
14 Friday 8th Jan 1986 BBC One Broadcast, Tommy Vance
15 Interview with Alan Byrne
16 *Black Rose,* copyright Adam Winstanley, used with permission
17 Interview with Alan Byrne
18 Interview with Alan Byrne
19 *The Rocker*, by Mark Putterford.
20 Interview with Alan Byrne
21 *Disc,* 1st July '72
22 Interview with Alan Byrne
23 Interview with Alan Byrne
24 *Black Rose,* copyright Adam Winstanley, used with permission
25 Friday Night BBC One Broadcast, Tommy Vance, 8th jan 1986
26 Interview with Alan Byrne
27 Interview with Alan Byrne
28 *Mercury – King Of Queen,* by Laura Jackson
29 *Black Rose,* Adam Winstanley, used with permission
30 *Record Mirror,* 29th Sept 1973
31 *Record Mirror,* 29th Sept 1973
32 *Record Mirror,* 29th Sept 1973
32 Jim Fitzpatrick website with permission
33 Interview with Alan Byrne
34 *Black Rose,* copyright Adam Winstanley, used with permission
35 Friday Night BBC One Broadcast, Tommy Vance, 8th jan 1986
36 unknown quote source, *Black Rose*
37 Interview with Alan Byrne
38 Interview with Alan Byrne

CHAPTER 3

1 Interview with Alan Byrne
2 Interview with Alan Byrne
3 Interview with Alan Byrne
4 Interview with Alan Byrne
5 Interview with Alan Byrne
6 Interview with Alan Byrne
7 Interview with Alan Byrne
8 Interview with Alan Byrne
9 Interview with Alan Byrne
10 Interview with Alan Byrne
11 Interview with Alan Byrne
12 Interview with Alan Byrne
13 *Hot Press,* Nigel Grainge with Liam Fay with permission
14 Interview with Alan Byrne
15 Interview with Alan Byrne
16 Interview with Alan Byrne
17 Interview with Alan Byrne
18 *Hot Press* Sept 2nd 1977, used with permission
19 Interview with Alan Byrne
20 Interview with Alan Byrne
21 Interview with Alan Byrne
22 *Record Mirror* 1977
23 Sleeve notes of tribute album *Spirit Of The Black Rose,* used with permission
24 Interview with Alan Byrne
25 Interview with Alan Byrne
26 Interview with Alan Byrne
27 *Hot Press,* used with permission
28 Interview with Alan Byrne
29 Interview with Alan Byrne
30 Interview with Alan Byrne

CHAPTER 4

1 Interview with Alan Byrne
2 Interview with Alan Byrne
3 Interview with Alan Byrne/Dawn Poole
4 Interview with Alan Byrne

5 Interview with Alan Byrne
6 *NME*, Nov 6th '76
7 Interview with Alan Byrne
8 Interview with Alan Byrne
9 Interview with Alan Byrne
10 Interview with Alan Byrne
11 Interview with Alan Byrne
12 Interview with Alan Byrne
13 Interview with Alan Byrne

CHAPTER 5
1 Interview Alan Byrne and Dawn Poole
2 Interview with Alan Byrne
3 Interview with Alan Byrne/Dawn Poole
4 Interview with Alan Byrne
5 Interview with Alan Byrne
6 Interview with Alan Byrne
7 *Thin Lizzy*, Larry Pryce
8 Interview with Alan Byrne

CHAPTER 6
1 *Mercury, King Of Queen,* by Laura Jackson
2 Interview with Alan Byrne
3 Interview with Alan Byrne
4 *The Rocker,* by Mark Putterford
5 *Mercury, King Of Queen,* by Laura Jackson
6 Interview with Alan Byrne
7 *Mercury, King Of Queen,* Laura Jackson
8 Interview with Alan Byrne
9 Tony Visconti website, used with permission
10 Interview with Alan Byrne
11 Interview with Alan Byrne
12 Tony Visconti website, used with permission
13 Tony Visconti website, used with permission
14 Interview with Alan Byrne
15 Interview with Alan Byrne
16 Interview with Alan Byrne
17 *Hot Press Yearbook 1991*, used with permission
18 *Sounds* Aug 27th '77
19 Interview with Alan Byrne
20 Interview with Alan Byrne

CHAPTER 7
1 Interview with Alan Byrne
2 Tony Visconti website, used with permission
3 Interview with Alan Byrne
4 Interview with Alan Byrne
5 *NME*, 27th May 1978
6 *The Rocker* by Mark Putterford
7 Interview with Alan Byrne
8 Interview with Alan Byrne
9 Interview with Alan Byrne
10 *The Rocker* by Mark Putterford
11 Interview with Alan Byrne
12 Interview with Alan Byrne
13 Interview with Alan Byrne
14 *The Rocker* by Mark Putterford
15 Interview with Alan Byrne
16 Interview with Alan Byrne
17 *NME*

CHAPTER 8
1 Interview with Alan Byrne
2 Visconti website, used with permission
3 *Recording World,* Apr '82, article by James Betteridge
4 TonyVisconti website, used with permission
5 TonyVisconti website, used with permission
6 Interview with Alan Byrne
7 Interview with Alan Byrne
8 Interview with Alan Byrne
9 *Record Mirror,* Sept 8th '79

10 Interview with Alan Byrne
11 Interview with Alan Byrne
12 Interview with Alan Byrne
13 Interview with Alan Byrne
14 *Melody Maker,* 27th Oct '79
15 Interview with Alan Byrne
16 Interview with Alan Byrne
17 Interview with Alan Byrne

CHAPTER 9
1 *Daily Mirror*
2 Interview with Alan Byrne
3 *Daily Mirror*
4 Interview with Alan Byrne
5 Interview with Alan Byrne
6 Interview with Alan Byrne
7 Interview with Alan Byrne
8 Interview with Alan Byrne
9 Interview with Alan Byrne
10 Interview with Alan Byrne
11 Interview with Alan Byrne
12 Interview with Alan Byrne
13 Interview with Alan Byrne
14 Interview with Alan Byrne
15 Interview with Alan Byrne
16 Interview with Alan Byrne
17 *Sounds*, 21 June 1980
18 Interview with Alan Byrne
19 Interview with Alan Byrne
20 Interview with Alan Byrne

CHAPTER 10
1 Interview with Alan Byrne
2 Interview with Alan Byrne
3 Interview with Alan Byrne
4 *Hot Press,* used with permission
5 Interview with Alan Byrne
6 *Sounds* 26th Jan '91
8 Interview with Alan Byrne
9 Interview with Alan Byrne
10 Interview with Alan Byrne
11 Interview with Alan Byrne

CHAPTER 11
1 Interview with Alan Byrne
2 Interview with Alan Byrne
3 *Sunday Tribune* mag, 27th June 1982
4 Interview with Alan Byrne
5 Interview with Alan Byrne
6 Interview with Alan Byrne
7 Interview with Alan Byrne
8 Friday Night Rock Show, BBC Radio 1, 8th Jan '86, with Tommy Vance
9 Interview with Alan Byrne
10 Interview with Alan Byrne
11 Interview with Alan Byrne
12 Interview with Alan Byrne
13 Interview with Alan Byrne
14 Interview with Alan Byrne
15 Interview with Alan Byrne
16 Interview with Alan Byrne

CHAPTER 12
1 *Daily Record,* 21st Jan/'83
2 Interview with Alan Byrne
3 Interview with Alan Byrne
4 Interview with Alan Byrne
5 Dawn Poole, used with permission
6 *Vintage Guitar,* June 1999 by Tony Nobles, used with permission
7 Jim Fitzpatrick website, used with permission

THIN LIZZY

[8] *Melody Maker,* March 93
[9] *Interview with Alan Byrne*
[10] *Interview with Alan Byrne*
[11] Sleeve notes of *Zoomclub* release
[12] Interview with Alan Byrne
[13] Interview with Alan Byrne
[14] Interview with Alan Byrne
[15] *Vintage Guitar* June 1999, used with permission
[16] TonyVisconti website, used with permission
[17] Interview with Alan Byrne
[18] Interview with Alan Byrne
[19] Interview with Alan Byrne
[20] Interview with Alan Byrne
[21] Interview with Alan Byrne
[22] Jim Fitz website, used with permission
[23] *Vintage Guitar* June 1999, used with permission
[24] Interview with Alan Byrne
[25] *Kerrang* Interview, Mark Putterford 26th July 1984.
[26] Interview with Alan Byrne
[27] Interview with Alan Byrne
[28] Interview with Alan Byrne
[29] Interview with Alan Byrne
[30] RTE Radio, 7/5/84 Fanning Rock Show
[31] *Kerrang* Interview with Mark Putterford, 26th July 1984
[32] Interview with Alan Byrne
[33] Interview with Alan Byrne
[34] Interview with Alan Byrne
[35] Interview with Alan Byrne
[36] Interview with Alan Byrne
[37] Interview with Alan Byrne
[38] Interview with Alan Byrne
[39] Interview with Alan Byrne
[40] *Kerrang* article by Derek Oliver 20th Sept 1984
[41] Interview with Alan Byrne
[42] *Black Rose,* used with permission
[43] Interview with Alan Byrne
[44] *Sounds* 12th Dec 1984 by Alan Pell
[45] Interview with Alan Byrne
[46] Interview with Alan Byrne
[47] Interview with Alan Byrne
[48] Interview with Alan Byrne
[49] Interview with Alan Byrne

CHAPTER 13
[1] Interview with Alan Byrne
[2] Interview with Alan Byrne
[3] Interview with Alan Byrne
[4] *Melody Maker* 11th May 1985
[5] Interview with Alan Byrne
[6] Interview with Alan Byrne

[7] Interview with Alan Byrne
[8] Interview with Alan Byrne
[9] Interview with Alan Byrne
[10] Interview with Alan Byrne
[11] Interview with Alan Byrne
[12] Interview with Alan Byrne
[13] Interview with Alan Byrne
[14] Interview with Alan Byrne
[15] Interview with Alan Byrne
[16] Interview with Alan Byrne
[17] Interview with Alan Byrne
[18] Interview with Alan Byrne
[19] Interview with Alan Byrne
[20] Interview with Alan Byrne
[21] *Kerrang,* Interview by Mark Putterford
[22] Interview with Alan Byrne
[23] Interview with Alan Byrne
[24] Interview with Alan Byrne
[25] Interview with Alan Byrne
[26] Interview with Alan Byrne
[27] Interview with Alan Byrne
[28] Interview with James McNair
[29] Interview with Alan Byrne
[30] Interview with Alan Byrne
[31] Interview with Alan Byrne
[32] Interview with Alan Byrne
[33] Interview with Alan Byrne
[34] Interview with Alan Byrne
[35] Interview with Alan Byrne
[36] Interview with Alan Byrne
[37] Interview with Alan Byrne
[38] Interview with Alan Byrne
[39] Interview with Alan Byrne
[40] Interviews with Alan Byrne
[41] Interview with Alan Byrne
[42] *Black Rose,* used with permission

CHAPTER 14
[1] Interview with Alan Byrne
[2] Interview with Alan Byrne
[3] Interview with Alan Byrne
[4] Interview with Alan Byrne
[5] Interview with Alan Byrne
[6] Interview with Alan Byrne
[7] Interview with Alan Byrne
[8] *Zoom Club* release sleeve notes, used with permission
[9] Interview with Alan Byrne
[10] Interview with Alan Byrne
[11] Interview with Alan Byrne

SAF, HELTER SKELTER and FIREFLY Books

Order Online

For the latest on Fire y, SAF and Helter Skelter titles, or to order books online, check our websites.

www.safpublishing.com
www.helterskelterbooks.com

You can also browse the full range of rock, pop, jazz and experimental music books we have available, as well as keeping up with our latest releases and special offers.

You can also contact us via email, and request a catalogue.

FIRE
FLY
PUBLISHING

www.safpublishing.com
www.helterskelterbooks.com